THE SOCIAL MEDIA HANDBOOK

WITHDRAWN
FOR SALE

The Social Media Handbook explores how social media are changing disciplinary understandings of the internet and our everyday lives. In addition to person-to-person social networking services like Facebook and Twitter, this volume considers a broad range of networked information services that support in-depth social interaction, community formation, and collaboration in the Web 2.0 era.

Rather than considering social media in terms of specific technologies, the chapters in this book engage topics across a range of research, techniques, practices, culture and society, and theories. These broader topics—including community, gender, fandom, disability, and journalism—are entryways through which students and faculty can explore ways of thinking about social media and find new paradigms for analysis.

Jeremy Hunsinger is an Assistant Professor in Communication Studies at Wilfrid Laurier University. He is co-editor of the *International Handbook of Virtual Learning Environments* and the *International Handbook of Internet Research*.

Theresa Senft is the author of *Camgirls: Celebrity & Community in the Age of Social Networks* and the co-author of *History of the Internet: A Chronology, 1843–Present*. Formerly a Senior Lecturer at the University of East London, Terri now teaches in the Global Liberal Studies Program at New York University.

Contributors: Axel Bruns, Francesca Coppa, Katie Ellis, Gerard Goggin, Alexander Halavais, Andrew Herman, Angus Johnston, Alice Marwick, Safiya Umoja Noble, Zizi Papacharissi, Toni Sant.

THE SOCIAL MEDIA HANDBOOK

Edited by Jeremy Hunsinger and Theresa Senft

Routledge
Taylor & Francis Group

NEW YORK AND LONDON

First published 2014
by Routledge
711 Third Avenue, New York, NY 10017

and by Routledge
2 Park Square, Milton Park, Abingdon, Oxfordshire OX14 4RN

First issued in paperback 2014

Routledge is an imprint of the Taylor and Francis Group, an informa business

Library of Congress Cataloging-in-Publication Data

The social media handbook / edited by Jeremy Hunsinger and
  Theresa Senft.
    pages cm
  Includes bibliographical references and index.
  1. Social media. I. Hunsinger, Jeremy. II. Senft, Theresa M., 1965–
  HM742.S6281963 2013
  302.23′1—dc23
  2013017330

ISBN 978-0-415-88680-2 (hbk)
ISBN 978-0-415-71441-9 (pbk)
ISBN 978-0-203-40761-5 (ebk)

Typeset in Bembo
by Apex CoVantage, LLC

To our editors and our colleagues, thank you for your patience.

CONTENTS

INTRODUCTION

Jeremy Hunsinger and Theresa Senft

This book examines how social media are changing the plural landscapes and disciplinary understandings of the internet and our everyday lives. The meaning of "social media" is a matter of debate: while some use the term quite narrowly to describe person-to-person relations on social networking services like Facebook and Twitter, others use the term to signal socialization aspects of Web 2.0 sites in general. In this book, social media means networked information services designed to support in-depth social interaction, community formation, collaborative opportunities and collaborative work (Bruns & Bahnisch, 2009). While the term social media arose in relation to the terms social software and Web 2.0, viewing social media as a web-oriented system forgets the many systems that people use every day that are not web based. Some elements of social media predate the Web 2.0 phenomena and continue today, such as parts of interactive television, socially playable video games, and virtual worlds/MMORPGs. This book explores the broad range of social media available today and provides insights into its use and understanding for a broad audience.

More and more users are drawn to social media every day, and that broad user base has made social media platforms into social and commercial successes. The observation that many scholars seem fascinated by and use social media in their day-to-day lives isn't particularly interesting. After all, the notion that people are gregarious by nature (and thus want to be with other people) is as old as Aristotle. What makes social media matter—the reason why both educators and students are pondering its meanings—is threefold. First, we are increasingly fascinated by social media's capacity to support and extend in-depth social interactions in ways that traverse the online and offline worlds, be they in-flesh meetings through online dating services, or government visits to our home after authorities locate "suspicious" messages sent from our account on Twitter. Second, while social media are increasingly seen as an ideal way to help existing communities engage in outreach (such as in political campaigns), they are just as often used to enable new and sometimes troubling "imagined communities" such as "pro-anorexia" and racist groups online. Third, while we acknowledge how social media makes valuable spaces for people to collaborate over distance, we feel these collaborations (and the "immaterial labor" that results) force us to reconsider older notions of work in a networked world.

Rather than considering social media in terms of specific technologies, this book is divided into introductory categories centering on topics that unite a range of research, techniques, practices, culture and society, and theories. The broader topics are not meant to cover all of the possibilities of studying social media but are imagined to be entryways through which students and faculty can explore ways of thinking about social media, find paradigms for analyzing social media, and consider alternative perspectives on social media. To that end, the categories are diverse but practical topics that are frequently taught in communications, information studies, media studies, and other disciplinary and interdisciplinary areas.

The contributions to this volume engage contemporary topics across a wide variety of disciplines and topics, but they all engage with the idea of social media in our culture and society. The book begins with a chapter by Jeremy Hunsinger that explores the technical and political sides of a debate about social media and infrastructures. It frames the debate through Operation Electronic Leviathan and Operation Encrypt Everything of the Canadian Pirate Party. This chapter introduces the background functioning of the internet as it relates to questions of neoliberalism and leviathanic politics.

In the second chapter of the book, Angus Johnston tackles the question of community in social media formations. From the dawn of the internet era, many worried that, as people spent more time online, "real" relationships would suffer, predicting increasing isolation and disconnectedness would follow. Internet users have always sought to build communities online, however, and with the rise of social media, those communities have grown ever more complex, more robust, and more diverse. Today, the boundaries between online and offline life continue to blur. This chapter charts two recent student activist events in New York City, using them as case studies to demonstrate how internet-based communities increasingly reshape our understanding of the concept of community itself.

In the book's third chapter, Andrew Herman engages the Facebook urge in his piece on the political economy of social media. Through a comparative analysis with mass media, he distinguishes qualities of social media's political economy that have lasting effects on the economics of social media use. He builds an argument that culminates in a thesis of differentiation based on the articulations and assemblages that are constituted through social media use as they differ from mass media use.

Chapter four considers art and performance in social media. Citing specific examples from the 1970s to the present, Toni Sant focuses on the nature of performativity as it applies to playing with online identities, performing in virtual worlds, participatory art, and fan art. Sant argues that at least one outcome of increased artistic production in social media venues has been the increasing democratization of notions of art itself.

In the fifth chapter, Alice Marwick considers how social media intersects with issues of gender, sex, and sexuality. Examining the controversies surrounding blogger Julia Allison, Marwick argues that social media both *reflects* and *produces* gender and sexuality in online venues. This chapter reads Allison's over-the-top femininity as a threatening reminder that gender is always performative in nature, and sees objections to her "shameless" self-promotion for "doing nothing" as illustrating how certain types of online participation are valued more than others, based on social norms of gender.

The sixth chapter is devoted to the theme of fan cultures. Here, Francesca Coppa provides both an extensive overview and argument about the transformations that fan cultures have had through the use of social media. She traces social networking from the analog to the digital histories of fandom and explains how the technologies relate and have empowered fandom in different ways. She focuses this history on the development of the ethos of participation, interaction, and creativity that she finds in fan cultures.

Teaching and learning in social media is the topic of Alexander Halavais in the seventh chapter of this book. His work engages the field of educational technologies through social media. Focusing on the notion of unbundled education or an education without walls, he argues that we can use social media to enable students to transform their processes of learning from a place-bound situated learning, to a model that parallels informal learning, or learning everywhere. He presents us with several perspectives on possible social media technologies that could enable that transformation.

Chapter eight considers the theme of race and social media. Here, Theresa Senft and Safiya Umoja Noble first detail the dominant narratives of race and representation on the internet to date, and then question those narratives by juxtaposing them with case studies drawn from social media. In particular, they focus on the reception of Franchesca Ramsey's viral YouTube video, "Sh★t White Girls Say to Black Girls," comparing it to other antiracist efforts, such as the blog *Stuff White People Like*. They argue that Ramsey's video "works" because it refuses to present race as a solid category of identity and uses performance to show how certain bodies become "racialized" while others remain invisible. They end by speaking about the limits of social media–generated viral humor as antiracist political practice.

In chapter nine, Katie Ellis and Gerard Goggin argue that social media should be open to all and that for some people with disabilities it is a social lifeline. Arguing for an explicit paradox in the nature of social media, Ellis and Goggin show that social media provides not only opportunities, but also enables new forms of life for people with certain disabilities. Their ideas open new areas for research and challenge the assumption that the disabled disappear in online environments.

The Arab Spring and the mythologies of democracy are the topics that are central to Zizi Papacharissi's paper on networked publics and private spheres. She analyzes the possibility that social media enable democratic action or at least the social imagination of democratic action. Her work engages the binary nature of the private and public in political spaces and how this might be used or directed into affective attachments and moments of expression that allow transformative politics.

Axel Bruns confronts social media and journalism in a time of crisis through his analysis of Twitter during a recent New Zealand earthquake. His example illustrates how journalists are now relying on social media to help them perform journalism. Equally as important, his analysis of the data around #eqnz provides students with another way of thinking about social media.

This book represents accessible arguments about the nature and history of social media. In it we seek to engage our readers in a debate about the explorations, considerations, and analyses that are possible in social media. We sought authors who would provide both theoretical and empirical depth based on case studies that illustrate the topic of their essay. This book is meant to be an active engagement and a tool to think with when thinking about social media.

Bibliography

Bruns, A., & Bahnisch, M. (2009). *Social media volume 1: State of the art.* Smart Services CRC. Retrieved from http://snurb.info/files/Social%20Media%20-%20State%20of%20the%20 Art%20-%20March%202009.pdf

1

INTERFACE AND INFRASTRUCTURE OF SOCIAL MEDIA

Jeremy Hunsinger

Operation Electronic Leviathan was started in 2012 by the Pirate Party of Canada as an informational campaign that would programmatically resist warrantless surveillance, oppressive intellectual property regimes, and internet censorship that are embedded in bills in the Canadian Parliament. However, the operation also recognizes that the government is not the only participant in the creation of the electronic leviathan; there are also private companies, such as Twitter, Facebook, and Google, amongst other more secretive firms, that have elements that could feed into the electronic leviathan, such as Blue Coat or The Gamma Group. The information and programmatic campaign of the Pirate Party was later renamed Operation Encrypt Everything. This new name de-emphasized the transformation of the neoliberal state into the neoliberal surveillance state. The foundational idea of these campaigns was to leverage social media—such as wikis, Facebook, and Reddit—to inform people about the many possible dangers of using the internet and social media. These campaigns were especially engaged in warning the public about using the internet without using the proper tools to protect themselves and their representations online. In short, the idea was to teach people to use the internet and social media safely.

The idea of the electronic leviathan places politics back in the leviathanic body, which in Hobbes was thought to be the Sovereign and its state, but in contemporary neoliberal capitalism, the locus of the leviathanic body is no longer only embodied in the Sovereign, but is also found as corporations and post-statist organizations (Dosse, 1998; Foucault, 1979, 2008; Hobbes, 1994). This new nature of the leviathan arose because the sovereign entity—whether it is a person, a virtual person like a corporation, or a state—exists as the mode of centralization and enclosure of power. In neoliberal capitalism, while the state still exists, it is arguable that the main centralizer of power is not the old form of leviathanic, centralized state, but instead is the plurality of corporations that constitutes that state, including those that exist or operate outside of that state, such as social media corporations.

Arguably, social media and the internet tend to decentralize power and disseminate it through the network. This decentralization caused conflict with the statist model of the leviathan, because the power embodied in the state seems to appear to disperse, recede, or even disappear in trans-statist social media. As the new corporate leviathans were enclosing the power of the internet and social media, states saw an opportunity to leverage those corporations to new ends. These new ends beget the theory of the electronic leviathan, which is a leviathanic body managed by corporations in service to the state interests, where the state interests are also remarkably centered on corporate interests. The electronic leviathans derive from state-tied social media corporations and seem to be able to concentrate and demonstrate sovereign power by providing a new means of censoring, behavior monitoring, and thus modulating that behavior in the population (Deibert, Palfrey, Rohozinski, & Zittrain, 2011; Deibert, Palfrey, Rohozinski, & Zittrain, 2008). This reconcentration is resisted by the democratic side of the general will of the population, and this resistance is supplemented by their technological capacity. The general will need not always be democratically oriented. As we have seen clearly in the past, the general will has been led toward both fascistic and authoritarian directions (Guattari, 1995; Rousseau, 1997). As social media might be thought of as a manifestation of the general will, perhaps we are heading down these dark paths once more.

There is an imagination of a public good that is driving the creation of these new regimes of surveillance and repression, and that is an imagination of a public serviced by market-driven corporations. As an example of this relationship, in the construction of these regimes governments are making some currently legal social media and internet practices into questions of torts, and thus into finable offenses, and transforming the legal relationship surrounding established internet practices into new profit centers for corporations who can now sue for the tort fines. This change of the law generates the new illegality. In attempting to curb this newly illegal action, our governments create a statutory system through which other parties can profit. This transformation of the legal system transforms the nature of sovereign-subject relations by mediating it with the interests of profit-centered content production on the internet. With that change, when you contribute your material to a social media corporation, who then claims rights to that material under contract with you, you could theoretically be sued for your own use of your own intellectual products in a way that is deeply problematic for you as a producer of intellectual property via social media. This problematization of your online actions comes into being because of the new regime the government is constructing and to which you, as a citizen, are consenting.

Our consent is also generated from our use of social media. Social media corporations develop the interfaces through which many people access internet services, but also access their friends, communities, and social networks. These social media interfaces become familiar and comfortable to us. These interfaces become so comfortable that when major changes happen, some users quit, rebel, or complain. These interfaces have become standardized and normal in our social media worlds. Similarly, the install base of internet infrastructures, such as the internet protocols, copper and fiber-optic networks, computers, server software, and networking hardware like hubs and switches, all tend not to change their operating parameters quickly, or at all. These systems and their software become standards and standardized in interface and infrastructure. This standardization provides for the possibilities embodied in the systems, but also provides for the system's limitations. That standardization is also what allows for the manifestation of the general will within and through the systems, and it is also what allows the creation of the electronic leviathan as a will toward governmentality generated between the sovereign will of the state as our consent to be governed and the market-driven will of the social media corporations as our consent to participate in social media.

This chapter is about how the interfaces and infrastructures of social media constrain and envelop our internet experiences. Throughout this chapter, we confront questions about the nature of the social media as interface and infrastructure that lead us to more strongly consider the necessity of actions such as Operation Electronic Leviathan.

The Nature of Internetworks, the World Wide Web, and Social Media

It is important to realize how the internet works at a basic level in order to understand the implications of social media interfaces and infrastructures in our everyday lives. The internet is a network of networks to which a computational device connected to local networks can send data encapsulated in a protocol to another computational device connected to a remote network (Cerf & Kahn, 2004; Virilio, 2000). These networks might be comprised of physical things, like copper wire or fiber-optic cabling, or they might be radio, laser, or, in humorous cases, they might even be comprised of pigeons (RFC 1149). To initiate the internet communication, the first computer creates an outgoing port by connecting the software that wants to connect to the remote machine to the networking protocol software stack on the local machine. This protocol stack starts with transmission control protocol (TCP), which takes the data stream from the application and breaks it into number chunks, which, combined with header information, are then encapsulated and addressed by internet protocol (IP). This TCP/IP data is then sent as a packet to the remote computer, which then receives it with its own incoming port. This port is connected to its TCP/IP stack, which is connected to the software trying to communicate to the remotely hosted software. This remote software to which we connect is usually called a daemon or a server. The TCP/IP stack upon initial receipt of the packet sends an acknowledgement of the receipt to the originating device. As the data travels from one machine to the other, and it is acknowledged and other data is likely sent back, it first passes through the local network that might be Ethernet, television cable, phone line, or fiber-optic cabling to its first point of connection to the internet. This connection is usually provided by the internet service provider (ISP). The internet service provider provides the initial destination routing information that allows the packet to travel along the internet backbones to its final destination. It provides the destination address using the domain name system (DNS), which also allows computers to translate from human meaningful names like zombo.com to its IP address 69.16.230.117. However, what happens on the server side does not necessarily map onto the physical IP address to where the packets arrive. Once it arrives at the IP address, the packet may be routed along a whole subnet of real and virtual machines. These machines may provide the information that allows the originating machine to construct the data that it requests. Frequently for social media sites, the huge virtual machines represented by their domain name, such as Facebook.com or Google.com, cut across geographic locations, national boundaries, and all kinds of other situatednesses that make it hard to understand all the implications of the data arriving at the requesting computer. What is clear though is that the connection between the receiving computer and the sending computer is not a direct connection, but a highly mediated connection that not only passes through the ISP and backbone networks of the internet, but passes through many different middle stations. These middle stations may manipulate the data, or otherwise change it, delete it, copy it, or log it, but also frequently do not. It is said that the internet routes around problematic networks, such as censored networks, and it does, but that does not mean that the internet infrastructure alone allows us to overcome those barriers in everyday life (Elmer-Dewitt, 1993).

We should not just think that this traffic is passing unnoticed either. Each machine that social media traffic passes through is owned by someone or some institution. Traffic on the internet is constantly monitored by both humans and machines. That monitoring feeds into a management regime that seeks to ensure that quality of service is guaranteed for those that can pay for those guarantees. It also seeks to manage the internet in order to prevent the design of the internet, which is fairly open, from lending itself to being exploited for malevolent use, or it even sometimes seeks to prevent the internet from being used for political, economic, or social dissent. This management of the internet should not be seen necessarily as the neutral management of apolitical businesses or professional engineers, because the neutrality is only an ideological construct floating in relation to the contexts of the medium. If you change the legal landscape, you can transform those businesses and engineers into police and political operatives. This is not what anyone would prefer until something causes it to become a political necessity, which would be the case in the creation of the Electronic Leviathan.

Thus we can posit the generation of an electronic leviathan scenario of corporate or state-based internet surveillance and control, but need we?

Most social media exists within this realm of questioning and worry. Social media exists mostly on the World Wide Web (WWW), though some of it operates through applications on mobile devices. There are a few social media systems that are older than the WWW or function differently than the WWW, such as Internet Relay Chat (IRC) and Skype. These are applications in their own right operating outside, though sometimes through, web browsers. Generally though, the web browser is the front-end interface of the WWW, which runs over hypertext transfer protocol (http) and connects to the http server, which is usually an Apache webserver (www.apache.org). Much of the WWW is generated from data from a wide variety of sources compiled on the fly or cached on the webserver. In social media, much of this data is generated by the users and then served back to them and their friends. In the beginning of the WWW, this dynamic content generation was very basic and not as interactive as social media has become. It is the interactivity that generates the sense of presence and thus community that enables most people to engage with social media. However, it is also this interactivity that encourages people to use it with their friends and communities.

This interactivity that is generated by the connection between computers is mediated in the interfaces of social media as the interfaces are mediations of data mediated by webservers to browsers, or via a similar process. Social media interfaces engage us through interactivity and the appearance of co-presence, community, and, in the end, the appearance of social connection. The interface, whether it is a computer screen, a terminal, or a mobile device screen, is the center of the appearance of personal and group interaction online. It is the center of the constructions of our subjectivity online and our distributed subjectivities online. In other words, the interfaces are places that we inhabit and that inhabit us as we imagine ourselves in them and using them, and their designers imagine us doing the same. This social imagination varies amongst groups but is important to note, because it is the interfaces and infrastructures of social media that now enable significant parts of our social imagination and with that significant parts of our social memory. The control of our social memories is control of us at a very basic level (Calvino, 2009).

Users might mistake the use of an interface and the knowledge of an interface with the use of a computer or computational literacy. However, it is more than literacy with social media and the internet; it is more than knowing and using; it is also a question of being. The focus on literacy is problematic, because while there are standards for interface design for each major operating system, there is no necessity for the familiarity with those interfaces to traverse all the possible software that could be run on the particular platform. Indeed, some software, such as keyloggers, viruses, or trojans, might not have a human accessible interface at all. The lack of a human accessible interface for many computer operations demonstrates that we need to be more aware of the computer's operations than just what is represented to us via the interfaces that we have. Social media primarily relies on the appearance of the human accessible interface as the mode of becoming complicit in the provision, sharing, and exploitation of the users' identity and online life as represented by their data. Users of social media provide their data to the social media services to share amongst their networks of users via that interface, but that interface is not the only place the data then exists, nor is it the only place that the data is changed and manipulated. However, that interface is the only interface that the user sees and interacts with, and, as such, the rest of the interfaces and infrastructures of social media are invisible to them (Hunsinger, 2009a; Star, 1999; Star & Ruhleder, 1994). The visibility of the human interface frequently occludes the imaginations of the other interfaces of the computational device, but those interfaces are just as important.

The centrality of the interface to human experience of computation not only allows us to portray data in compelling ways, but also allows us to hide data in interesting ways (Dourish, 2004). Social media industries rely upon the collection of large amounts of data that the users never see, but the human experience of social media is all about the presentation of social interaction online and thus the provision of data by users to other users through the social media service. Users co-construct their ignorance of the industry side of social media much like they co-construct their ignorance of other cultural industries (Adorno, 1996, 2001). According to Adorno, users construct a relationship with the image on the screen for cinema and its production techniques that allows them to ignore the work that produced that image. This ignorance of the 'hidden' operations of social media parallels the ignorance toward other interface/screen technologies. The knowledge present behind the interface, but through the interface, is precisely what this chapter is meant to address. However, even gaining the knowledge of the infrastructure and interfaces of social media frequently fails to overcome the willful ignorance of that knowledge that we require to engage in social media.

"Don't be evil" was the informal corporate motto for the Google corporation (Vaidhyanathan, 2012). If this motto is needed, then we must be aware that there is a great deal of possible evil to be done. What sort of evil is it though? Arguably it is an evil like any other that engages in the devaluation, damage, or destruction of something valued. In the case of social media, what is valued is information and our representation through information. Most specifically, we value the relationships that information represents. A picture, for instance, represents an enormous amount of information about a person, whereas clicking the "like" button on a service such as Facebook might represent very little information, or even counter-information. However, the capacity to transform this little valued information shared with friends into a marketable informational commodity is the key element of social media services. Some services transform the market by being a subscription service, but other services are free. This begets the idea attributed to Andrew Lewis (Blue_beetle on Metafilter) that "if you are not paying for it, you are not the customer, you are the product being sold." As the product, you become the marketable product comprised of information that you have put online via a wide variety of services, not only social media, but, if you think about it, you probably have constructed hundreds of digital or data "ghosts" that are representations of you that exist as data that are owned by someone else. Previously we have seen that some states have thought that these data ghosts could possibly be unified into a model of your actions (Lockwood & Coley, 2012; Suarez, 2010; Waldby, 2000).

One such example of this model was the Total Information Awareness (TIA) program of the US government's Defense Advanced Research Projects Agency (DARPA), which has since been decommissioned. DARPA, in the form of ARPA, was the group that originally funded the networks and research that became the internet (Vaidhyanathan, 2012). However, that older institutional history does not participate strongly in the current commercial internet on which current social media is founded. This brings us back to the leviathan model; contemporary neoliberal capitalism is corporate leviathanism (Hunsinger, 2009b). The leviathan is traditionally considered as the body politic that unites the many individualistic interests, transforming the "nasty, brutish, and short" world into a collective that can seek a common goal while suppressing many of our individual goals (Hobbes, 1994). But contemporarily governments are in a neoliberal phase, and as such they are less interested in forming collectives that seek sovereign goals (Foucault, 2008). Instead, governments are seeking to manage populations and to modulate behaviors of individuals in a controlled society (Deleuze, 1992; Foucault, 2003). This construction of the neoliberal body politic allows the creation of a space of sub-politics, and it is in this space that the new corporate leviathans flourish (Beck, 1997; Hunsinger, 2009b). Corporate leviathans are frequently still funded by governments, but it is the unity of the two leviathanic bodies through the internet and social media that brings about the electronic leviathan.

Leviathans unite individuals into collectives to pursue common goals under a sovereign position, but also in that process they unite power, capital, and social control into systems of modulation which require interaction from people (Hunsinger, 2009b). Interactions online can be tracked for a myriad of reasons, and the question presented by the laws that Operation Electronic Leviathan resists is the tracking by government and corporations in the service of capital and thus in the service of profit. They promote these tactics contrary to government interests and capital interests in your data. They want you to be aware that you have private interest that you can maintain if you take the proper precautions online. You can encrypt your data so that the intermediaries and secondary interests that have access to it cannot read it. You can also browse the internet anonymously via Tor (https://www.torproject.org) or instead not participate in companies like Facebook, but participate in organizations such as Diaspora (https://joindiaspora.com). You can also learn more deeply about your computer and the internet and learn not to allow the default configuration of your computer to determine your abilities to control your information, but to use a protective hosts file such as the one at http://someonewhocares.org/hosts/. The broader idea is that if everyone takes personal responsibility for their data, their online subjectivities represented as the data traces they leave, and their data ghosts, then those people will be able to develop toward a sense of sovereignty that allows them to resist the leviathans.

But is sovereignty over your data really a form of sovereignty, or is it merely a projection of your distributed subjectivities coming to be informed within the sphere of performative computational and networked literacy? This possible manifestation of subjectivity more likely exempts one from the general will as the general will becomes complicit in the creation of the corporate leviathan (Rousseau, 1997). Practices such as online purchasing, participation in corporate social media campaigns, and similar elements of promotional cultures help to legitimate, thus symbolize our consent to the corporate leviathans. It is unclear if even active, well-informed participation can prevent the interests of capital and profit from undermining and/or repurposing the data that you have already made available. As we saw earlier, even if you try to be informed and try to take appropriate action, the interfaces of social media and the infrastructures they rely on discourage you. These services promote a co-construction of invisibility of operation and ignorance of the infrastructure through the interfaces. Even if you become informed and try to take control of your information, your friends might loosen that control and give your information away through their actions. The solution though is not to hyper-individuate oneself and become a digital hermit, rather it is to share your tips and techniques and concerns with your friends. This sharing of information that informs each other is precisely the basis of building a trust-based online community which can substantiate a general will that might resist the leviathanic social media constructs.

But if you do not construct networks of trust, you, as a digital subject to the electronic leviathans of neoliberal corporate capitalism, will have already become complicit in your own exploitation by creation through almost any action of a data ghost of you. You create such a thing both by your performance in social media and also through the absence of performance when performance is expected. The change in performativity in social media that one would operationalize if one pursued the model of Operation Encrypt Everything would also create traces that the electronic leviathans can operationalize into marketable commodities. Presence and absence from social media are both meaningful for data analysis of you and your data ghosts.

The form that this data ghost takes is comprised of digital traces or footprints that you make online via social media and similar services. It is a presence that exists whether you are there or not, representing you to your friends, but also representing you to anyone who has access to the information it constructs about you. It is comprised as much by your presence and preferences as by the places you are not present, because the absence constructs the likelihood of presence elsewhere. The data ghost is a being of likelihoods, much like your existence in a myriad of actuarial tables is defined in likelihoods. Your perpetual performance or nonperformance of what is expected changes the likelihoods of future performance, which is why absence is just as important as presence, and absten-tion is as important as participation in constructing your online existence or lack thereof as a data ghost.

In some contexts, your data ghost also has agency to act even beyond its capac-ity to represent. That is to say some institutions, organizations, or people have constituted the capacity to act independently into data ghosts. For instance, in an effort to create the appearance of activity in some unused profiles, Facebook has had them "like" things that they may have been inclined to like in the past (Meisler, 2012; Taylor, 2012). Some of these profiles have been people who have died, and the posthumous posting demonstrates clearly that your data ghosts will continue acting after you have passed away. But beyond such simple constructs as Facebook acting on your behalf, you also have the possibility of creating alterna-tive ghosts in the machines of social media that will act on your behalf. You can manipulate the interfaces and infrastructures for purposes that might undermine the constructions of your data ghosts (Steinhart, 2007; Suarez, 2010; Waldby, 2000).

If the first goal of this chapter is to make you aware of your digital existence in the interfaces and infrastructures of the social media, then the second goal is to make you aware of how that plays in regards to the larger contexts of your life. That is not to say that you should not use social media, because you probably should if it is important in your life. It is to say that social media use has to be con-sidered in relation to the larger picture of what you and your peers using social media are constructing and for whom you are building it. As mentioned earlier, social media operates much like other cultural industries: it uses glamour and style to entice you and social connections surrounding it to keep you involved. The end of that involvement is profit. It is profit with you as product.

In contemporary hard science fiction, there is a mode of resistance to being objectified as a product. In Daniel Suarez's books *Daemon* and *Freedom,* the con-struction of agential software systems represent the interests of a few people at first, but through dissemination through diverse communities, the interests spread until the numbers of people involved grow into something more both socially and politically. At first, the system of government that was introduced in those books as a result of technological systems was similar to a demagogic democ-racy. This form of demagoguery is more or less a popularity contest made into a computational system. It is frequently found on Facebook or Slashdot.org and operates to give some people more power over others. In the book, slowly this popularity regime is dissolved into systems of knowledge where the decentral-ized system of judgment surrounding people enabled those that performed well in their community and encouraged community members to perform their role better. This was all mediated by a large user-oriented social media display built into glasses. Unsurprisingly, we could do everything in Suarez's books with today's technology. A similar system empowers the police in the book *Rule 34* by Charles Stross. While not rising to the status of electronic leviathan, the police manage-ment augmented reality system described in that book was constrained by legal, practical, and human capacities, enabling a somewhat dysfunctional bureaucracy to function in the context of the technical system. The technical system enabled the dysfunctional police protocols as much as it enabled actual police work. This back-and-forth between the good possibilities and the bad possibilities of social media is embedded in the openness of its design or lack of openness, as the case may be.

Arguments about the infrastructure and functioning of the internet and social media suggest that much of its design and function maps onto late 1960s and early 1970s bureaucratic governance models (Hunsinger, 2009c; Salus, 1995). Much of engineering design is built upon prior understandings that have developed over time and constrained the imaginations of the possible, while opening other possibilities. Realizing the parallels between human bureaucratic systems and the technical system of the internet does provide some insights into the basic operation problematics of social media as indicated in *Rule 34, Daemon,* and *Freedom* above.

The failures of the network system of social media parallels the failures of human society. We exist within a plurality of nations, states, societies, cultures, institutions, communities, friendships, and roles. Individually some of those social systems inherently conflict with each other and cause conflict when mediated by third parties. For instance, many people who play sports have seen other players on their team, or not on their team, in various modes of dress or undress. That is common in relation to many sports, but when you mediate the sports, suddenly the generalized expectation is that we will not see people undressed or partly undressed on TV or via social media. Some groups in society would find such a visual experience to be shocking; others would not, but in either case it would generally be unexpected. Similarly, one does not expect to learn of a good friend's wedding via social media prior to actually being invited via post or e-mail; it would symbolically indicate that the friendship might not be as close as expected. In formal communication via social media, which is not really most social media's foremost design goal, there is the same problematic norm structure, where the assumptions of address and propriety are lost within the system, so as to cause some people minor discomfort. This discomfiture is part of the problem of managing social media expectations, and is accounted for in the design of the infrastructure and interface. Even if it is little accounted for, it does indicate that there is a separation between the "social" in social media and the "social" in society. This difference is part of the expectations and general will of the users of social media and its difference from that of the general will of the larger society. This difference is important because it highlights the plurality of possible wills, which, as indicated earlier, can take positive directions toward democracy and freedom and negative directions toward demagoguery, fascism, and perhaps authoritarianism. Both directions are entirely possible within the constraints of social media, as I am sure we all have felt that some of our social media "friends" have at one time or another pushed toward the negative side of the general will, espousing things that would possibly lead to problematic futures.

The general complicity with the tendency toward internet despotism or internet fascism in social media should be resisted and organized against, much like it has been organized against in other media. This is part of the message of Operation Electronic Leviathan. If someone is going to remove the means through which you can pursue currently permissible actions in social media—through censorship, through monitoring of content, by changing their legality, or similar actions—then you as a user have choices that could lead you away from that social media, or you could act to change that social media and related users through an informational campaign.

The problem with the legal changes is not so much that they are changing the landscape, but it is how they are changing the landscape. They are changing the landscape in a way that allows people to do things as they do now to be fined, possibly bankrupted, or imprisoned or maybe worse if we let property rights trump other rights. The current outcome is worse than merely banning the activity altogether, because it transforms the legal system of torts from a punitive one to a profitable one, and that is deeply problematic for any democratic legal system.

Conclusion

The space for analysis and investigation in interface studies is quite broad in relation to social media. As discussed above, the World Wide Web is the standard interface for many of the services, but there are a plurality of possible alternatives. Future analysis of interface matters can investigate whether they encourage or discourage the development of electronic leviathans, online democracies, or other political constructs. Alternatively, future research might consider the relations between interface and standards in order to discern the structuring capacities of social media. Do social media interfaces and infrastructure provide for more or less political, ethical, or social actions? Or perhaps the interface encourages or discourages creativity in some minimal or profound way; we can surely see the creativity of hackers in resolving their problems of interface and infrastructure.

In regard to the argument surrounding infrastructure, people research infrastructure and standards in a myriad of ways that open up all kinds of questions about rationality, technical systems development, democratic and antidemocratic discourse in standards decisions, and so on. And infrastructure itself is hard for many people to think about because it is seemingly invisible, though it is an invisible structuring force beyond the invisible basis. This is why we must, as scholars and concerned citizens, look beyond the interface, to the operations of the system. We must open the black box of social media in order to consider its broader effect on our lives, not just as they appear to be constructed to us and by us in the media, but also how our lives are being constructed by those interfaces and infrastructures. We should be concerned with not merely our unmediated subjectivity, but also the distributed subjectivity of our social network and the hyper-mediated subjectivity of our data ghosts. Only with a critical eye toward it all can we make informed decisions about our use of social media and the internet.

Bibliography

Adorno, T. W. (1996). *Minima Moralia* (New edition ed.). Verso Press.

Adorno, T. W. (2001). *The culture industry: Selected essays on mass culture* (2nd ed.). Routledge.

Beck, U. (1997). *The reinvention of politics: Rethinking modernity in the global social order.* Polity Press.

Calvino, I. (2009). World memory. In *The complete Cosmicomics* (pp. 365–372). Penguin Classics.

Cerf, V., & Kahn, R. (2004). What is the internet? In M. N. Cooper (Ed.), *Open architecture as communication policy.* Stanford, CT: Center for Internet and Society Stanford Law School.

Deibert, R., Palfrey, J., Rohozinski, R., & Zittrain, J. (2011). *Access contested: Security, identity, and resistance in Asian cyberspace.* The MIT Press.

Deibert, R. J., Palfrey, J. G., Rohozinski, R., & Zittrain, J. (2008). *Access denied: The practice and policy of global internet filtering (Information Revolution and Global Politics).* The MIT Press.

Deleuze, G. (1992). Postscript on the societies of control. *October, 59*(4), 3–7.

Dosse, F. (1998). *History of structuralism: The rising sign 1945–1966.* University of Minnesota Press.

Dourish, P. (2004). *Where the action is: The foundations of embodied interaction.* The MIT Press.

Elmer-Dewitt, P. (1993). First nation in cyberspace. *Time, 6,* 62–64.

Foucault, M. (1979). *Discipline and punish* (A. Sheridan, Trans.). Vantage.

Foucault, M. (2003). *"Society must be defended": Lectures at the Collège de France, 1975–1976.* Picador.

Foucault, M. (2008). *The birth of biopolitics: Lectures at the Collège de France, 1978–1979.* Palgrave Macmillan.

Guattari, F. (1995). *Chaosophy (foreign agents).* Semiotext(e).

Hobbes, T. (1994). *Leviathan: With selected variants from the Latin edition of 1668.* Hackett.

Hunsinger, J. (2009a). Introducing learning infrastructures: Invisibility, context, and governance. *Learning Inquiry, 3*(3), 111–114.

Hunsinger, J. (2009b). Knowledge and cultural production in the context of contemporary capitalism: A response to Wittkower. *Fast Capitalism, 4*(1).

Hunsinger, J. (2009c). Toward nomadological cyberinfrastructures. In J. Hunsinger, L. Klastrup, & M. Allen (Eds.), *International handbook of internet research.* Springer.

Lockwood, D., & Coley, R. (2012). *Cloud time* (Reprint ed.). O Books, John Hunt.

Meisler, B. (2012). Why are dead people liking stuff on Facebook? Retrieved December 29, 2012, from http://readwrite.com/2012/12/11/why-are-dead-people-liking-stuff-on-facebook

Rousseau, J.-J. (1997). *Rousseau: "The social contract" and other later political writings.* Cambridge University Press.

Salus, P. H. (1995). *Casting the net: From ARPANET to internet and beyond.* Addison-Wesley Professional.

Star, S. L. (1999). The ethnography of infrastructure. *American Behavioral Scientist, 43*(3), 377.

Star, S. L., & Ruhleder, K. (1994). Steps towards an ecology of infrastructure: Complex problems in design and access for large-scale collaborative systems. *Proceedings of the 1994 ACM conference on Computer Supported Cooperative Work.*

Steinhart, E. (2007). Survival as a digital ghost. *Minds and Machines, 17*(3), 261–271.

Suarez, D. (2010). *Freedom.* Dutton.

Taylor, L. C. (2012, December 12). Why are dead people "liking" stuff on Facebook? *Toronto Star.*

Vaidhyanathan, S. (2012). *The Googlization of everything: (And why we should worry).* University of California Press.

Virilio, P. (2000). *The information bomb.* Verso.

Waldby, C. (2000). *The visible human project: Informatic bodies and posthuman medicine.* Routledge.

2

COMMUNITY AND SOCIAL MEDIA

Angus Johnston

Introduction

On the evening of February 18, 2009, a planned dance party hosted by a student activist group at New York University turned without public warning into a building occupation. As many as a hundred students took over a dining hall space on the third floor of NYU's Kimmel Hall, presenting a variety of demands to the administration.

The occupiers had a Twitter feed and a website, and they broadcast intermittently from within the occupation via livecam, but for them building and sustaining community among themselves was a more pressing concern than connecting with communities beyond their barricades. One student, however, barricaded inside the dining hall with his laptop, had little else to do. Charlie Eisenhood was a reporter for the campus newspaper *NYU Local,* and over the next two days he emerged as one of the most important links between the occupiers and an increasingly fascinated outside world.

Eisenhood would ultimately liveblog from within Kimmel Hall for more than twenty-nine consecutive hours, nearly the entire length of the occupation. (He left Kimmel to sleep in the early hours of February 20, and the occupiers were rousted at noon that day.) His blogging was cited by the *New York Times, Gawker,* and other sites as a crucial resource for understanding the occupation as it unfolded.

Eisenhood's presence within the occupation generated controversy among his hosts. Some objected to his reporting of what they considered sensitive information, and others objected to his public assessments of the action itself. He was excluded from observing negotiations and organizing meetings, and many occupiers refused to talk to him. (A proposal that he be asked to leave the dining hall was raised and rejected on February 19.)

As isolated as Eisenhood may have been, however, he wasn't writing in a vac-
uum. Hundreds of people, from the NYU community and beyond, left comments
on his liveblog in the twenty-nine hours he was embedded in the occupation—
some responding to his writing, others reacting to the occupation itself. Many
provided their own insights and information from their perspectives outside the
building. Some used the platform to converse with each other, and Eisenhood
took time to answer their questions and respond to their analyses.

Meanwhile, journalists and bloggers picked up Eisenhood's reporting and
expanded upon it, and he replied to what they wrote as well. Observers within
and without NYU shared his information on Twitter and Facebook. His liveblog
even served as a way for Eisenhood to communicate with the occupiers as their
relationship became strained—at one point early on he posted, "I just ate a sugar
packet. I have no food," and then, nine minutes later, "somebody gave me a vegan
chocolate chip cookie."

A little less than two months later and eight blocks uptown, activists at The
New School staged an occupation of their own. Early in the morning of April 10,
about two dozen students entered a vacant university building at 65 Fifth Avenue,
barricading themselves inside. This time there were no journalists on hand, no
Twitter feed, no livecam. (An occupation blog was established, but it was updated
infrequently and tersely.)

With little direct communication between the New School occupiers and the
outside world, other online communities rushed in to fill the information vac-
uum. Some of these were encouraged by the occupiers' allies, while others were
mobilized by the work of journalists or through unrelated social networks. An
activist Facebook group was the first place to publicly announce the occupation;
it was first mentioned on Twitter at 6:46 a.m. At 7:26 a nonstudent activist relayed
a request via Twitter that supporters bring cameras to the scene to document
police activity, a request that would be heavily retweeted that morning. Fifteen
minutes later, the occupation acquired a hashtag—#NSIE, for "New School In
Exile," the name of an activist organization informally linked to the occupiers.

At 8:09 a.m. a Twitter user with no connection to The New School, the occupation, or activist politics tweeted that the "New School protests outside my apt
looks like a murder scene." This was the first eyewitness report on the event, and
it was followed six minutes later by a photo of a banner hanging from the roof of
65 Fifth Avenue. This first tweeted visual image of the action came nearly an hour
before the first media outlet tweeted about the story.

By ten o'clock, four and a half hours after the occupation had begun in secrecy,
it was all over social media. A New School student newspaper was liveblogging the
event, an NYU paper was covering the story on its site, and tweets were coming in
at a rate of about one a minute. In the next hour local office workers, alerted to the
excitement, began posting aerial photographs taken from their windows—including one that provided activists with their first evidence that police were massing
on the building's roof for possible entry. (These photos were taken and shared for

the amusement of the workers' friends and colleagues, but were quickly uncovered and shared by activists and journalists via Twitter's search function.)

By eleven o'clock there had been at least 132 tweets about the occupation, including a rooftop photograph of police attempting to gain access to the building and several reports of arrests from passersby—all of these coming before those developments had been noted on television, radio news, or on journalism websites. There had still been no tweets from self-identified occupiers or organizers, and only one link, at eleven o'clock exactly, to the occupiers' blog.

The first firm confirmation of earlier reports of arrests at the occupation came in the form of a photograph of a protester in handcuffs taken by an onlooker and tweeted at 11:12 a.m. A protest supporter tweeted an eyewitness report of arrests two minutes later, and the first media confirmation of arrests came twenty-five minutes after that.

The New York Times did not mention the story on social media until 11:21 a.m., tweeting a link to its own coverage fifty-two minutes after someone else had, and nearly two hours after the first student newspaper linked to their own reporting on the site. By then police were in the building conducting arrests—the *Times* had spent the morning covering the story and being quoted and cited throughout Twitter for it, but they themselves only arrived at the social media party as it was being shut down.

Just a few years ago, people looking to learn about a breaking event online would have gravitated to one of a very short list of online spaces, and stayed there. Back then, an "online community" was a simple, straightforward thing—a place one went online to connect with like-minded people. Today, however, online communities aren't bounded by virtual geography any more than they are by physical geography, and they emerge and transform and disperse in ways that are confounding to understand, and even more so to influence.

In each of these two occupations, a cohesive community of activists set out to intervene in the life of the university community and urban community in which they lived through a political act. Each time, however, they found their intervention shaped and refracted through the responses of other communities—offline and virtual—that mobilized as a response. These communities deployed in response to the activists' work, but they did so according to their own interests, their own traditions, and their own internal dynamics. Although each occupation was short lived, they both took place in the context of longer-term community formations and affiliations. To understand socially mediated communal moments such as these we need to understand what community is, how it works, and how it has evolved online.

The Idea of Community and Its Variations

The concept of "community" is itself in need of critical interrogation, as it can imply a coherence and unidirectionality that is alien to our lived experience (Wilson & Peterson, 2002). In an era in which the typical—or at least the stereotypical—human community was a small town, it seemed natural to take such towns as representative models, and scholarly research sites, for community studies. Accordingly, early theoretical work tended to proceed from the premise that communities were bounded and discrete. But humans, as social animals embedded in complex webs of relationships, exist simultaneously within multiple communities whose boundaries are ill defined, shifting, and flexible. Even small towns see arrivals and departures, are embedded in larger social spaces, and respond to developments outside their borders. Just as no individual exists in isolation or stasis, the same can be said of the communities in which they reside.

In a highly influential 1986 article, McMillan and Chavis foregrounded a subjective "sense of community" in place of geographical or similarly empirical definitions, approaching the concept of community from an affective rather than a spatial perspective. In their work they described a sense of community as consisting of four elements: membership, influence, integration and fulfillment of needs, and shared emotional connection. They further described community membership as being based on boundaries, emotional safety, a sense of belonging and identification, personal investment, and a common symbol system.

By emphasizing community based in lived subjective experience rather than its objective markers (residency, employment, organizational membership, and so on), McMillan and Chavis emphasized both the slipperiness of community identification and its centrality to our understanding of self and social relations. A community is more than a group to which we belong, they argued. It's a group to which we feel a sense of belonging.

Another challenge to earlier conceptions of communities as grounded in geography came with the publication of Benedict Anderson's *Imagined Communities* (1983). Anderson explored the ways in which national identities are constructed among populations so large as to largely preclude direct relationships among their members, arguing that media play a decisive role in bringing such imagined communities into being. National communities are real, he suggested, but they are only real because, and only become real when, their members come to see them as real. The explanatory power of Anderson's argument was such that his conception was quickly adopted beyond the bounds of his original examples, including—as we shall see—in discussions of the at-a-distance communities fostered by online social media.

Early Internet Communities: Discrete Spaces

When the US Department of Defense chose to fund the development of the internet in the 1960s as a mechanism for linking up academic, scientific, and government/military researchers, the term "community" wasn't commonly used to describe its character—the ARPANET network was seen as professional rather than social. But from the network's earliest days, its users found ways (some sanctioned, some not) to use the technology to facilitate personal connections.

One of the most visible early examples of this impulse has proven one of the most robust, influential, and persistent structures for building online community: the e-mail listserve. E-mail itself predated the creation of ARPANET, but it took on its modern form (and acquired the now-ubiquitous @ symbol) through ARPANET protocols implemented in 1972. The earliest informal mailing lists appeared almost immediately thereafter, and the first ongoing topical list—a science fiction fan list called SF-LOVERS—appeared the following year. With the emergence of the listserve, e-mail expanded from a one-on-one communication tool to a virtual site for larger-scale discussion, debate, and connection.

Internet communities' potential took a huge step forward with the creation of Usenet in 1980. Designed as an infrastructure for creating sites of discussion of various specific topics, Usenet was an agglomeration of "newsgroups" in which users could post queries and comments for public view and reply to those posted by others. In its earliest years Usenet organization was quite haphazard, but in 1987's "Great Renaming" a new structure was imposed on the chaos. There would be seven primary hierarchies—"comp.*" for computer discussions, "sci.*" for the sciences, "rec.*" for recreation and entertainment, and "news.*" for discussion of Usenet itself, along with "misc.*" for miscellaneous topics, "soc.*" for social issues, and "talk.*" for controversial subjects. Thus, "sci.physics" would be a site for physics discussion, "comp.os.windows.ms" would be for questions regarding the Microsoft Windows operating system, and "talk.abortion" would be for arguing about abortion policy.

Each newsgroup under these "Big 7" hierarchies was subject to regulation by the large internet site administrators whose responsibility it was to keep traffic moving. Shortly thereafter an eighth hierarchy, "alt.*" for alternative, was established to allow the creation of newsgroups without the approval or oversight of top administrators. Thus, with the promulgation of the Big 7 and the "alt.*" hierarchy, the universe of dedicated sites for topical discussion online expanded to encompass the entire range of human activity, from "sci.archaeology.mesoamerican" to "rec.aquaria.freshwater.plants" to "alt.recovery.addiction."

In the late 1980s and early 1990s, while Usenet grew in scope and size, other homes for online community sprung up and matured. One could engage in real-time text conversation on an Internet Relay Chat (IRC) channel, connect to a Bulletin Board System (BBS) to e-mail, chat, or play games, or enter into the rickety text-based virtual world of a Multi-User Domain (MUD).

Increasingly, with the growing availability of modems, one could do all this from home over a telephone line. This not only enhanced the intimacy and ubiquity of the online experience, it tethered it to physical location more strongly than before. Bulletin Board Systems, for instance, tended to attract communities within specific cities, since connecting to them from further away required a long-distance phone call. As a result, each BBS would develop a character and a set of interests that reflected the city in which it was based, and would—in a pivotal development for online communities—become a site for the facilitation of offline connections on an increasingly large scale.

Usenet and BBSs shaped online community in different ways, but each facilitated an online life that was richer, more immersive, and more complex than those that had gone before. Crucially, where science fiction had imagined "cyberspace" as a hallucinatory environment remote from and unconnected to offline life, as the world of the cyber was instantiated in practice it quickly became clear that cyberspaces were plural, not singular, and that they were in actuality "continuous with and embedded in other social spaces," enmeshed in the "mundane social structures and relations" that preceded them (Miller & Slater, 2000). These developments also complicated arguments suggesting that societal shifts in the second half of the twentieth century—including the rise of the internet itself—had produced a pulling back from community and an increase in social isolation (Putnam, 2000).

In a 1994 dissertation that became a 2000 book, communication studies scholar Nancy Baym examined the online community that emerged in and around the Usenet newsgroup "rec.arts.tv.soaps" (RATS), a site for soap opera fans of which Baym herself was a member. In her research, Baym documented the strong relationships that developed among RATS participants, the community mores that shaped interactions within it, and the various ways in which dyadic and group relationships formed there spilled over into other online and offline venues.

As Baym was chronicling RATS, a researcher named Howard Rheingold was participating in a San Francisco–based BBS known as the WELL. As Rheingold later wrote of that experience, "It became clear to me . . . that I was participating in the self-design of a new kind of culture. I watched the community's social contracts stretch and change as . . . norms were established, challenged, changed, re-established, re-challenged, in a kind of speeded-up social evolution." Rheingold's thoughts echoed those of A. R. Stone, who argued that virtual communities were "social spaces where people met face-to-face, but under new definitions of both 'meet' and 'face' " (Stone, 1991, p. 85).

The Shift from Internet Spaces to Online Social Networks

The early 1990s saw a huge explosion in the number of people who were living their lives online, with the huge growth in popularity of the America Online (AOL) commercial internet service and the mass adoption of the World Wide Web. The proliferation of the web, and a concomitant expansion of online connectivity, didn't just boost the internet's population, it also played a dramatic role in expanding the geographical reach of the online world. In 1990 the total number of internet users worldwide was estimated at less than three million people, with only a few hundred thousand of them outside the United States. The world's internet population would expand tenfold by the end of that decade, with the US portion dropping below half of the total for the first time. Today there are nearly two and a half billion people with internet access—a thousand times as many as there were in 1990—and barely 10 percent of them live in the United States. This transformation has profound implications for community formation online.

If early internet spaces had been largely conversational, the web facilitated the development of spaces that replicated the broadcast model of old media. These "one to many" sites existed to speak to an audience, not to converse within a community. Even in older spaces, moreover, increased membership often weakened community bonds. As Clay Shirky argued in 2002, at a certain size a community stops being a community and turns into an audience. Conversing transforms into broadcasting as "speaking to" turns into "talking at," while mutuality is replaced by particularity.

Yet even as the web appeared to diminish the internet's capacity for fostering community, the sheer volume of people going online provided new opportunities for those interested in connecting diasporic communities of individuals scattered or displaced from a previous shared homeland. Members of a diaspora share not only a common heritage and culture, but also common experiences of dislocation and of at least partial outsiderdom in their communities of residence. By fostering geographically dispersed communities among the diasporic, the internet facilitates both the reconstruction of community formations and the development of novel communities of shared interest and concern.

As the web saw the emergence of social networking platforms like Friendster, Myspace, and Facebook, a perception grew that the internet was becoming less a mechanism for strangers to connect around common interests or geography and more a place in which people focused on enhancing, expanding, or managing their preexisting relationships. As one researcher wrote in 2006 of his undergraduate students, "Rather than turning to the internet to become members of specifically online communities, they were using it as infrastructure to communicate with a geographically distributed network of friends and family" (Gochenour, 2006).

In 1997 Quentin Jones described an online community as a "virtual settlement" meeting four conditions: it must be interactive, must include more than two participants, must incorporate a common/public space in which its members can meet, and must provide for sustained membership over time (in Gruzd, Wellman, & Takhteyev, 2011). While this definition has undeniable value in exploring communities grounded in individual sites, it has less obvious applicability to the sprawling, open-ended online existence Gochenour describes above.

The days when internet content providers would simply set up forums or bulletin boards or chat rooms and wait for people to populate them ended in the early years of the new century. Today, the social media spaces that break huge tend to be flexible, customizable, and open templates within which people can create and play with a variety of environments—some lasting, some ephemeral, all fluid and malleable, and ideally interconnected with others. With the rise of these individualized spaces, the very concept of the social network has come in for reevaluation (Wellman, 2001).

As each new component of the online world has sprung into being, the older manifestations of online community have persisted. ARPANET was shut down for good in 1990, but listserves remain. Usenet is mostly a ghost town these days, but its structure lives on in a hundred thousand web forums. The current online world exists as an agglomeration of all its prior iterations, each existing simultaneously, all overlapping, and continuing to evolve.

Catching Up with Virtual Communities

In 1993 I was part of one online community: the AOL chat rooms. In 1994 I found another: the Usenet newsgroup "alt.folklore.urban," AFU, for the discussion of urban legends. My participation in AFU led me to an invite-only mailing list created by a self-selected group of the newsgroup's readers, and for years after that AFU and its private mailing list were my primary online homes.

Today, if you were to ask me to describe what my online home is, I'd be stumped. I'm on Twitter, with two separate accounts. I'm on Facebook, with six hundred friends and dozens of pages "liked," some active and some not. I've got a website that receives about a thousand visitors a day, some small percentage of whom leave comments. I read other people's blogs, and comment on their sites. I send and receive e-mails and texts, some of which, through embedded URLs, send me off to explore. Facebook manages the commenting systems of many blogs, facilitating serendipitous interactions with old friends in unfamiliar locales. I'm on an online dating site, I have a YouTube account, and I follow a few dozen Tumblrs when I remember.

And none of these are walled off from the others. Friends from the AFU mailing list comment on my website. I share links to blog posts via Tumblr. I stumble across blog commenters on Twitter, and friend them on Facebook. "Real world" connections lead to online ones, and vice versa—I honestly have no idea whether I first "met" some of my friends on- or offline, and for an ever-growing number of others, our first meetings in each sphere were essentially simultaneous.

It has taken internet researchers a while to catch up to these developments. I am by no means unusual in having had my formative online experiences in the discrete, bounded, purposive virtual spaces of the late twentieth century internet, and those experiences have provided researchers with a familiar framework for understanding online community. But today's online communities are unbounded. They overlap and blur and cross-pollinate. They include spaces that wink in and out of existence and others we visit intensely for a short time, then leave, then return to months later, picking up where we left off. All this means that the contours and boundaries of our online lives are increasingly personal, idiosyncratic, and unsettled. Some have argued that those online lives have been stripped of some of the richness of "true" lived experience, while others contemplate the possibility that, as they merge with the ones we live offline, they may come to more and more resemble our lives as we lived them before an online world existed at all (Wellman, 2001).

This suggests a second and perhaps no less important reason why it has taken community scholars some time to catch up to technological advancements. The newest social media platforms don't just blur distinctions between offline and online relationships, they trouble already sociologically baffling concepts like "friendship." On the first generation of social media sites—Friendster, Myspace, LiveJournal, Facebook—friendship tended to be fluid but largely reciprocal. The same decision that made you a part of someone's Facebook circle made them a part of yours. Now, with sites like Twitter and Tumblr, however, that reciprocality has been broken—I can bring you into my Twitter feed without the precondition that you bring me into yours.

Some people argue that by bringing people together in a public space in such great numbers, without the requirement of mutualism in their relations, services like Twitter permit "imagined community." Others worry over the continuing blurred distinctions between communities and audiences (Shirky, 2002.) Still others insist that tools such as hashtags and @ delineations on Twitter work in such a way to allow mass mediated audiences to coexist on the same plane as localized, narrow, often intense community affiliations, and immediate, intimate communal spaces.

And then there are those who note that offline communities too are working to create audiences on the internet, pointing out that because every bowling team and book club and protest action is now only a click away from having its own blog and Tumblr and Facebook page and Formspring profile, it's now possible for everyone with internet access to greet guests in their own personal online living room.

The Community Context of the 2009 Occupations

The students who staged the dining hall occupation at New York University in February 2009 had a variety of things in common. They were enrolled at NYU (for the most part, though some had come in from other local colleges). They were undergraduates, at least temporarily New Yorkers, and members of a more or less cohesive political left. Some of these shared affiliations had been expressed as personal relationships before the occupation began—through friendships, shared classes, organizational memberships. But they were not a discrete and uncomplicated community—some knew others well, others less so. Some collective values were widely shared within the group; others were more contested.

It was the occupation itself that made them into a physical community, albeit one with an ever-shifting membership (some activists left over the course of the occupation, while others on two occasions were able to make their way past police and campus security to join the group). And that community had as one of its first tasks the project of governing itself, establishing its responses to events as they unfolded, and communicating with the outside world.

Charlie Eisenhood would have, in other circumstances, seen himself and been seen as uncomplicatedly part of that community. He was, like the occupiers, a student. He shared demographic commonalities and many political and social commitments with them. But because he was in the room as a journalist, not an occupier, he was simultaneously a part of the community (like them hungry, worried, looking for companionship) and excluded from it (distrusted, excluded from meetings).

In a similar occupation forty years earlier, an earlier generation's Eisenhood would have been far more isolated. Cut off from contact with the outside world, able to observe but not report, he would have been dependent on the group's goodwill to a much greater extent, both practically and psychologically—bound to their community until he left their space and, returning to the campus paper's newsroom to write and file his story, reentered his own. Because of the existence of the online, however, Eisenhood was able not merely to connect up with his own preexisting communities (at his newspaper, among his friends, and beyond) while in the room, but to bring new communities into being in real time.

And while his presence complicated the occupiers' relationship with the university, the police, the media, and their student and nonstudent allies and enemies beyond the walls of Kimmel Hall, it also complicated the political narrative that cast the occupation as a single, unitary community of its own. When Eisenhood described disagreements among the occupiers, or even the varying ways in which they responded to him, he made their rhetorical posture of unanimity harder to sustain. At the same time, however, he served the function of humanizing and softening their presentation to an audience whose opinions might well be decisive in determining how the university and police were likely to respond to their provocations.

If the story of the February NYU occupation is the story of how a complex, amorphous, but largely singular community—the community of the occupiers, their supporters, and their embedded student journalist—can be created in response to a precipitating event, the story of the April New School occupation is the story of how widely disparate communities with little or no direct interaction can nonetheless powerfully influence each other, and of how that influence can be amplified by social media.

We know very little about the community that existed within the April 2009 New School occupation. They conducted their action largely behind closed doors, the handful of blog posts they sent out were sloganeering and exhortative, they created no livestream and posed for few photos, and they had no Charlie Eisenhood on board to create a public record of their brief time inside 65 Fifth Avenue.

If the NYU occupation was forced to reckon with the consequences of an action mounted in full public view, then the New School action illustrated some possible effects of a strategy of radical obscurity. No narrative voice emerged from their occupation, no first-person story, and so the crowds observing them in person and from afar were constructed as their audience, not invited to join their community. Where Eisenhood received nearly a thousand comments on his liveblog, the New School occupiers received just a handful. Several of those pled for connection—"what exactly can others outside to do to help," read one, and "IS EVERYONE OK?" read another—but none received any response.

Even as the occupiers stood disinclined or unable to foster a sense of community with their supporters and potential supporters online, though, members of other communities mobilized for their own purposes, and those mobilizations shaped the course of the occupation itself. A New School student newspaper rolled out a liveblog, as did my own StudentActivism.net.

At the same time, other communities roused themselves to connect on Twitter and Facebook. Passersby photographed arrestees on the street, confirming for remote observers that arrests were taking place long before the media reported it. Office dwellers shared photos of police attempting to gain access to the occupation from the roof, giving any occupiers and their supporters vital information about the developing situation.

They did so not to help the occupation, of course. They had no investment in the occupation and little interest in the occupiers or their cause. It's even likely that some of those who posted photos of the police on the roof would have refrained from doing so if the cops had asked. Rather, the photos were posted by individuals to their own social circles, and it's only because those postings were public (because, in turn, the boundaries of our communities are porous and blurred, which means that posting privately excludes friends as well as strangers) that they were able to be adopted and repurposed by others.

That repurposing isn't shocking to us from our vantage point in the twenty-first century. In fact, it's mundane. Our private lives are lived in semipublic now, and we anticipate and plan (imperfectly) for the possibility that what we create for our own communities will find its way to others. In the same way, we now regard the slippage between our online and offline lives as predictable and unexceptional. We can't always predict it, and we don't always like it, but we know and understand that cyberspace exists in the real world and vice versa.

This complexity, this blurring of the borders of community and the lines between the online and offline worlds, is nowhere more visible than in one tiny moment I mentioned in the introduction to this chapter. Alone at his keyboard, isolated from a group whose members had recently chastised and shamed him, Charlie Eisenhood blogged that he was hungry and cranky. In response, someone in the room—we don't know who, because Eisenhood didn't say—brought him a single vegan chocolate chip cookie and made him happy. Happy because he was a little less hungry, but also, it seems plausible to suggest, happy because he had been accepted, if only conditionally, into the occupiers' circle. Happy because he had been heard. Happy because he had, in some sense, been befriended.

Bibliography

Anderson, B. (1983). *Imagined communities: Reflections on the origin and spread of nationalism.* London: Verso.

Baym, Nancy K. (2000). *Tune in, log on: Soaps, fandom, and online community.* Thousand Oaks, CA: Sage.

Gochenour, P. H. (2006). Distributed communities and nodal subjects. *New Media & Society, 8*(1), 33–51.

Gruzd, A., Wellman, B., & Takhteyev, Y. (2011). Imagining Twitter as an imagined community. *American Behavioral Scientist, Special Issue on Imagined Communities, 55*(10), 1294–1318.

Jones, Q. (1997).Virtual-communities, virtual settlements & cyber-archaeology: A theoretical outline. *Journal of Computer Mediated Communication, 3*(3).

McMillan, D. W., & Chavis, D. M. (1986). Sense of community: A definition and theory. *Journal of Community Psychology, 14,* 6–23.

Miller, D., & Slater, D. (2000). *The internet: An ethnographic approach.* Oxford; New York: Berg.

Putnam, R. (2000). *Bowling alone.* New York: Simon & Schuster.

Rheingold, H. (1993). *The virtual community: Homesteading on the electronic frontier.* Reading, MA: Addison-Wesley.

Shirky, C. (2002, April 6). Communities, audiences, and scale. *Clay Shirky's writings about the internet: Networks, economics, and culture.* Retrieved July 29, 2013 from http://shirky.com/writings/community_scale.html

Stone, A. R. (1991) Will the real body please stand up? Boundary stories about virtual cultures. In M. Benedikt (Ed.), *Cyberspace: First steps,* 96–113. Cawmbridge, MA: MIT Press.

Wellman, B. (2001). Physical place and cyber-place: The rise of networked individualism. *International Journal for Urban and Regional Research, 25,* 227–252.

Wilson, S. M., & Peterson, L. C. (2002). The anthropology of online communities. *Annual Review of Anthropology, 31*(1), 449–467.

3

PRODUCTION, CONSUMPTION, AND LABOR IN THE SOCIAL MEDIA MODE OF COMMUNICATION AND PRODUCTION

Andrew Herman

I. Introduction: The Ubiquity of the Facebook Urge

In this chapter we will explore recent developments in the critical analysis of culture, media, and communication in order to construct a conceptual framework for understanding how social media technologies simultaneously constitute a *mode of communication* that creates symbolic value and sustains socially shared meaning, as well as a *mode of production* that creates material value or capital out of the symbolic value of meaning (Fisher, 2012). In so doing, we will highlight how social media embody contradictions between the imperatives of operating as modes of communication, on the one hand, and production, on the other, that illuminate the structures and relations of power that cohere around the activities of production, consumption, and labor.

In this first section we will evoke the central framing issues of the chapter that emerge from viewing Facebook and social networking sites in general as modes of communication and production (cf. boyd & Ellison, 2007). In the second section we will explore the different ways in which the critical analysis of media, communication, and culture have approached media forms and practices in terms of production, consumption, and labor in what I term the "mass media mode of communication and production." In the third section, we examine the emergence of the interactive digital media, the internet, and "Web 2.0" technologies. In conclusion, we briefly consider the impact of the mobile internet on the social media mode of communication and production.

The urge—indeed the necessity—of communicating to others about ourselves and lives on an everyday basis—and having such communication entail a reciprocal recognition—is a fundamental foundation of personal and social identity in the contemporary world (cf. Bauman, 2000, 2007; Giddens, 1991; Taylor, 1992; for the centrality of media forms and practices in shaping identity formation, see Couldry,

2012). Without such communicative practices, we would not have a coherent sense of who we are and would not be able to conduct ourselves in everyday life. At any given moment in the day, hundreds of millions of Facebook exchanges take place. An individual posts an image, comment, or link; the person's Facebook friends see it appear in their news feed; some take note and "like" it; some of these friends are motivated beyond simply signifying their pleasure to commenting on it, sparking discussion; and some share the original post on their own page, possibly setting the dynamic of communication and sociality into motion again. As mundane and ephemeral as such activities are, they comprise the primary reason why people inhabit the communicative space of sociality that Facebook as a platform, portal, and application interface affords its users. Facebook provides both the capacity and the opportunity for individual users to evoke and express their personal thoughts and feelings about the myriad discrete moments that comprise the ebb and flow of their everyday life to whomever they wish to include in their network of Facebook friends (privacy settings permitting, of course).

The point to keep in mind here is how ubiquitous Facebook has become as a social networking site in terms of being one of the dominant modalities of quotidian communication in the world. In its second quarter filings for 2012 to the US Securities and Exchange Commission, Facebook claimed it had 955 million individual accounts (although it admitted that upwards of eighty million may be "false") (Reuters, 2012). That is, if Facebook's numbers are reasonably accurate, almost one of every seven people on the planet has a Facebook account (Protalinski, 2012). Facebook dwarfs all other internet sites and social media platforms in terms of the amount of time people spend on the site: during May 2012, users spent an average of over 410 minutes per month, or about thirteen minutes per user day. Overall, Facebook accounts for one in every seven minutes spent online from every desktop or laptop in the world (Protalinski, 2011b).

As a paradigmatic social media form and practice, Facebook operates as a mode of making meaning (communication) that is deployed and structured to also make money (production). As such, it renders the power and freedom to communicate very contingent upon its technological affordances as code, protocol, interface, social network, and, last but certainly not least, a commercial enterprise that seeks to "monetize" our communicative sociality. Moreover, in our compulsion to be present on Facebook (as well as Twitter or Pinterest or Tumblr or Reddit) and to embrace its possibilities of communication and sociality, we run the risk of forgetting about the relations of power that determine whose property our communication and sociality is to command.

II. Production, Consumption, Labor in the "Mass" Media Mode of Communication and Production

Production. Consumption. Labor. These seem like foreign words and strange concepts to be associated with our everyday experience of social media. Considering the avidity with which we engage in social media practices and the pleasures of self-expression and sociability that are part and parcel of inhabiting their spaces, it seems incongruous to think of such activity as having such "crass" commercial dimensions to them. However, it is impossible to understand their psychic pleasures and social rewards without examining them through the lens of such concepts.

To understand the centrality of production, consumption, and labor to social media, we need to go back to a prior era in media history—that of the "mass media" of radio, television, newspapers, magazines, "Hollywood" film, and so on—that dominated media practices and spaces for most of the twentieth century before the spread of the internet, the World Wide Web, and other digital media forms.

As John Durham Peters (2010) points out, all media forms from the spoken word to the tweet have three essential elements that characterize their distinctiveness: a message, a means of creating and conveying that message, and a set of agents who create, convey, and consume the message. In other words, all media can be classified according to their "what," "how," and "by/to whom." In terms of defining the mass media,

> communication differentiates into distinct roles: content must adapt to the fact of addressing strangers; the delivery device multiplies both messages and opportunities of reception, the audience expands to include strangers, and content must be adapted accordingly. The relationship between participants becomes loosely coupled, distanced or otherwise problematic. Increased differentiation of author (who sends) from audience (who receives) is an artifact of the increased complexity of mass media. (p. 267)

This basic model of "mass media," as it emerged in the decades between the world wars, viewed communication as a distinctive process of transporting (in the case of print or film) or transmitting (in the case of broadcast media such as radio or television) media content in the form of discrete media artifacts unidirectionally from a central, singular source—such as a broadcast radio network or a major metropolitan newspaper company—to a broad audience of receivers of that content. In this framework there is a clear break between those who produce media content and those who consume it. Authors must address content to a generalized other of potential consumers and allow for a great deal of flexibility in terms of the spatiotemporal occasion of reception and consumption (i.e., the movie theater, car radio, or living room television).

What is missing from the preceding take on mass media is the consideration of "labor," which is provided by critical analysis of mass media and communication rooted, broadly speaking, in the Marxist tradition of political economy and cultural analysis. The critical analysis of mass media first emerged with the work of the Frankfurt School of Critical Theory, especially in the work of Theodor Adorno and Max Horkheimer (2007; Cook, 1996). Their contributions to critical media and cultural studies are many, but the concept of theirs that I want to deploy here is that of the "culture industry." Adorno and Horkheimer accepted the basic premise of the mass media model in terms of message, means, and agents. However, rather than looking at the world of film, radio, newspapers, popular fiction, and television as simply a world of popular entertainment, they emphasized the institutionally organized production of mass culture as a capitalist enterprise. The artifacts and experiences of mass culture were, first and foremost, commodities that were mass produced to be mass consumed by mass audience in order to maximize profit and the accumulation of capital by the industrial organizations—such as Hollywood movie studios, record companies, and radio and television broadcast networks—that governed their production.

For Adorno and Horkheimer, as well as for a generation of Marxist political economists of communication who followed in their wake in the last quarter of the twentieth century (Garnham, 1990, 2000; Markusen, 2005; Mosco, 2009), the *commodification* of communication and culture was paramount in understanding mass media as being constitutive of social relations of power in capitalist society. In essence, commodification is the very simple process of "transforming things valued for their use into marketable products that are valued for what they can bring in exchange" (Mosco, 2009, p. 127). Commodification, therefore, entails turning cultural practices into objects that can be sold for a profit.

There are three aspects of the commodification of culture and its organization along the lines of a capitalist industry that are salient for understanding just how radically different social media *appear* to be from the dominant mass media of the twentieth century: the first has to do with the impact of the organizational logic of the culture industry upon the form of cultural products (and, by implication, the subjectivity or "consciousness" of their consumers); the second has to do with the activity and "labor" of the audience; and the third has to do with the spatio-temporal dimensions of cultural production and consumption.

By subjecting the process and product of communication to commodification and profit maximization, the corporate organization of the media industry instituted what is termed a "Fordist" model of cultural production and consumption, a term based on the organizational logic of Henry Ford's assembly line method of mass production. Newspapers, popular fiction, movies, and radio and television broadcasts were subjected to economies of scale of mass production, producing standardized cultural goods *en masse* that, in turn, could be efficiently distributed to be consumed on a mass basis. Moreover, as with all capitalist industries from agriculture and extraction to manufacturing and finance, there is an inevitable tendency for the productive and distributive capacities of the media industry to be concentrated and centralized in fewer and larger corporate hands through the elimination of competing firms through acquisitions and mergers. This accumulation of corporate power over cultural production led to a proliferation of cultural commodities that, below the surface appearance of profusion and abundance, offered a smaller and smaller range of choice in terms of content and ideology (cf. McChesney, 2008).

One of the weaknesses of the culture industry analytic was the presumption that the consumers or "audiences" of mass media were passive in their reception and use of cultural commodities. However, in working through the logic of the commodification of communication and culture, the political economy perspective also addressed the question of audience activity in ways that are also crucial to understanding the social media as modes of production and communication. The political economy perspective's key and enduring insight in this regard involves the concept of the "audience commodity."

As originally developed by the Canadian communication scholar Dallas Smythe (1977, 1978), the "audience commodity" refers to the organizational processes of the media industries that turn the consumers of media content into commodities themselves. In Smythe's original formulation, the Fordist organization of mass media also entailed a parallel rationalization and colonization of "free" or "leisure" time of consumers. Broadcast television, in particular for Smythe, was organized around capturing the attention of the viewers as an audience during their non-waged or "free time" so that they could be packaged and sold to advertisers. The content of television programming, for Smythe, was literally immaterial to the way that television worked as a means of production and mode of capital accumulation. The content of any given show was simply a "free lunch" to entice viewers to watch advertising. Through ever more sophisticated regimes of tracking and measuring audience characteristics and viewing habits, media companies are able to turn the audience into a commodity that is sold to the marketers and advertisers (Bermejo, 2009). Moreover, Smythe argued, the audience commodity was the most important commodity produced through broadcast television as the programming commodity itself was subsidiary to the imperative of turning the audience into a product. The time spent in front of the television set, for example, *was not leisure but labor* as the audience worked to produce profit for media companies (by watching the programming) and their advertisers (by buying their products). Thus, watching time became work time to the extent that exposure to advertising could be turned into attention and desire for what was being advertised.[1] Mosco (2009) succinctly summarizes Smythe's analytical contribution:

> Media firms use their programming to construct audiences; advertisers pay media companies for access to these audiences; audiences are thereby delivered to advertisers. Such an argument *broadens the space* [my emphasis] within which media commodification takes place beyond the immediate process by which media companies produce [content] to include advertisers or capital in general. The process of commodification thoroughly integrates the media industries into the total capitalist economy not by creating ideologically saturated products but by producing audiences, en masse, an in specific demographically desirable forms, for advertisers. (p. 137)

One of the more important analytical innovations that emerged from Smythe's conceptualization of the audience commodity was an emphasis on the spatiotemporal dimensions of media production and consumption. At issue here is not simply the production of cultural commodities by media corporations, but the insinuation of the imperatives of commodification into the circuit of cultural production and consumption as a whole. Thus, implicit in the concept of the audience commodity is a distinct understanding of the spatial and temporal organization of mass media forms and practices.

Broadly speaking, in the Fordist model of twentieth century industrial capitalism, there is clear differentiation of places of work and production from the places and times of "leisure" and consumption (Antonio & Bonanno, 2000; Harvey, 1991). Denizens of the Fordist regimes of production and consumption go to the public world of work in one place for a circumscribed amount of time to return to the private sphere of home, domesticity, and neighborhood in another place for the rest of the day. Money was earned in one place and spent for consumption another.

The structure and flow of mass media forms and practices was organized around a parallel spatial and temporal logic, which John Thompson (1995) has termed the "structured break" (p. 23) between media production and reception in mass communication. Spatially, there is distinct differentiation between the places where television shows, newspapers, films, popular music recordings, and so on are created and assembled and the places where they are encountered and used by consumers. So, too, the moments at which such goods are consumed are differentiated as well. Mass-produced cultural commodities are produced in one particular set of places and times to be consumed at a very different set of places and times. Commodities circulate unidirectionally and linearly in terms of form and content from sites of production to sites of consumption, from producer to consumer, publisher to reader, and broadcaster to audience.

At the foundation of this spatiotemporal arrangement of media production and consumption—as well as the "labor" embodied in the work of the audience commodity—was the discrete separation of creators and authors of media texts, the texts themselves, and the recipients and consumers of those texts. Yet in order for mass media to work as successfully as a mode of communication and mode of production, there needed to be a structured dynamic in which the author, text, and audience came together in order to integrate the making of meaning and the making of money. In order to understand how this dynamic works, first in mass media and then in social media, I would like to introduce three new concepts into our conceptual apparatus: *articulation, assemblage,* and *flow.*

The concepts of "articulation" and "assemblage" have a very rich and nuanced philosophical grounding in critical theory and cultural studies, a full consideration of which is well beyond the scope of this essay (cf. De Landa, 2006; Taylor, 2009; Wise, 2012). Perhaps the clearest exposition of these two concepts can be found in Slack and Wise (2007). Their definitions of these concepts is meant to illuminate how all (media) technologies are material and cultural in composition, spatial and temporal in constitution, symbolic and psychic in meaning, and profoundly social as well as deeply personal in practice. "Articulation" refers to how the ontology or identity of any technology is "understood as the contingent connection of different elements that, when connected in particular way, form a specific unity" (Slack & Wise, 2007, p. 107). These elements include what we typically think of as being "technology" in terms of "material things," but also encompass discourses, narratives, ideologies, cultural values, organizations, and social practices, as well as states of affect and embodiment.

According to Slack and Wise (2007), the concept of assemblage adds depth to the structural connective tissue of discrete elements in an articulation by highlighting their spatial and dynamic quality. "The concept of assemblage," they write,

> might best be understood by thinking about the term "constellation." . . . A constellation of heavenly bodies like the Big Dipper, for example, takes a particular form: It selects, draws together, stakes out, and envelops a territory. . . . However, once drawn in this form, the constellation exhibits some tenacity; it doesn't simply appear and disappear. In this sense, then, an assemblage is a particular constellation of articulations that selects, draws together, stakes out and envelops a territory that exhibits some tenacity and effectivity. (p. 129)

We can now approach mass media as a dynamic assemblage that, for our purposes here, is comprised of two imbricated articulations. The first is the structure and logic of mass media that was laid out by Peters, that is, as a set of media forms and practices constituted by a particular relationship between message or content, means of channel, and agents or characters. Mass media texts are produced by strangers (media professionals) for other strangers (consumers) in a durable form that can be distributed and received in a variety of spatial and temporal contexts. The second articulation entails how this arrangement of message, means, and agents is governed by the organizational and financial imperatives of capital accumulation. Mass media texts are replicable commodities produced on large scale, subject to the logic of profit maximization, and characterized by a clear spatial and temporal differentiation between production and consumption. That said, the consumers of mass media are not passive recipients of cultural commodities, as they work actively to produce value as the "audience commodity."

The dynamic dimension of these mass media articulations as part of an assemblage that, as Slack and Wise say, "selects, draws together, stakes out, and envelops a territory" can be evoked by the concept of "flow." There are three registers of scale at which flow animates media assemblages. The first entails the way media assemblages organize the movement of cultural artifacts and media texts as part of what Manuel Castells (1996) has termed a coherent "space of flows" that is able to suture together what has been sundered by the "structured break" (Thompson, 1995) between the agents, places, and times of production and consumption.

Whether the means of movement is transmission (for television and radio) or transportation (for print and film), institutional actors must organize the flow of media texts as commodities to facilitate and maximize their purchase, reception, and consumption.

The second register of flow pertains to the creation of the audience through consumption of the texts and, thereby, creating the conditions for production of the audience commodity. In his classic work *Television: Technology and Cultural Form,* Raymond Williams (1974) deployed the concept of "flow" in order to understand how television was part of a larger articulation that he termed *mobile privatization,* whereby television, suburbanization, and automobility worked with one another to constitute the new consumer-citizens of the postwar Fordist era. For Williams, increased mobility between work and home via new modes of transportation (i.e., the automobile) and the separation and sequestration of the public sphere of work and the private sphere of the domestic lead to a "home centered way of living" (Morley, 2001).

The flows of the media texts and commodities (first register of flow) and of consumer-citizens (the second register of flow) run in tandem with one another and eventually converge in space and time, thereby giving the mass media assemblage its shape and tenacity. The former traces a path from sites of institutional production to sites of consumption, while the latter tracks the consumer-citizens from places of waged work to the very same places of consumption, where the domestic abode was—until the age of mobile media—paramount. In the spatio-temporal locus where the flows of commodities and consumers converge, there is a third register of flow that organizes the experience of consumption. Here, these flows become constituted as an apparatus of the capture of time (time spent watching television) and space (the living room or the family room or bedroom) when and where attention is fixed upon the screen and the "audience" as subject and agent is instantiated.

In other words, media texts, contexts, and consumers are organized so to maximize attention and engagement. For example, Williams argued that there was temporal logic to the way that the broadcast schedule of programing was organized to mirror the structure and activities of the everyday life. Daytime programming (melodramas, talk shows, game shows, etc.) was structured so as to be relevant to women in their domestic duties, and "prime-time" (news, drama, sitcoms, etc.) was intended to occupy the wage earners of the household and their family from dinnertime to bedtime (cf. Boddy, 2004; Spigel, 1992). As Oswald and Packer (2012) point out, these flows act as "a metaphor of movement in which audiences are moved through media content while their bodies are fixed in space" (p. 276). As media texts move through the household and across the screen, the viewers actively engage the texts while watching, becoming "audiences" that are commodified. Thus did the imbricated registers of flow of television as mass media comprise the territory of the suburban landed consumer and the ethos of the audience as commodity.

III. From Mass Media to Social Media as Articulation and Assemblage

With the emergence of social media as a distinctive articulation of modes of communication and production, each of the principal elements of the twentieth century broadcast model of mass media mode of communication and production—the Fordist industrial logic of production and consumption; the nature of "audience" activity and labor, and the spatiotemporal articulations of production and consumption as an assemblage with its specific registers of flow—become radically transformed. Or, at least, that is the way that social media is often characterized, celebrated, and studied. The extent to which such a characterization is warranted is the subject of the rest of the chapter.

The primary features of what we are calling the social media mode of production were first announced to the world in 2005 as the wonderful world of "Web 2.0" with great acclaim by internet millionaire and "evangelist" Tim O'Reilly and then enthusiastically affirmed by the digerati and the popular media. O'Reilly (2005) contrasted the internet and associated digital media forms as we had known it (Web 1.0) with the internet as it was coming to be (Web 2.0). Web 1.0 was characterized by a structure of the production and consumption of content that was very similar to the broadcast model, except that one "web surfed" from website to website rather than "channel surfed" from station to station (Johnson, 1997). In both cases, the content that was consumed was predetermined by the producer and exactly the same for every person who visited the site, just as it was for anybody who watched the same television show. The unidirectional relationship of power over content between "sender" and "receiver" was still predominant, although the internet browser allowed for considerably more "choice" in terms of variety of content and time of consumption than did the television, cable box, and remote, and one could move "hypertextually" through a multiplicity of links within and between websites.

In contrast, O'Reilly argued that new web-based applications and protocols—such as blogs, wikis, podcasting, "folksonomies," social bookmarking, photo sharing sites such as Flickr, video sharing sites such as YouTube, and, last but not least, the newfangled social networking sites such as Myspace and Friendster—created a rather different experience for the consumer/receiver. Web 2.0 is based upon an "architecture of participation" that increasingly allowed for the blurring of the boundaries between producer and consumer.

We cannot underestimate just how significant this purported transformation of the relationship between the agents of communication in terms of production and consumption (as well as sending and receiving) was in the popular imaginary of the internet and digital culture at the time. YouTube, one of the hottest new websites and applications of the first decade of the twentieth century, branded itself through the trademark slogan of "Broadcast Yourself." By the end of 2006, the image of the computer user as a creator of media content had become so widespread that *Time* magazine named the denizen of the brave new world of Web 2.0 "Person of the Year" (Grossman, 2006). Web 2.0 was considered to be as revolutionary and revelatory as, say, discovering a new constellation.

However, all hyperbole aside, there is no question that something significant was happening to the everyday experience of cultural production and consumption afforded by the technological capacities of digital media and new internet applications, which heralded the emergence of social media as a distinctive mode of communication and mode of production. All of the aforementioned Web 2.0 applications and platforms allowed individuals to play an active role in the circuit of cultural production and consumption in heretofore unique ways and, in so doing, reconfigured the dominant characteristics of the broadcast model of the culture industry.

One of the key academic texts of the period that helped to define these changes within critical media studies was Henry Jenkins's *Convergence Culture: Where Old and New Media Collide* (2006). Jenkins argued that the emergence of new digital media allowed for a "participatory culture" of media production and consumption that radically undermined the distinction between the traditional organizations that produced media content and the audience that consumed such content. "The term participatory culture," Jenkins (2006) wrote, "contrasts with older notions of passive media spectatorship. Rather than talking about media producers and consumers occupying separate roles, we might see them as participants who interact with each other according to a new set of rules that none of us fully understand" (p. 3).

It is important at this juncture to point out that the audience or spectator or readers of mass culture were never as passive as the culture industry analytic presumed. The field of cultural studies in large part emerged out of research into the myriad ways in which popular music subcultures, television news audiences, or readers of romance fiction (to name a few canonical examples) comprised a group of consumers who were very much active cultural agents in terms of interpretation and appropriation (mode of communication) of media content in everyday life (Fiske, 1993; Jenkins, 1992). In this regard, cultural studies is foundational in terms of understanding the social media as mode of communication *and* mode of production.

But the technological affordances of Web 2.0 apps and programs allowed for a set of quotidian media practices that extended the capacity of users to act as newly empowered cultural agents in materially significant ways. Jenkins (2006), Livingstone (1999, 2003), and Cover (2006) identified two principal axes of empowerment of the emergent social media mode of production: the first axis is that content *creation,* and the second is that content distribution. The increasing salience of "user generated content" in digital culture is evident across a variety of applications and platforms, where there are greater or lesser capacities for users to become content creators either as individuals (e.g., blogs, image macros such as LOLcats, chattel or avatars in MMORPGs) or in collaboration with others (such as FOSS, wikis, or social news sites such as Reddit). For some scholars such as Napoli (2010), however, the most significant reconfiguration of the power relationships between media producers and consumers was less about user-generated content (UGC) and more about the enhanced capacity of users to distribute content, whether it was created by themselves or by traditional media corporations (i.e., "pirated" software, music, film, television, etc.). The broadcast model of mass communication was characterized by a one-to-many relationship between sender as producer and receiver as consumer. With the emergence of the social web, we moved to a many-to-many (or select few to select few in the case of the "narrow casting" of YouTube; cf. Kim, 2012) dynamic of the circulation of media content. Be this as it may, the networked and interactive nature of the UGC process cannot be underemphasized. What is fundamentally different in the social media mode of communication and production is the fact that the text or artifact can be created, modified, supplemented, and appropriated as part of a dynamic process of interactivity and networked collaboration.

However, what these notions of Web 2.0, or participatory media culture, or "produsage" (Bruns, 2008) end to obviate in the elision of producer and consumer is the question of labor. The audience, as it was known and loved in the broadcast model of the culture industry, may have been displaced by what Bruns terms the "produser," but the activity is still very much a source of value to be monetized and accumulated as wealth and capital by new media corporations and the owners of social network sites.

Accordingly, some scholars argue that the figure of the producers of social media and their interactive labors should be seen as "co-creators" of value (see Arvidsson, 2008; Banks & Humphreys, 2008; Zwick, Bonsu, & Darmody, 2008). What does it mean to speak of the "co-creation" of value? In the mass media mode of communication and production, consumers seek pleasure and meaning in media commodities whose material parameters as artifacts are fixed. The activity of consumers is located primarily in the act of interpretation and contextualization of a cultural commodity that is "finished" in terms of its form and content. With the emergence of user-generated content where consumer becomes a producer, their agency entails the direct production of use and exchange value that is manifested in their social media (inter)activity. Of course, this creation of value does not occur *ex nihilio,* as the productivity and creativity depends upon the socio-technical affordances of the code, interface design, and extensibility of any social media app or platform. This interdependency of user and social media platform (and its owners) is one reason why Zwick et al. (2008), Arvidsson (2008), and others called the productivity of producers the "*co-creation* of value."

However, if one steps back from this rather obvious dimension of the "co-creation" of value though UGC by producers and attempts to locate this activity within the social media mode of production, then some deeper—and perhaps darker—dimensions of interplay of production, consumption, and labor in the world of social media become apparent. Co-creation does not solely inhabit the spatiotemporal configuration of this or that social media application or platform, such as Facebook or Twitter. Rather, it is one distinctive articulation within an emergent social media assemblage.

This assemblage is characterized by three discrete articulations that give rise to new dynamics of flow. First, as Andrejevic (2011) argues, digital media in general and social media in particular allow for ever-increasing "de-differentiation" between the space and time of work and labor and that of leisure and play. Melissa Gregg (2011), for example, has ethnographically examined the way in which the world of work increasingly invades and colonizes time and space away from the workplace per se. Second, with the emergence of UGC, the ontological distinction between the media text or cultural commodity and the consumer becomes increasingly irrelevant as the spaces and times of production and consumption converge to the point of collapse. Finally, as Fisher (2012) and Terranova (2012) argue, with the emergence of information-based capitalism, all communication increasingly becomes "monetized" and subsumed within the logic of capital accumulation. Every status update posted to Facebook, every hashtagged event circulated in Twitter, every avocation or hobby "pinned" on Pinterest, or every photo posted on Instagram become grist for the analytics of big data that serve to turn your social life into potential target market.

The next step in the evolution of the social media mode of production is its increasing mobility. In spite of all the affordances of Web 2.0, prior to the development of wireless internet connectivity and mobile internet devices such as the laptop, notebook, and smartphone, the internet was still was characterized by the static location of communication as production and consumption. With the internet gone mobile and wireless, as Oswald and Packer (2012) argue, the dynamics of flow shift significantly: the media environment is no longer devoted to keeping viewers fixed on one transmission but rather fixed in transmission through multiple screens that guide subjects through all of time and space (p. 277).

Note

1. The publication of Smythe's piece was followed by a long debate among media scholars as to whether or not what the audience did was actually labor in the traditional Marxist sense of producing "surplus value," or if it was simply a way of realizing surplus value produced elsewhere (cf. Jhally, 1982; Jhally & Livant, 1986; Livant, 1982). But one does not need to disappear down the rabbit hole of Marxist theories of surplus value to appreciate the insight that Smythe had about the central role played by audiences in the capital accumulation process aside from consumption itself (cf. Bermejo, 2009; Caraway, 2011; Meehan, 1984; Mosco & Kaye, 2000; Napoli, 2003, 2010).

Bibliography

Andrejevic, M. (2011). Social network exploitation. In Z. Papacharissi (Ed.), *A networked self: Identity, community, and culture on social network sites* (pp. 82–101). New York: Routledge.

Antonio, R., & Bonanno, A. (2000) Globalization, transnationalism, and the end of the American century. *American Studies, 41*(2/3), 33–77.

Arvidsson, A. (2008). The ethical economy of customer coproduction. *Journal of Macromarketing, 28*(4), 326–338.

Banks, J., & Humphreys, S. (2008). The labour of user co-creators: Emergent social network markets? *Convergence, 14*(4), 401–418.

Bauman, Z. (2000). *Liquid modernity.* Cambridge, UK: Polity.

——— (2007). *Consuming life.* Cambridge, UK: Polity

Bermejo, F. (2009). Audience manufacture in historical perspective: From broadcasting to Google. *New Media and Society, 11*(1–2), 133–154.

Boddy, W. (2004). Interactive television and advertising form in contemporary US television. In L. Spigel and J. Olsson (Eds.), *Television after TV: Essays on a medium in transition* (pp. 113–132). Durham, NC: Duke University Press.

boyd, d. m., & Ellison, N. B. (2007). Social network sites: Definition, history, and scholarship. *Journal of Computer-Mediated Communication, 13*(1), article 11. http://jcmc.indiana.edu/vol13/issue1/boyd.ellison.html

Bruns, A. (2008). *Blogs, Wikipedia, Second Life, and beyond: From production to produsage.* New York: Peter Lang.

Caraway, B. (2011). Audience labour in the new media environment: A Marxian revisiting of the audience commodity. *Media, Culture, and Society, 33*(5), 693–708.

Castells, M. (1996). *The Rise of the network society, the information age: Economy, society and culture Vol. I.* Cambridge, MA: Blackwell.

Cohen, N.S. (2008). The valorization of surveillance: Towards a political economy of Facebook. *Democratic Communiqué, 22*(1), 5–22.

Cook, D. (1996). *The culture industry revisited: Theodor A. Adorno on mass culture.* Lanham, MD: Rowman and Littlefield.

Couldry, N. (2012). *Media, society, world: Social theory and digital media practice.* Cambridge, UK: Polity.

Cover, R. (2006). Audience inter/active: Interactive media, narrative control & reconceiving audience history. *New Media & Society, 8*(1), 139–158.

De Landa, M. (2006). *A new philosophy of society: Assemblage theory and social complexity.* New York: Continuum.

Fisher, E. (2012). How less alienation creates more exploitation? Audience labour on social network sites. *tripleC, 10*(2), 171–183

Fiske, J. (1993). *Power plays, power works.* New York: Verso.

Garnham, N. (1990). *Capitalism and communication: Global culture and the economics of information.* London: Sage.

Garnham, N. (2000). *Emancipation, the media and modernity: Arguments about media and social theory.* New York: Oxford University Press.

Giddens, A. (1991). *Modernity and self-identity: Self and society in the late modern age.* Stanford, CA: Stanford University Press.

Gregg, M. (2011). *Work's intimacy.* Cambridge, MA: Basil Blackwell.

Grossman, L. (2006, December 25). You—yes, you—yre TIME's person of the year. *TIME Magazine.* Retreived from http://www.time.com/time/magazine/article/0,9171,1570810,00.html

Harvey, D. (1991) *The condition of postmodernity: An enquiry into the origins of cultural change.* Cambridge, UK: Blackwell.

Horkheimer, M., & Adorno, T. (2007). *Dialectic of enlightenment.* Stanford, CA: Stanford University Press.

Jenkins, H. (1992). *Textual poachers: Television fans & participatory culture.* New York: Routledge.

——— (2006). *Convergence culture: Where old and new media collide.* Cambridge, MA: MIT Press.

Jhally, S. (1982). Probing the blindspot: The audience commodity. *Canadian Journal of Political and Social Theory, 6*(1–2), 204–210.

Jhally, S., & Livant, B. (1986). Watching as working: The valorization of audience consciousness. *Journal of Communication, 36*, 124–143.

Johnson, S. (1997). *Interface culture: How new technology transforms the way we create and communicate.* New York: Basic.

Kim, J. (2012). The institutionalization of YouTube: From user-generated content to professionally generated content. *Media Culture Society, 34*(1), 53–67.

Livant, B. (1979). The audience commodity: On the blindspot debate. *Canadian Journal of Political and Social Theory, 3*(1), 91–106.

Livant, B. (1982). Working at watching: A reply to Sut Jhally. *Canadian Journal of Political and Social Theory, 6*(1–2), 211–215.

Livingstone, S. (1999). New media, new audiences? *New Media & Society, 1*(1), 59–66.

Livingstone, S. (2003). The changing nature of audiences: From the mass audience to the interactive media user. In A. Valdivia (Ed.), *The Blackwell companion to media research* (pp. 337–359). Oxford: Blackwell.

Markusen, A. (2005). Communicating political economy. *Review of Radical Political Economics, 37*(3), 269–280.

McChesney, R. (2008). *The political economy of media: Enduring issues, emerging dilemmas.* New York: Monthly Review Press.

Meehan, E. (1984) Towards a third vision of an information society. *Media, Culture & Society 6*(3), 257–77.

Morley, D. (2001). *Home territories: Media, mobility and identity.* New York: Routledge.

Mosco, V. (2009). *The political economy of communication* (2nd ed.). Thousand Oaks, CA: Sage.

Mosco, V., & Kaye, L. (2000). Questioning the concept of the audience. In I. Hagen & J. Wasko (Eds.), *Consuming audiences? Production and reception in media research* (pp. 31–46). Cresskill, NJ: Hampton Press.

Murdock, G. (1978). Blindspots about Western Marxism: A reply to Dallas Smythe. *Canadian Journal of Political and Social Theory, 2*(2), 109–119.

Napoli, P. (2003). *Audience economics: Media institutions and the audience marketplace.* New York: Columbia University Press.

——— (2010). Revisiting "mass communication" and the "work" of the audience in the new media environment. *Media, Culture & Society, 32*(3), 505–516.

O'Reilly, T. (2005). What is Web 2.0: Design patterns and business models for the next generation of software. Retrieved August 31, 2012, from http://oreilly.com/web2/archive/what-is-web-20.html

Oswald, K. & Packer, J. (2012). Flow and mobile media: Broadcast fixity to digital fluidity. In J. Packer & S. Wiley (Eds.), *Communication matters: Materialist approaches to media, mobility and networks* (pp. 276–287). New York: Routledge.

Peters, J. D. (2010). Mass media. In W.J.T. Mitchell & M. Hansen (Eds.), *Critical terms for media studies* (pp. 266–279). Chicago: University of Chicago Press.

Protalinski, E. (2011a, September 28). Facebook is destroying Google in time spent online (chart). Retrieved August 28, 2012, from *ZDNet* website: http://www.zdnet.com/blog/facebook/facebook-is-destroying-google-in-time-spent-online-chart/4183

Protalinski, E. (2011b, December 27). Facebook accounts for 1 in every 7 online minutes. Retrieved on August 28, 2012 from *ZDNet* website: http://www.zdnet.com/blog/facebook/facebook-accounts-for-1-in-every-7-online-minutes/6639

Protalinski, E. (2012, May 8). Smartphones beat computers for Facebook time. Retrieved August 28, 2012, from *ZDNet* website: http://www.zdnet.com/blog/facebook/smartphones-beat-computers-for-facebook-time/12705

Reuters.(2012,August 2).Facebook has as many as 83 million questionable accounts.Retrieved August 17, 2012, from *The Globe and Mail* website: http://www.theglobeandmail.com/technology/tech-news/facebook-has-as-many-as-83-million-questionable-accounts/article4457596/?service=print

Slack, J., & Wise, G. (2007). Culture + Technology: A primer. New York: Peter Lang.

Smythe, D. (1977). Communications: Blindspot of Western Marxism. *Canadian Journal of Political and Social Theory, 1*(3), 1–27.

Smythe, D. (1978). A rejoinder to Graham Murdock. *Canadian Journal of Political and Social Theory, 2*(2), 120–129.

Spigel, L. (1992). *Make room for TV: Television and the family ideal in postwar America.* Chicago: University of Chicago Press, 1992

Taylor, C. (1992). *Sources of the self: The making of modern identity.* Cambridge, MA: Harvard University Press.

Taylor, T. L. (2009). The assemblage of play. *Games and Culture, 4*(4), 331–339.

Terranova, T. (2012) Free labor. In T. Scholz (Ed.), *The internet as factory and playground.* New York: Routledge.

Thompson, J. (1995). *The media and modernity: A social theory of the media.* Palo Alto, CA: Stanford University Press.

Williams, R. (1974). *Television: Technology and cultural form.* New York: Routledge.

Wise, G. (2012) Attention and assemblage in a clickable world. In J. Packer & S. Wiley (Eds.), *Communication matters: Materialist approaches to media, mobility and networks* (pp. 159–172). New York: Routledge.

Zwick, D., Bonsu, S., & Darmody, A. (2008). Putting consumers to work: "Co-creation" and new marketing govern-mentality. *Journal of Consumer Culture, 8*(2), 163–196.

4

ART, PERFORMANCE, AND SOCIAL MEDIA

Toni Sant

Hamlet (Facebook News Feed Edition) (2008) written by Sarah Schmelling and photoshopped by Angela Liao is an excellent work to look at more closely in relation to the central focus of this chapter.[1] This is an example of internet art that involves performance and revolves around a social networking website in ways that are exclusive to the piece, which also exists outside the original social medium within which it was created. It employs elements unique to Facebook and similar social networking sites while juxtaposing others from diverse sources that include dramatic literature and online performance. This work also employs aspects of appropriation that came to the fore very prominently in conceptual and pop art during the twentieth century.

While Schmelling's take on *Hamlet* is not a live performance, it utilizes performative elements in presenting the main points of the play as a Facebook News Feed, which is familiar to all members of the world's most popular online social networking website. In collaboration with graphic designer Liao, Schmelling made it seem that William Shakespeare had logged on to his own Facebook News Feed, where the main characters and events in *Hamlet* appear in reverse chronological order. Even someone who is not a Facebook user, but familiar with the general plot and character of *Hamlet,* will instantly recognize that Schmelling and Lioa's collaboration have appropriated the main elements of the famous play. In this way, this work echoes the level of playfulness introduced to *Hamlet* on the internet by Stuart Harris and the Hamnet Players using internet relay chat (IRC) in the early 1990s (Danet, 2001). Further performative engagement with similar works on the internet is not uncommon, ranging from reinterpretations of live performance in online virtual worlds like Second Life (Sant, 2009, pp. 149–161) to the Royal Shakespeare Company's reimagining of *Romeo and Juliet* on Twitter in a 2010 production called *Such Tweet Sorrow* through usernames like @julietcap16,

@romeo_mo, and @LaurenceFriar, as well as webcam or phonecam video clips on YouTube by 94Juliet.[2]

In the latter half of the twentieth century, the general notion of performance was broadened beyond cultural presentations based on communal rituals to include personal(ized?) behavior as performance. This came about mostly through the influential work of Erving Goffman (1959) on the presentation of self in everyday life: a social theory presenting everyone as a performer and ordinary everyday situations as performances. This theory runs in tandem with the controversial argument implicit in conceptual art that everyone is (or can be considered) an artist. This idea was popularized by German artist Joseph Beuys (1975) insisting that creativity is all around us and not simply the purview of conventional artists. The democratization of art became a major issue in the art world in the latter half of the twentieth century.

By the end of the 1990s, with the rise of digital media technology, anyone able to get their hands on audiovisual equipment hooked up to the internet could potentially present works of art, with varying degrees of competence, to audiences hitherto unavailable to them. It was also possible for the creators of such works to add value to their creations through criteria that were no longer the exclusive domain of art impresarios, critics, or other figures of authority. Still, it took the institutions of art about two decades to start warming up to this concept enough to start embracing it fully. In 2010, the Guggenheim Museum collaborated with YouTube to organize a worldwide contest called *Play Biennial,* which was open to everyone.[3] This Guggenheim program now continues under the title *YouTube Play: A Biennial of Creative Video.*[4] This is a prominent example of how art and performance can reach new audiences through social media, but this aspect is only one way that the democratization of art has come to be an essential element of everyday culture.

Not all works of internet art or online performance involve social media. Both forms, however, employ considerable use of social media, particularly virtual worlds and social networking sites. While readers of this book will already be familiar with most of the virtual worlds and social media networks discussed here, the use of these online environments for art and performance has not yet reached mainstream audiences.

Performing in Virtual Worlds

The history of art and performance on social media goes back to the first years of text-based social networking platforms like MUD, MOO, and IRC. As I've pointed out elsewhere, an understanding of the histories of such work is highly useful in approaching similar work in the 3-D massively multiuser online role-playing games—commonly known as MMORPGs—that have evolved along with high-speed broadband connections and faster processors on computers (Sant, 2008). Online performance brings about an evaluation of the relationship between the designated performers and their audience, particularly the potential for interactive experiences and alternative narratives through improvisation. There have been further developments since then, primarily in the use of 3-D MMORPGs such as Second Life, World of Warcraft, and The Sims, among others.

This is just one aspect of the broader practice known as Networked Art, which predates the internet in terms of the interplay between performance/art and social media (Saper, 2001). Maria Chatzichristodoulou (2010) explains that the field of Networked Art has a specific performance format, which she proposes to call cybertheaters—a term borrowed from the Russian kinetic arts group Dvizjenije who used it in a different context in 1967. Cybertheaters operate in a range of "broad and diverse" environments and "other practitioners / theorists use different terms to refer to techno-performative practices"(Chatzichristodoulou, 2006). In the context of creative works discussed in this chapter, cybertheaters seem an appropriate way to classify this type of artistic pursuit. An alternative term is Desktop Theater, proposed by Adriene Jenik and Lisa Brenneis as both the name for their cybertheater company as well as the term for any "intentional theater-like activity [that] wafts through the layers of unintentional drama and surreal banality encountered in online visual chat rooms" (Jenik, 2001, p. 95). Interestingly, the term *desktop theater* was coined for works created in an online chat environment populated by 2-D graphics called The Palace: a short-lived evolutionary step between the text-based chat rooms that mushroomed throughout the 1990s and the rise of 3-D virtual worlds during the first decade of the twenty-first century.[5]

Avatars

When you first enter an online virtual world, your avatar—that is, the way you appear online—is the most important thing. Once you log into an MMORPG you instantly activate the possibility of being someone else, playing the role you have created for and through your avatar. The mechanics of any specific virtual world—its physics or game engine and expected or acceptable behavior—are the rules that enable you to operate within the online environment. Beyond this, whatever role you choose for your avatar is an identity performance. As digital artist Mark Stephen Meadows (2008) puts it, "A rule is a function of mechanics. A role is a function of theatre" (p. 34). The fact that Meadows, who is not directly involved in any of the performance arts, sees "theater" as an essential part of all avatars builds on the broader idea of performance in everyday life introduced by Goffman.

In attempting to understand avatar behavior in online virtual worlds, it is useful to distinguish between the two basic types of online identity performance: role-play and real-play. Most MMORPG avatars role-play. Most avatars have a different name than their user, but it most often still tells you something about the user, even if it reinforces the way a user wants to be perceived. This is also possible in text-based online virtual worlds. To some degree or other, the 3-D representation looks different from the person operating it, enabling the user to perform a role that is as close or as different from their known self as they make their avatar appear. By contrast, real-play involves avatars or other online representations whose name is identical to the one the user uses offline. With real-play, the avatar is usually as faithful a representation of the way the user looks in everyday life, as much as possible. To be clear, however, all avatars have the potential to enable real-play for their users. If an exchange based on ordinary reality occurs between Second Life players who know exactly who is behind the avatar they see on their screens, then the suspension of disbelief that is essential in successful role-play is disengaged temporarily to enable real-play between the users. In this way, the relationship between users and their avatars is similar to that between actors and their roles. For the sake of the user's mental sanity, it is essential to ensure that the role of the avatar in role-play does not take control of the user's life as a person. The cautionary tale for this can be seen on a large visible scale with celebrities and typecast actors, who are always seen as their constructed persona before they are seen for the person they are beneath the superimposed layers of identity.

It is significant to note that Second Life offers its users a function that most other 3-D MMORPGs do not or offer only indirectly: the possibility to create completely new or personalized narratives. This basic idea has attracted creative interest in virtual worlds since the days of text-based chat environments like IRC, MUDs, and MOOs, which were also designed as extensible spaces rather than prescribed gaming environments. Meadows (2008) sees this as a function of identity performance, claiming that "virtual worlds are interactive narratives, and the avatars are actors in a kind of street theater where the audience helps improvise the plot" (p. 67). The connection with street theater is a common observation for this type of activity (Danet, 2001, p.100; Jenik, 2001, p.100). More than this, without referring directly to it, Meadows invokes an established form of interactive performance established by Brazilian theater-maker Augusto Boal known as Forum Theater. In this form of theater, members of the audience are encouraged to become "spect-actors" and invited within the performance space to take over the role of the protagonist with the aim of changing the outcome of the plot. This is one of Boal's (1979) techniques in the Theater of the Oppressed, where theater is seen as a rehearsal for social change. Equally, "an Avatar can be seen as a rehearsal mechanism we can use to figure out the important stuff in real life" (Meadows, 2008, p. 72). This shows that this virtual world can be used to remodel offline experiences rather than just serve to model experiences from everyday life into Second Life and other extensible virtual worlds.

Playing with Identity

A distinction between role-play and real-play was made earlier in this chapter to say that in most online virtual worlds involving avatars in MMORPG environments, role-play is more common than real-play. The opposite is true, of course, on social networking sites like Facebook, Twitter, and others, with some interesting exceptions.

In picking a username on social media sites, most people don't think they are creating a fictional character but a version of themselves that is close to their true self, or at least an image of themselves they have for themselves and/or want others to see. Scholarly activity related to this aspect of social media is slowly growing. Two such studies (Birnbaum, 2009; Salimkhan, Manago, & Greenfield, 2010) cite Goffman as one of the basic theorists whose work informs such elaborations. It is fairly evident that the construction of a virtual self for online interactions is merely another iteration of the way we endeavor to present ourselves in everyday life. Conversely, to create a fictional character online, especially one intended to deceive others that this is not someone in role-play, is an exercise in what performance theorist Richard Schechner (1993) calls "dark play" (pp. 36–39), following anthropologist Clifford Geertz's (1975) elaboration on Jeremy Bentham's concept "deep play" (pp. 432–433). In this way, Schechner (2002) sees "much of role-playing over the internet" as a kind of dark play related to "assuming a new or alternative identity . . . masking, cloaking one's ordinary self" (pp. 108–109). The possibility of playing with our everyday identities is among the most intriguing facets of online performance. A famous *New Yorker* cartoon by Peter Steiner (1993) depicts a dog sitting at a computer terminal, saying to another dog, "On the Internet, nobody knows you're a dog" (p. 61). At a relatively early juncture in the spread of internet communication for social purposes, the cartoon highlights the possibilities of performing an identity other than one's own; you can be perceived to be as whoever you say you are online.

Social Networking Sites

Although Facebook became the most popular social networking site by the beginning of the 2010s, during the previous two decades a number of other social networking sites played a significant part both in the presentation of art and performance created elsewhere, as well as in providing a new channel for performance/art.

The earliest type of social networking sites were online forums or bulletin boards with threaded discussions on, most often, preselected topics. It was in this social media format, for example, that the work of performance artist Annie Sprinkle was first exposed online by fellow artist Frank Moore on a bulletin board system in the late 1980s, several years before it was possible to easily watch either still or moving images of her work (Sant, 2011, pp. 105–106). As with other media technology, adult entertainment and erotic art have led the way with innovation in social media, particularly in enabling other forms of art and performance to make use of the technology for other ends. When the first live online chat channels were incorporated into the sessions of live art on the internet presented by New York–based arts presenter Franklin Furnace through Pseudo.com in 1997, similar technology had already been in relatively wide use on sex sites for several months.

Even so, Pseudo.com started out in 1994 as the text-based chat service provider to subscribers of the now-defunct Prodigy online service. Within less than five years, it evolved from a text-based, multiple chat-room outpost to a multichannel video webcasting network. All this was based on experience that the organization's founders had with ChatRadio before Pseudo, wherein people on the 1050 AM frequency in New York City could text chat with hosts of live broadcasts. As audio and video delivery through the internet evolved, Pseudo embraced the new technology and positioned itself as the world's first internet-based broadcasting company. Within this new structure, Pseudo gave an online platform to a number of performance producers, via its Performance Channel. This went on until the company succumbed along with other web content pioneers when the so-called dot-com bubble burst at the turn of the century.[6]

Other related activities were also taking place at around this time, with considerably smaller corporate aspirations. The DIY culture inherent in authoring content for the web, the removal of a controlling intermediary in the form of a publisher, film director or television producer, camera crew, editor, and so on brings to the fore the drive for the democratization of art. The ease of duplication built into most digital technologies makes it possible to distribute ourselves as copies, making our mark, or at least leaving our trace, in places most people could not access as easily before the internet made it all possible.

Since 2000 most computers have come with standard plug-and-play USB ports. Webcams and other peripheral media devices are easily connected to computers through these ports. Many laptops and even desktop computers, such as the iMac, have had preinstalled webcams embedded in the screen frame since around 2005, making webcams even more ubiquitous. And now, almost all mobile phones are also cameras and in many cases capable of capturing video, often live broadcasting these images too. It is therefore understandable that photo and video websites have arisen as a multimedia subset of the broader reaching social media networking sites. The foremost sites in this category include Flickr and Picasa for photos and YouTube and Vimeo for video. Each of these sites has large numbers of art and performance-related stills or clips making it hard for creative endeavors of particular individuals to stand out above those of others, unless mitigated through older media platforms such as newsprint or broadcasting.

Prior to all this, back when online communities formed around bulletin board systems, members often included artists and performers, but it was with the rise of the World Wide Web in the early 1990s that creative activities came to the fore beyond the earlier forms of online social media. Howard Rheingold (1994) and Stacy Horn (1998), among others, have chronicled the stories of these pioneering online communities, which had names like The WELL and ECHO, in books that have since become classics of internet culture. The number of overall users involved in such activities was miniscule compared to the overall numbers on social networking sites like Facebook and Twitter a decade or so later. Nevertheless, while it can be argued that art and performance abound on these massive social networking sites, the level of engagement by both producers and followers is noticeably and understandably not at the same level of intensity as it was, and still is, on smaller networks such as deviantART.[7] Moreover, the commitment by those involved in the community contrasts sharply with that of specialized social networking sites for art and performance and the various wikis, blogs, and Ning sites created by and for specific subcultures or artists, performers, and their audiences, admirers, and imitators/emulators.

Participatory Art

Participation is an essential element for the survival and growth of social media. Through the new ways afforded by the internet to reach audiences that were previously inaccessible (or at least not as easy to reach), social media are predicated by the participation of the audiences in ways that are not simply based on action and reaction, but rather collective action as interaction.

By around 2009, most artists had come to realize that communicating with their target audience and loyal admirers was best done through online social media. Almost every artist now has a presence on one or more social media sites from Facebook and Twitter to Google+ as well as less broad reaching platforms, like Myspace, ReverbNation, and many others. However, very few make any special effort to interact with their fans. British singer-songwriter Imogen Heap is one who has integrated social media in her practice in remarkable ways. She has an active studio webcam connected to Ustream, maintains her blog with regular observations, photos, and videos while she is on tour, and encourages her fans to communicate with her by suggesting ideas for new works or simply to communicate with her. For her fourth album, she asked her fans to take part in the composition of the songs. This approach is known as crowdsourcing and forms the basis for the success behind projects like *Wikipedia* and other collaborative displays of collective knowledge.

On March 14, 2011, Heap asked fans through Facebook and Twitter to send in sounds from their everyday lives. Seven sounds of a match being struck came on the very first day so she decided that this was how the song would begin. Her brother sent her a heartbeat recording of her newborn niece Robin from his phone. The heartbeat was almost perfectly in time with a piano riff she had already written, and so she decided to speed it up slightly and merge the two together. Eventually she added the sound of someone's stove-top clicks, a bicycle, and other sounds. She then sang the first thing that came to her head as she played back the whole thing to her brother on her studio webcam. All this was established as the first part of the song. The next day she asked the fans to send in words for the lyrics. She combined some of these with the story of a man escaping the earthquake in Japan, which she read in a newspaper on that day. She also invited musicians to send her solos to consider including in the song; she received about four hundred solos. The result was a song called *Lifeline,* which she released on iTunes in April 2011, but it was also readily available through her website and via the social sound platform SoundCloud. Other songs followed in subsequent months toward the making of her *Heapsongs* album over a period of about three years.[8]

Fan Art

Another significant aspect of participatory creativity is known as fan art. This type of activity involves works created by fans based on established work they admire. It is also a large part of the creativity that can been commonly seen in social media environments. As Henry Jenkins (1992) has observed, fan art has "inescapable relations with other forms of cultural production and other social identities" (p. 3). This gives rise to work that deviates from the original in some way or other, sometimes subverting conventional sexual orientation, gender, or racial configurations. This extends the life of the original work well beyond that intended by its originator.

This type of creative activity is quite prevalent in social media environments and may seem to be the predominant approach in many cases. Close observation of fan art on social media sites brings up one of Marshall McLuhan's assertions in observing new media whereby any new medium that is still in its infancy takes some time to absorb the qualities of the proceeding media before finding and establishing its own aesthetic qualities. This is part of a process that Bolter and Grusin (1999) call remediation. Although media theorists like Lev Manovich (2001, 2013) have attempted to identify what aesthetic elements are unique/indigenous to the internet and the digital technologies associated with it, the medium is arguably not mature enough to enable the full identification of the essential qualities that make remarkable online performance/art different from works in other media. Is the internet just a new way to perform and make art, or is this a new medium with formal and aesthetic possibilities of its own? Particularly with social media, attempts to answer this crucial question cannot yield a satisfactory answer yet. It is not unlike what it must have been like to ask anyone to identify the aesthetic elements of cinema a century ago, before the significant contributions of filmmakers discussed by the groundbreaking theorists of film, including Arnheim, Eisenstein, Kracauer, and Kuleshov (Stam, 2000).

Blogging is one feature of the internet that is remarkably different from anything else in previous media forms. Scott Rosenberg's 2009 book *Say Everything: How Blogging Began, What It's Becoming, and Why It Matters* provides an interesting history of blogging, in its various forms, since 1994. As social media content becomes easier to produce, there is a tendency to forget what a significant impact blogging had on underground culture and the democratization of art before the rise of behemoth networks like Myspace, Facebook, and Twitter. Blogs, including formats before the popularization of the term, as well as photo blogs and video blogs, were the first accessible way for artists and performers to reach their online audiences without any significant intermediaries. It is this freedom to communicate as "solo bootstrappers of their own stream of self-expression . . . the least dependent on others to publish their words" (Rosenberg, 2009, p. 326) that places bloggers and blogging at the forefront of what is different with the internet from previous media.

Access for All

As a device for self-expression, blogging simultaneously provides a platform for writing and reading, both private and public, depending on the personal desires of the writers and readers. Above all, it moves away from previous broadcasting molds and offers narrowcasting as a viable model for audience interaction. Narrowcasting is a long-established variation on broadcasting. Various democratic countries encourage local governments to require local cable television operators to provide equipment, facilities, and channel space for public, educational, and government access on local cable systems as compensation for the cable companies' use of local rights-of-way such as publicly owned city streets and buildings.[9] In many cases, this applies to radio too. The primary resources for such public access services often come from cable companies, but city or county administration funds are frequently provided to strengthen the resources available for the access. This mass communication model consists of video programming produced on all creative and technical levels by community volunteers, sometimes assisted by trained professionals. Narrowcasting lets programmers target particular segments of their local community.

When done right, public access serves a wide range of individuals and community-based nonprofit organizations who do not have the resources, tools, or staff to fully utilize the electronic media. Their work usually benefits children, the elderly, the homeless, the disabled, immigrants, minorities, artists, educators, religious organizations, and others who are otherwise underrepresented in the mainstream commercial media. Within this framework, anyone with the time and inclination to do so can be a provider as well as a recipient of information, participating in a public debate via cable television. Many cable access facilities teach media literacy and video production through a pool of volunteers who create community-based programs and help others needing assistance. Most of them do it on a nondiscriminatory basis, at low or no cost. Video production facilities and equipment have been available for public use this way for quite some time, and now several such centers are upgrading their operations to include social media dissemination, particularly through channels on sites like YouTube and Vimeo. This work is now an essential part of ensuring that Beuys' declaration about the democratization of art goes beyond the equivocal rhetoric to truly enable anyone to make art.

Other Considerations

We can understand how the internet is different from broadcasting via other media by distinguishing between the technical terms *push* and *fetch*. The process of fetching involves a request for data from another computer or bank of computers. On the contrary, when data is sent without a request being made, whether directly or indirectly, the process employs push technology. Push was one of the internet buzzwords around 1997 when it was first being presented as a unique feature of new media technology that was entering the mainstream at that time. However, it is hardly ever mentioned now except perhaps as a setting on mobile devices. The concept is very prevalent in enhanced formats through portal integration, dynamic HTML, XML, and other developments in delivering a personalized online experience. The basic concept of push can be compared to the function of more established media technologies. Both radio and television broadcasting are built on a push model. Each channel pushes its programs to the listeners/viewers. For the most part, social media are based on a fetch model. A page or other content is usually not delivered until a user requests it, by adding a user as a friend or following someone's feed. The use of push technologies, however, is utilized to keep you updated with information over the internet, and for the delivery of e-mail and advertising. You receive e-mail and adverts whether you ask for them or not. Nevertheless, the concept of push is establishing an ever-growing presence in social media, and this is certainly not outside the realm of art and performance.

In 2011, for a hip-hop version of Shakespeare's *Much Ado About Nothing* by the Q Brothers called *Funk It Up About Nothin'*, on a wide-ranging tour that started at the Chicago Shakespeare Theatre (January–February 2011) and ended at the Royal Stratford East in London (April 2011), the Q Brothers actively encouraged their audiences to keep their mobile phones on and use them during the show.[10] For this performance, audience members were invited to use a special hashtag to post their comments so that performers could respond live online and in person at the theater. This most certainly flies in the face of conventional live theater where actors and other performers have always considered phones and other mobile devices an undesirable presence in the theater. London newspaper the *Evening Standard* (Tuesday, April 12, 2011) reported Stratford East's artistic director Kerry Michael saying this was a move against the "formal and stale" air that theatergoing has commonly acquired over the years.

In other ways, this can also be seen as another nod in the direction of the democratization of art. This level of engagement can eventually lead to what can be considered a dematerialization not just of art but also of the originating artist. The long history of fakes, forgeries, and imitations in art has come to a point where not only the work can be passed on as made by an established artist but also the artist themselves can be impersonated to a high level of credibility. A clear example of this can be seen in the evolution of a work of art called *Truisms* by visual artist Jenny Holzer. This work was originally exhibited as a large poster at

Franklin Furnace in New York, in 1978. The poster contained a long list of truisms such as "abuse of power comes as no surprise," "boredom makes you do crazy things," "eating too much is criminal," and "even your family can betray you." In 1995, Holzer made a web project based on this artwork. She called it *Please Change Beliefs* and invited internet users to alter her list of truisms by leaving comments for her and other online visitors to read. More than ten years later, this was available online as part of äda'web, an online art project established in February 1995 to provide contemporary artists with a station from which they can engage in a dialogue with internet users.[11] On May 30, 2007, Holzer's *Truisms* was developed for yet another electronic platform: Twitter. The now iconic phrases and variations on them gathered since *Please Change Beliefs* were now open to Twitter users to forward (with or without comments or alterations) or reply to the @jennyholzer Twitter profile with appropriate or inappropriate responses.[12] Jenny Holzer did not create this Twitter account, nor does she control it or seem to mind that it exists.[13] It also had more than 34,500 followers by the end of 2011, which is most certainly more than ever saw it when it was first displayed at Franklin Furnace in 1978, and most likely far more than the number of people who engaged with it through äda'web.

Although quite peculiar in its engagement of social media, this work clearly involves the input, albeit indirectly, of a professional artist, who had already established herself outside social media, feeding on genealogies of performance and art history, which can be traced back in time. It is also fan art. Following the frameworks established by Goffman and Beuys, art and performances created by ordinary people contrast starkly in terms of their history. Is this the mark of a radical shift in the production and dissemination of art and performance? Has the lowering of cost and skill barriers signaled the arrival of a new chapter in art and performance history where patrons matter less than they ever did and carefully honed skills are no longer a necessary prerequisite for the communication of creativity? Is the relative democratization of dissemination a significant game changer with what art and performances reach audiences that they previously could not and would not reach? Or is this just the next step in the gradual evolution of reality television, from the favorite home movies shows all the way to elevating ordinary people to celebrities, where they are merely known for being famous and not for any other particularly notable quality?

As we have seen, social media is part of the mode of production and dissemination for art and performance. While the production part is an almost inevitable element of the creative process, the dissemination aspect has more in common with other modes of communication. Twitter and Facebook provide ways for communities to communicate with each other easily over a distance and collectively without necessarily excluding others who may want, or may be wanted, to join in. Several major museums, to mention just one instance of this practice, now rely on social media to expand their audiences and maintain interest in their permanent or touring collections. However, it is not unlikely that as the networks become more and more crowded with undesirables, from people to adverts, better-filtered social media will be the platforms of choice for like-minded producers and consumers of art and performance to gather for further explorations into the various forms of creativity.

Notes

1. Available at http://www.angelfire.com/art2/antwerplettuce/hamlet.html.
2. See www.suchtweetsorrow.com (accessed October 30, 2011).
3. See www.youtube.com/user/playbiennial (accessed October 30, 2011).
4. See www.guggenheim.org/new-york/interact/participate/youtube-play (accessed October 30, 2011).
5. For more about The Palace, see Jim Bumgardner, "Palace Stuff," available at www. jbum.com/palacestuff.html. See also www.thepalace.com (both websites accessed October 30, 2011).
6. For a history of Pseudo Programs Inc., see Sant (2011), pp. 118–120. For a broader context on the collapse of the information economy at the end of the twentieth century, see Lowenstein, R. (2004). *Origins of the crash: The great bubble and its undoing*. New York: Penguin Press; see also Abramson, B. (2005). *Digital phoenix: Why the information economy collapsed and how it will rise again*. Cambridge, MA: MIT Press.
7. Available at www.deviantart.com (accessed October 30, 2011).
8. See www.imogenheap.com/heapsongs/ (accessed October 30, 2011).
9. In the United States, the federal Cable and Telecommunications Acts of 1984, 1992, and 1996 provide for this. The Alliance for Community Media, a resources advocacy organization for community-based media access active since 1976, reports that through cable TV access centers, thousands of community groups and over one million individuals produce more than twenty thousand hours of new local programming each week in the United States: this amounts to more than all programs produced by the four major networks (CBS, NBC, ABC, and Fox) and PBS combined. See www. alliancecm.org (accessed October 30, 2011).
10. See http://www.chicagoshakes.com/funk (accessed October 30, 2011).
11. The project is archived through the website of the Walker Art Center in Minneapolis, Minnesota—http://adaweb.walkerart.org (accessed October 30, 2011).
12. See http://www.twitter.com/jennyholzer (accessed October 30, 2011).
13. This was revealed in October 2008 by Kathryn Born, Chicago correspondent for the blog *Bad at Sport*. See http://badatsports.com/2008/jenny-holzer-is-not-on-twitter-kathryn-born-does-actual-investigative-journalism/ (accessed October 30, 2011).

Recommended Readings

Chatzichristodoulou, M., Jefferies, J., & Zerihan, R. (Eds.). (2009). *Interfaces of Performance*. Farnham, UK: Ashgate.

Danet, B. (2001). *Cyberpl@y: Communicating Online*. Oxford: Berg.

Dixon, S. (2007). *Digital Performance: A History of New Media in Theater, Dance, Performance Art, and Installation*. Cambridge, MA; London: MIT Press.

Garde-Hansen, J., Hoskins, A., & Reading, A. (Eds.). (2009). *Save as . . . Digital Memories*. Basingstoke, UK: Palgrave Macmillan.

Graham, B., & Cook, S. (2010). *Rethinking Curating: Art after New Media*. Cambridge, MA; London: MIT Press.

Jenik, A. (2001). Desktop Theater Keyboard Catharsis and the Masking of Roundheads. *The Drama Review, 45*(3), 95–112.

Sant, T. (2011). *Franklin Furnace and the Spirit of the Avant-Garde: A History of the Future.* Bristol, UK: Intellect.

Saper, C. J. (2001). *Networked Art.* Minneapolis: University of Minnesota Press.

Schmelling, S. (2009). *Ophelia Joined the Group Maidens Who Don't Float: Classic Lit Signs on to Facebook.* Plume.

Schrum, S. A. (Ed.). (1999). *Theatre in Cyberspace: Issues of Teaching, Acting and Directing.* New York: P. Lang.

Senft, T. M. (2008). *Camgirls: Celebrity & Community in the Age of Social Networks.* New York; Oxford: P. Lang.

Turkle, S. (1997). *Life on the Screen: Identity in the Age of the Internet* (1st ed.). New York: Simon & Schuster.

Walser, R. (1991). Elements of a Cyberspace Playhouse. In S. K. Helsel & J. P. Roth (Eds.), *Virtual Reality: Theory, Practice, and Promise* (pp. 51–64). Westport, CT: Meckler.

Bibliography

Beuys, J. (1975). *Jeder mensch ein kunstler.* Berlin: Ullstein Buchverlage GmbH.

Birnbaum, M. G. (2009). *Taking Goffman on a Tour of Facebook: College Students and the Presentation of Self in a Mediated Digital Environment.* (Doctoral dissertation). University of Arizona, Tucson, AZ.

Boal, A. (1979). *The Theatre of the Oppressed.* London: Pluto Press.

Bolter, J. D., & Grusin, R. A. (1999). *Remediation: Understanding New Media.* London: MIT Press.

Chatzichristodoulou, M. (2006). Cyber Theaters: Emergent, Hybrid, Networked Performance Practices. In *Sklunk!* Available at http://www.sklunk.net/cybertheaters (accessed October 30, 2011).

Chatzichristodoulou, M. (2010). *Cybertheaters: Emergent Networked Performance Practices.* (Doctoral dissertation). Goldsmiths, University of London.

Danet, B. (2001). *Cyberpl@y: Communicating Online.* Oxford: Berg.

Geertz, C. (1975). *The Interpretation of Culture: Selected Essays.* London: Hutchinson.

Goffman, E. (1959). *The Presentation of Self in Everyday Life.* New York: Doubleday Anchor Books.

Horn, S. (1998). *Cyberville?: Clicks, Culture, and the Creation of an Online Town.* New York: Warner Books.

Jenik, A. (2001). Desktop Theater Keyboard Catharsis and the Masking of Roundheads. *The Drama Review, 45*(3), 95–112.

Jenkins, H. (1992). *Textual Poachers: Television Fans and Participatory Culture.* London: Routledge.

Manovich, L. (2001). *The Language of New Media.* Cambridge, MA: MIT Press.

Manovich, L. (2013). *Software Takes Command.* London: Bloomsbury Academic.

Meadows, M. S. (2008). *I, Avatar: The Culture and Consequence of Having a Second Life.* Berkeley, CA: New Riders.

Rheingold, H. (1994). *The Virtual Community: Finding Connection in a Computerized World.* London: Secker & Warburg.

Rosenberg, S. (2009). *Say Everything: How Blogging Began, What It's Becoming, and Why It Matters.* New York: Three Rivers Press.

Salimkhan, G., Manago, A., & Greenfield, P. (2010). The Construction of the Virtual Self on MySpace. *Cyberpsychology: Journal of Psychosocial Research on Cyberspace* 4 (1). Available at http://cyberpsychology.eu/view.php?cisloclanku=2010050203&article=1

Sant, T. (2008). A Second Life for Online Performance: Understanding Present Developments Through an Historical Context. *International Journal of Performance Arts and Digital Media, 4*(1), 69–79.

Sant, T. (2009). Performance in Second Life: Some Possibilities for Learning and Teaching. In J. Molka-Danielsen & M. Deutschmann (Eds.), *Learning and Teaching in the Virtual World of Second Life*. Trondheim, Norway: Tapir Academic Press.

Sant, T. (2011). *Franklin Furnace & the Spirit of the Avant-Garde: A History of the Future.* Bristol, UK: Intellect; Chicago: University of Chicago Press.

Schechner, R. (1993). *The Future of Ritual: Writings on Culture and Performance.* London: Routledge.

Schechner, R. (2002). *Performance Studies: An Introduction.* London: Routledge.

Stam, R. (2000). *Film Theory: An Introduction.* Malden, MA: Blackwell.

Steiner, P. (1993, July 5). On the Internet, Nobody Knows You're a Dog (cartoon). *The New Yorker, 69*(20), 61.

5

GENDER, SEXUALITY, AND SOCIAL MEDIA

Alice Marwick

Introduction

Julia Allison (real name: Julia Allison Baugher) is a twenty-nine-year-old blogger and personality who describes herself as "personally and professionally a handful." She rose to micro-fame as the dating columnist for *Time Out New York,* barraged the media gossip blog *Gawker* into covering her social life, and is now a syndicated columnist with the *Chicago Tribune.* Although Allison is not a technologist, she is a fixture at New York and San Francisco tech parties and conferences, and appeared on the cover of *Wired* to illustrate their story on internet fame. She is also a "professional talking head" and has appeared on hundreds of cable news programs, talk shows, and radio programs. Allison is primarily known for blogging continuous photographs, links, and tweets about herself, and chronicling her love life, social events, insecurity, issues with friends and family, and travel. She presents herself as very attractive and usually appears in photographs with full makeup, a dress, and her fluffy white dog. The bio on her website states:

> Julia has a Facebook account, a Myspace page, a Flickr, a Twitter, a Friend-feed, four Tumblrs, three Movable Type blogs, two Vimeos, one YouTube and a photogenic white shih-tzu named Marshmallow.[1] (Allison, 2009)

Allison's fame has resulted primarily from sharing intimate, personal information through social media. As Paris Hilton achieved fame by manipulating celebrity tabloids and gossip television, Julia Allison has become famous by leveraging Web 2.0 technologies.

Allison also receives a staggering amount of negative attention, mostly focused on her personal life, looks, and weight. A blog called *Reblogging NonSociety,*[2] founded in January 2009, responds almost daily to every piece of content Julia posts. It refers to her as "Donkey" and describes her as "[an] annoying piece of internet trash" and "another dumb trashy gold digger with a Tumblr" (Juliaspublicist, 2010; Partypants, 2010). Allison was named the third "Most hated person on the Internet" by *Radar* magazine, and *Gawker* wrote a vitriolic "Field Guide to Julia Allison" that poked fun at her popularity and sex life. The hatred shown toward Julia seems so out of proportion to her actual activities that *Gawker* eventually questioned the motives of the individuals behind the *Reblogging* site (Lawson, 2010a, 2010b). Maureen Henderson, after profiling Julia for *Forbes,* found the many negative comments on her story similarly inexplicable: "The idea that someone folks are calling a 'fraud' and an 'awful person' still merits a website focused on bashing her even as readers reiterate that she lacks substance or career success is just so damn weird in a Web 2.0 way" (Henderson, 2011).

Julia's detractors claim the negativity—which has included calling and e-mailing Julia's boyfriends, employers, and family members—is justified because Allison is a singularly awful person and a noxious representative of the worst of Web 2.0. Wendy Atterberry (2010) summed up on the popular women's blog *The Frisky:*

> Julia represents so much of what is icky about blogging and social networking. She is shamelessly narcissistic and vain, having posted thousands of photos of herself over the years and staging incredible, over-the-top "photo shoots" simply to post on her blog. . . . She's utterly obnoxious, and in a time when so many people are hurting financially, she gloats about expensive non-stop vacations, exorbitant gifts from boyfriends, and how many homes her parents own. It's gross.

Much of the hatred leveraged against Allison is rooted in expectations of appropriate behavior on social media. Allison uses the logics of celebrity culture to project a strategically "feminine" persona by sharing highly personal information and using digital imagery and reoccurring identity markers. However, she is working within a deeply gendered context that privileges "masculine" behaviors and closely polices female self-presentation. Social media technologies like Twitter, Foursquare, Facebook, and YouTube are spaces and tools that facilitate communication. Rather than presuming these technologies to be gender neutral, scholarship has demonstrated that information technologies can perpetuate norms of masculinity, business, and engineering (Hofmann, 1999; Kendall, 2002). Gender is produced and reproduced in social media both by software and the user interaction that takes place online. Looking at online communication as *gendered* reveals patterns in the types of communication that are encouraged and discouraged. Understanding how Julia uses social media to produce a gendered identity can help to explain some of the negativity she experiences, demonstrating how social media both *reflects* and *produces* gender.

Understanding Sex and Gender

While the terms "sex," "gender," and "sexuality" are often thought of as synonymous, they are actually quite distinct. The differences between the common understandings of these terms and how researchers think about them yields key insights about the social functioning of gender.

Sex is the biological state that corresponds to what we might call a "man" or a "woman." This might seem to be a simple distinction, but the biology of sex is actually very complicated, as chronicled by biologist Anne Fausto-Sterling. Fausto-Sterling (2000) argues that the binary system in which everyone's sexual organs neatly fit into one of two categories is deeply influenced by our social understanding of gender. Because conventional conceptions of gender are binary, the type of liminality represented by, say, hermaphroditism is hard to understand. We expect a pregnancy to result in a boy or a girl, or for someone to be a man *or* a woman. For people to inhabit both, or neither, of those two spaces is highly threatening to social order. While "sex" is often explained as biological, fixed, and immutable, it is actually socially constructed (West & Zimmerman, 1987).

"Gender," then, is the social understanding of how sex should be experienced and how sex manifests in behavior, personality, preferences, capabilities, and so forth. A person with male sex organs is expected to embody a masculine gender. While sex and gender are presumed to be biologically connected, we can understand gender as a socioculturally specific set of norms that are mapped onto a category of "sex" (Kessler & McKenna, 1978; Lorber, 1994). Gender is historical. It is produced by media and popular culture (Gauntlett, 2008; Van Zoonen, 1994). It is taught by family, schools, peer groups, and nation-states (Goffman, 1977). It is reinforced through songs, sayings, admonition, slang, language, fashion, and discourse (Cameron, 1998; Cameron & Kulick, 2003). And it is deeply ingrained. The violence, discrimination, and hatred shown toward transgendered individuals, people who experience disconnection between their biological sex and their gender, demonstrates that understanding gender as changeable or liminal threatens many assumptions considered biological or "natural" (Stryker, 2006).

Gender is a system of classification that values male-gendered things more than female-related things. This system plays out on the bodies of men and women and in constructing hierarchies of everything from colors (pink vs. blue) to academic departments (English vs. Math) to electronic gadgets and websites. Given this inequality, the universalized "male" body and experience is often constructed as average or normal, while female-gendered experiences are conceptualized as variations from the norm (Goffman, 1977). Technology has been criticized for this *male normativity* due to the disproportionate number of men and women involved in technical design and engineering (Faulkner, 2000; Hossfeld, 1990). Similarly, *heteronormativity* is the presumption of heterosexuality unless explicitly stated otherwise. Valuing some experiences as normal or natural, while stigmatizing others as pathological or deviant, is the process of establishing and maintaining social norms. *Normative* gender behavior is that which adheres to the dominant understanding of masculine men and feminine women; nonnormative behavior does not follow these social scripts (Shapiro, 2010).

"Sexuality" is an individual expression and understanding of desire. While, like gender, this is often viewed as binary (homosexual *or* heterosexual), in reality sexuality is often experienced as fluid. Bisexuality, pansexuality, and other forms of desire are often marginalized or written out of mainstream discourse, but they certainly exist (Sedgwick, 2008). The term "queer" can be used as an umbrella term for nonnormative expressions of sexuality, including practices like polyamory and BDSM. While queer is often used as a synonym for "gay or lesbian," it is decidedly not the same (Bristow, 1997). The popularity of queer as an umbrella term is in part driven by a desire to reject the confines of a strictly binary approach to male/female or gay/straight identity.

Despite extensive research undermining the binary concept of gender and framing gender as a social construction (Crawley, Foley, & Shehan, 2008; Goffman, 1977; Kessler & McKenna, 1978; Lorber, 1994), dominant discourses around gender and sexuality tend to a model in which sex and gender are fixed, unchanging, intimately intertwined, and based on biology.

Performing Gender Online

The theorist Judith Butler (1990) conceptualized gender as a performance. She maintained that popular understandings of gender and sexuality came to be through discourse and social processes. She argued that gender was *performative*, in that it is produced through millions of individual actions, rather than something that comes naturally to men and women. A woman sashaying down the street wearing high heels is performing femininity (as is a drag queen doing the same thing). Performances that adhere to normative understandings of gender and sexuality are sanctioned, while those that do not are admonished (for example, a boy "throwing like a girl") (Lorber, 1994).

In the 1990s, many internet scholars drew from Butler and other queer theorists to understand online identity. Academics like Sandy Stone (1996) and Sherry Turkle (1995) were fascinated by the idea that online spaces, like multiuser text games, bulletin boards, and chat rooms, made it possible for people to communicate without corporeal cues like appearance or voice. The *disembodiment hypothesis* held that internet users, liberated from the constraints of the flesh, would actively choose which gender or sexuality to "be," possibly creating alternate identities nothing like their own (Wynn & Katz, 1997). The ability of users to self-consciously adopt and play with different gender identities would reveal the choices involved in the production of gender, breaking down binaries and encouraging fluidity in sexuality and gender expression. As Sherry Turkle (1995) has written, "like transgressive gender practices in real life, by breaking the conventions, [online gender play] dramatizes our attachment to them" (p. 212).

Donna Haraway's (1985) cyborg emerged as the preferred metaphor of this new way of looking at identity. Her widely cited essay "A Manifesto for Cyborgs" conceptualized *the cyborg subject,* a new way of being and thinking about oneself that incorporated both "nature" and "technology." Rather than seeing the two concepts as intrinsically opposed, the cyborg simultaneously embodied both, proving the dichotomy false. Haraway's cyborg was a complicated political move that allowed the creation of other types of subject positions that were rooted in strategic commonality rather than biology, such as "queer politics" or "women of color."

Haraway's cyborg was widely adopted by a branch of unrelentingly positive cyber-theory (Kirkup et al., 2000; Terry & Calvert, 1997; Wolmark, 1999). *Cyborg feminism* (also known as cyberfeminism) argued that "technoscience" was potentially liberating for women, even to the extent that technical prostheses could be used to enhance their capabilities. Some cyberfeminists held that technologies like the internet were intrinsically suited to women's ways of thinking and being (Plant, 1998). This body of theory was a reaction to a strain of 1970s and 1980s feminism that maintained that Western computer technologies were intrinsically patriarchal, embodying masculine ideologies, and often leveraged by men to control women. Cyborg feminists instead argued that contemporary technology, particularly the internet, could be a space for organizing, theorizing, sharing experiences, and understanding oneself with tremendous potential for women (Wajcman, 2007). These *cyberfeminists* depended on an essentialist view of male and female capabilities, in that community building and nurturing were portrayed as something women are inherently good at (Van Zoonen, 2001).

This essentialist view of gender and technology still surfaces every once in a while. For example, claims that women's participation in Facebook is due to their superior multitasking or social skills may seem better than its alternative (e.g., women are unsuited to complex technical work), yet they still perpetrate an understanding of gender differences as innate and rooted in biological and psychological underpinnings.

Rather than taking an essentialist position, contemporary gender theorists focus on behavior that is encouraged, discouraged, rewarded, or prohibited and how it maps to ideal understandings of "men," "women," "feminine," and "masculine" (and evaluations like "stud," "slut," "queer," "tranny," and so forth). In other words, in particular environments, certain behavior in women is *encouraged* while the same behavior in men is *discouraged.* The meaning of "masculine" or "feminine" is reinforced every time a woman is rewarded for being polite and ladylike—in other words, appropriately hewing to a gender norm—or a man is denigrated for being a pussy or a weakling for not embodying ideal understandings of masculinity appropriately (Lorber, 1994). This happens both online, and off.

Clearly, the internet has not brought about a decoupling of sex and gender, a breakdown in the gender binary, or an end to patriarchal heterosexism. This is due to a variety of factors, including the mainstreaming of internet technologies since the 1990s, social media's emphasis on maintaining a "real" online identity, and the structural nature of sexism. In the next sections, I look at how, rather than breaking down gender, internet technologies *produce* it.

Social Media as Gendered Technology

In the nascent field of science and technology studies (STS), the link between gender and technology has been extensively examined (Cowan, 1985; Lerman, Oldenziel, & Mohun, 2003; Wajcman, 1991). Writers have analyzed how the design and deployment of technology can, knowingly or unknowingly, perpetrate sexist or exclusionary gender politics. For instance, Rachel Weber (1997) analyzed how military jet cockpits were originally built to accommodate the fifth to ninety-fifth percentile of male bodies, which resulted in excluding more than three-quarters of eligible women who did not meet the height and weight requirements. The presumption of male normativity was built directly into the technology with the result of furthering unequal employment practices.

While people use social technologies in many ways unintended by their designers and developers, it is important to look at those which are loaded with assumptions about gender and sexuality. Grindr, a locative app for gay men, presumes a model of gay male sexuality in which gay men are physically attractive, live in crowded urban areas, and enjoy casual, frequent "hook ups." While this model of behavior is different from the predominant heterosexual script, it does not reflect the experiences of all gay men. In rural areas with lower populations, gay men often use Grindr to find other gay men in the area, for friendship, support, or long-term relationships (Mowlabocus, 2010).

Social shopping sites like Polyvore and Pinterest, which are targeted at teenage girls and twentysomething women, presume that their users are interested in clothes and makeup. Although Polyvore, for example, has 6.6 million users (Jacobs, 2010), it has no features that let girls discuss anything other than collages made of images pulled from magazines and catalogs of purchasable goods. Pinterest, which lets users "bookmark" interesting things they find around the web, sets up default lists for new users that include "For the Home," "My Style," "Products I Love," "Favorite Places & Spaces," and "Books worth Reading." Pinterest assumes that its users are interested in homemaking, fashion, decorating, shopping, and books, but not sports, science, politics, or activism. Not only is its user model overtly feminine, she is a feminine *consumer*. As Liesbet van Zoonen wrote in 2001, the commodification of online space produces a normative model of woman as a shopper.

The Online and the Offline

It is difficult to define whether online social processes originate from the technological substrate or the social substrate. Is the expression of gender and sexuality online influenced by the technology being used, the people using it, "society" at large, or all of these?

Susan Herring is a linguist who has studied computer-mediated discourse for two decades, focusing on male and female communication styles. Her research in the 1990s found that online *asynchronous* communication tends to follow typical gendered communication styles. She wrote that on academic discussion lists, women were more polite and supportive than men, who tended to be confrontational, assertive, and adversarial in a way that often discouraged women from participating (Herring, 1993, 1996). More recent research on teen chat rooms found that teens used stereotypical gender markers in both their conversation and their profile photos. Kapidzic and Herring (2011) suggested that these gender stereotypes "are perceived by the teens who employ them to serve useful purposes" (p. 3). Elsewhere, Herring has argued that the online realm is hostile to women, especially women speaking critically of men, who are often subject to intimidation and harassment. On the other hand, she found evidence that computer mediated communication (CMC) encouraged female camaraderie and support (Herring, 2004). She concludes that gender difference is intrinsic to language: it "still employs politeness to symbolize femininity, and assertiveness to symbolize masculinity," (Herring, 2004, p. 220) and the gender inequality in larger society makes it impossible to pin down the cause of online harassment.

It is important not to take a technologically determinist attitude towards gender, which assumes that certain technical architectures intrinsically produce gendered affects. These explanations of online behavior assume that technology prescribes a certain user action. But neither should we adhere to strictly social constructivist models of technology, which argue that human actors and human action shape technology (Brey, 1997; MacKenzie & Wajcman, 1985; Pinch & Bijker, 1984; Winner, 1993). Rather, it is necessary to understand the relationship between the technological affordances of a system and the cultural behavior reinforced by the community using the system. The importance of understanding the social dimension is demonstrated by the immense contextual differences between different groups of users of the same technology. While Herring (1999) found widespread sexual harassment on Internet Relay Chat, other researchers worked with data that did not exhibit this type of sexism (Danet, Ruedenberg-Wright, & Rosenbaum-Tamari, 1997; O'Neill & Martin, 2003).

In lieu of positing certain technologies as more suited to quintessentially *male* behaviors or ways of thinking, technologies—and social media specifically—can be examined for how they reward or discourage patterns of behavior that adhere to predominant notions of gender. This differs between social contexts, as concepts of gender are fluid. The expectation of propriety for a young woman, for instance, is not only dependent on her class, race, religion, sexuality, and location (among other things), it has changed considerably in the last fifty years. It is radically different for a teenage girl to express aggression in predominantly white middle-class neighborhoods, which encourage young women to suppress anger, than it is in poor Black and Latino communities, where girls are explicitly expected to stand up for themselves verbally and physically (Ness, 2010).

Because contemporary social media is embedded within daily life, it draws from the same dynamics present in day-to-day interaction. For example, Julie Cupples and Lee Thompson (2010) analyze how the mobile phone is leveraged to reinforce a heterosexual "script" of high school, which allows young women to express agency over their romantic and sexual assignations in a way that maintains the fiction of status quo gender relations. Although the mobile phone may not intrinsically be gendered, it is used within the gendered framework of high school as part of the work of heterosexuality and gender.

Online Participation

Recently, social media has been celebrated for facilitating greater cultural participation and creativity (Jenkins, 2006; Lessig, 2004). Social media sites like Twitter and YouTube have purportedly led to the emergence of a "free culture" where individuals are empowered to engage in cultural production, using raw materials ranging from homemade videos to mainstream television characters to create new culture, memes, and humor. At its best, this culture of memes, mash-ups, and creative political activism allows for civic engagement and fun creative acts. But while this culture may resist dominant paradigms of economics, ownership, or intellectual property, it often hews to conventionally sexist tropes.

For example, the meme "Tits or GTFO" (Get the F★★★ Out) originated on a web forum called 4chan, which is both crude and influential. When a self-identified woman or girl posts something on 4chan, another forum member may retort "tits or GTFO": either post a picture of breasts, or get the heck out of the forum. This meme systematically discredits women's contributions by reducing their value to that of a sex object. And it has gained in popularity, moving beyond 4chan's /b/ board into mainstream internet culture.

While members of forums like Reddit or Digg often claim that memes like "Tits or GTFO" are funny jokes done for the "lolz" and that anyone who complains is humorless, this joke reinforces male entitlement and conventional gender stereotypes while normalizing egregiously sexist behavior. Even though such sites typically claim that they make fun of everyone, meme humor is disproportionately targeted at women, sexual minorities, and people of color. "Tits or GTFO" requires women who enjoy message board culture to either play along to be accepted as "one of the guys" (knowing that at any time the meme can be leveraged against her) or stop participating altogether. This has the effect of normalizing misogyny and reinforcing all-male spaces.

Of course, there are many other types of social media besides message boards. While Digg, 4chan, and Reddit are used mostly by men, most social network site users are women; this is true on Facebook, Flickr, LiveJournal, Tumblr, Twitter, and YouTube (Chappell, 2011; Lenhart, 2009; Lenhart, Purcell, Smith, & Zickuhr, 2010). But mere equality of use does not indicate equality of participation. While both men and women use *Wikipedia,* 87 percent of *Wikipedia* contributors identify as male (LaVallee, 2009). Male students are more likely than female students to create, edit, and distribute digital video over YouTube or Facebook (Vedantham, 2011). However, the Pew Internet and American Life Project found no discernible differences in user-generated content by gender *except* remixing, which was *most* likely among teen girls (Lenhart et al., 2010).

One explanation for these differences is that user-generated content is often clustered by gender. Researchers have consistently shown that similar numbers of men and women maintain a blog, about 14 percent of internet users (Lenhart et al., 2010). While the number of male and female bloggers is roughly equivalent, they tend to blog about different things. Overwhelmingly, certain types of blogs are written and read by women (food, fashion, parenting), while others (technology, politics) are written and run by men (Chittenden, 2010; Hindman, 2009; Meraz, 2008). Although the technologies are the same, the norms and mores of the people using them differ. This suggests that gender is experienced differently both on and within different social media sites. Moreover, these genres are valued differently. When blogs began gaining popularity, Herring et al. argued that "blogging" was just a new term for online "journaling" and "diarying," activities that girls and women had been participating in for a decade. This division systematically devalued female content creation online, as the "blog" was framed as a masculine context and linked to politics, civic engagement, and journalism, whereas the "diary" or "journal" was personal and often frivolous (Herring, Kouper, Scheidt, & Wright, 2004).

In order to understand the backlash against Julia Allison, it is worth examining both her use of technology and the social context in which she blogs.

Julia Allison

In some ways, Julia Allison's use of social media is in keeping with the ideals of participation, creativity, and self-expression espoused by academics, tech bloggers, and entrepreneurs alike. She blogs, tweets, and uploads digital pictures daily. She writes columns about technology, takes video of herself lip-synching, and stages photo shoots for her lifestream. She uses Tumblr, Twitter, and Vimeo to express herself, create content, and propagate it widely. To understand why Julia provokes such vehement reactions, we must explore two things. How does Julia express, perform, and produce gender? Do the gender norms that she espouses clash with those of the sociotechnical infrastructure in which she is working?

First, Julia's self-presentation is not simply normatively feminine. She posts frequent digital self-portraits, which are uniformly flattering and formally posed, drawing from celebrity and tabloid culture in which women are supposed to look put together in photographs. Allison wears very feminine makeup, clothing, and accessories, such as hot-pink party dresses, glittery high heels, and lip gloss. She frequently photographs herself with her small dog and feminine iconography like cupcakes, tiaras, and pink accessories. Allison's use of over-the-top gender markers are normally displayed only by young girls, beauty pageant contestants, or for camp, ironic affect. Allison's detractors often point to her use of these markers as a mark of her "immaturity" or "desperation" for violating the norms of age-appropriate femininity. And unlike Gala Darling, a fashion blogger who self-consciously plays with ultrafeminine iconography, or burlesque star Dita Von Teese, who affects a 1940s-cum-Bettie Page retro persona, Allison displays little irony or self-consciousness about her appearance. As a result, her gender presentation does not conform to either feminine propriety or ironic feminist reclamation.

Second, Allison talks primarily about herself, her romantic life, and fashion. She illustrates that the line between acceptable information sharing and "TMI" (too much information) is deeply gendered. Using social media for self-disclosure increases online status *up to a point,* after which the person is typically categorized as an "attention whore," "oversharer," or "desperate." Anthony Hoffman's (2009) critical discourse analysis of media coverage about oversharing found that the term was overwhelmingly negative, applied primarily to women, and had "the effect of creating a devalued subclass of information sharing online," mostly comprised of "sex and romance, intimate relationships, parenthood and reproduction, and so on" (p. 71). Allison's detractors demonstrate a similar pattern of normative judgment around information sharing. Her discussions of her dating life, desire to get married and Sex and the City–esque fantasies of urban life are labeled as "desperate" or "delusional" because these topics are seen as silly or irrelevant. That these are historically, intrinsically *feminine* topics is not coincidental.

Third, Allison represents a focus on appearance, possessions, and girlishness that is antithetical to the dominant values of the technology scene. She is overtly feminine and openly courts attention, using her image to attract and maintain her audience. But Allison's success threatens the myths that underlie social media production. Allison's strategic use of her appearance undermines the ideal of egalitarianism highly valued in Silicon Valley. Claims that Silicon Valley is a meritocracy, where the best succeed and anyone can enter, justify the great wealth accrued by young entrepreneurs at companies like Microsoft and Facebook. In many ways, Silicon Valley is actually a closed network with predominantly male funding and mentoring.

Like many other aspects of the tech industry, the companies designing and producing social media tend to be predominantly male. Only 3 percent of tech companies and 1.9 percent of high-tech companies are founded by women, and women-founded business receive venture capital at far lower rates than men (Robb & Coleman, 2009). This maintains despite recent studies that have found virtually no differences between female and male entrepreneurs in terms of education, wealth, or technical knowledge (Cohoon, Wadhwa, & Mitchell, 2010). According to the US Bureau of Labor Statistics, women make up 19 percent of hardware engineers, 21 percent of software engineers, and 22 percent of computer programmers. Overall, computer and mathematical professions are 75 percent male (Dines, 2009; National Center for Women and Information Technology,

2007). In Free/Open Source software development, researchers estimate that only about 1.5 percent of contributors are women (Holliger, 2007; Nafus, Leach, & Krieger, 2006). While some of these numbers can be explained by the lack of women in computer science, this in turn begs the question of why there are so few women in computer science, and why that number has decreased since the 1980s (National Center for Women and Information Technology, 2010). Professional roles in software development that do attract women, such as project management, marketing, graphic design, human resources, and public relations are lower status in the tech industry, often dismissed as not "real" tech jobs or framed in opposition to the more masculine work of programming.

Feminist scholars have argued that the exclusion of women from the social conditions under which technology is produced profoundly affects how such companies conceptualize and build technology (Faulkner, 2001; Wajcman, 1991, 2007). The majority of popular social media technologies are produced by American technologists in San Francisco or Silicon Valley, including Facebook, Twitter, YouTube, Instagram, Blogger, WordPress, Apple, and Google, with a few companies like Foursquare and Tumblr in New York. Mass media theorists have thoroughly explored how the culture and economies of Hollywood and New York affect how movies, television, and news are produced (Gitlin, 2000; Paterson & Domingo, 2008). Similarly, the values of the rarified tech professionals who build social media are reflected in software. For instance, Facebook's emphasis on "transparency" reflects a privileged position where one does not need to worry about being "outed," targeted by the government for political reasons, or being stalked by an abusive partner (boyd, 2011). The entrepreneurial climate of social software start-ups is deeply related to social media's focus on the individual as the unit of interaction, emphasis on visibility and publicity, and quantified measurement of social status, reputation, and other social metrics (Marwick, 2010).

While women in Silicon Valley are frequently judged on their appearance, Julia's assessment and presentation of herself as attractive invites a backlash, implying that a woman should not be the one to make that judgment. Ironically, Julia presenting herself as an object suggests an agented subjectivity that threatens the male-dominated social hierarchy.[3] Her success jeopardizes the idea that attention is *earned* in some measurable way, devaluing her accomplishments as irrelevant. Julia's case demonstrates that certain types of online participation are valued more than others, based on social norms of gender that are specific and contextual. These gendered norms are reinforced through the primarily male production context of Web 2.0.

Conclusion and Future Research

Julia Allison proves that all social media participation is not created equal. Just as "blogs" were valued while "journals" were not, technologies that facilitate stereotypically "male" ways of interaction and expression are valued more highly than those that are considered feminine. Julia's primary blogging platform is Tumblr, which primarily involves the curating and display of images and short texts. Tumblr is very popular among high school and college-age women, thus it is often seen as a "feminine" technology just as, say, Quora, a question-and-answer platform primarily used by male technologists, is considered a "masculine" one. These values are reinforced and reinscribed by the bloggers, journalists, venture capitalists, and technology conferences who promote social media companies and young entrepreneurs as role models.

The expression of gender and sexuality through social media is influenced in several ways. First, it is influenced by each individual user's social context. Different countries, regions, income levels, race and ethnicities, and sexualities deem different behavior on social media to be acceptable. Ilana Gershon (2010) calls these differences "idioms of practice" and finds that they vary even among different social groups of the same race, class, gender, and location. As a result, when examining social media use, we must account both for variance of use among user groups and look closely at the "offline" social contexts of different user groups.

Second, gender expression is influenced by the context in which the technology is produced, whether that is the US military or Silicon Valley. Typically, founders create products for *themselves;* if founders are primarily young white men, a large number of technologies will be designed for that demographic group. When young African American and Latino teenagers began using Twitter to talk to celebrities and for verbal jokes and games, many (wealthy, mostly white) technology pundits were taken by surprise by what they saw as an incorrect use of the service (Belton, 2011). The norms of Twitter had been formulated by its first users, members of the technology scene. The normative judgment on technological practice was determined by the social context of the creators. If the creators are primarily male, software will value and reward male-gendered practice.

Third, technologies may incorporate values and norms before anyone uses the software. On many different social network sites, for instance, users are required to use a "real name" to use the service, incorporating an ideal of transparency directly into the software. This ideal has two purposes. First, requiring "real names" creates more accurate user data, which can be sold to marketing and data-mining companies. Second, it is rooted in a particular Silicon Valley belief that computers will flatten hierarchy and increase democracy, making pseudonymity or anonymity unnecessary (Raynes-Goldie, 2010).

The relationship between gender and technology is complicated, since gender is a tremendously important social construct that exists throughout society and between social actors. Since the 1990s boom in cyberfeminism, gender and social media has fallen out of fashion as an object of study. More research is needed on social media and gender, especially examining particular types of software; the relationship between the social practice of users and their gendered social practices on websites; and the prevalence of overt sexism and harassment in social media spaces. This chapter serves as a call for others to engage in this research agenda.

Notes

1. Although this quotes directly from Julia's online bio, her dog is named Lily.
2. The original name of the blog was "Reblogging Julia Allison." When Julia co-founded the site *NonSociety,* the name of the blog was changed. The current name of the blog is *Reblogging Donkey,* based on the writers' nickname for Julia. The site's various moves and name changes are due primarily to threats of legal action by Julia's father.
3. Not insignificantly, she also angers women who wish to be judged on their accomplishments rather than looks.

Recommended Readings

Goffman, E. (1977). The arrangement between the sexes. *Theory and Society, 4*(3), 301–331.
Haraway, D. (1985). A manifesto for cyborgs: Science, technology, and socialist feminism in the 1980's. *Socialist Review, 80,* 65–108.
Lorber, J. (1994). Night to his day: The social construction of gender. In *Paradoxes of gender* (pp. 13–36). New Haven, CT: Yale University Press.
O'Riordan, K., & Phillips, D. J. (2007). *Queer online: Media technology & sexuality.* New York: Peter Lang Publishing.
Plant, S. (1998). *Zeros + ones: Digital women + the new technoculture.* London: Fourth Estate.
Shapiro, E. (2010). *Gender circuits: Bodies and identities in a technological age.* New York: Routledge.
Van Doorn, N., & Van Zoonen, L. (2009). Theorizing gender and the internet: Past, present and future. In A. Chadwick & P. N. Howard (Eds.), *Routledge handbook of internet politics* (pp. 261–274). New York: Routledge.
Wajcman, J. (2007). From women and technology to gendered technoscience. *Information, Communication & Society, 10*(3), 287–298.
West, C., & Zimmerman, D. H. (1987). Doing gender. *Gender & society, 1*(2), 125.

Bibliography

Allison, J. (2009). Bio—Julia Allison. *JuliaAllison.com.* Retrieved August 25, 2011, from http://juliaallison.com/bio.html
Atterberry, W. (2010, March 24). Julia Allison quits the internet, writing about your personal life online, a cautionary tale. *The Frisky.* Retrieved March 25, 2010, from http://www.thefrisky.com/post/246-writing-about-your-personal-life-online-a-cautionary-tale/
Belton, D. (2011, January 18). Black people still on Twitter! ★Clutches Pearls★. *The Black Snob.* Retrieved August 26, 2011, from http://blacksnob.com/snob_blog/2011/1/18/black-people-still-on-twitter-clutches-pearls.html
boyd, d. (2011, August 4). "Real Names" policies are an abuse of power. *Apophenia.* Retrieved August 26, 2011, from http://www.zephoria.org/thoughts/archives/2011/08/04/real-names.html
Brey, P. (1997). Philosophy of technology meets social constructivism. *Society for Philosophy and Technology, 2*(3–4). Retrieved from http://scholar.lib.vt.edu/ejournals/SPT/v2_n3n4html/brey.html
Bristow, J. (1997). *Sexuality.* New York: Routledge.
Butler, J. (1990). *Gender trouble: Feminism and the subversion of identity.* New York: Routledge.
Cameron, D. (1998). *The feminist critique of language: A reader.* New York: Routledge.
Cameron, D., & Kulick, D. (2003). *Language and sexuality.* Cambridge: Cambridge University Press.

Chappell, B. (2011). *2011 social network analysis data.* Ignite Social Media. Retrieved from http://www.ignitesocialmedia.com/social-media-stats/2011-social-network-analysis -report/

Chittenden, T. (2010). Digital dressing up: Modelling female teen identity in the discursive spaces of the fashion blogosphere. *Journal of Youth Studies, 13*(4), 505–520.

Cohoon, J. M. G., Wadhwa, V., & Mitchell, L. (2010). *Are successful women entrepreneurs different from men?* Kansas City, MO: Ewing Marion Kauffman Foundation. Retrieved from http://www.kauffman.org/uploadedFiles/successful_women_entrepreneurs_5-10.pdf

Cowan, R. S. (1985). *More work for mother: The ironies of household technology from the open hearth to the microwave.* New York: Basic Books.

Crawley, S. L., Foley, L. J., & Shehan, C. L. (2008). *Gendering bodies.* New York: Rowman & Littlefield Publishers.

Cupples, J., & Thompson, L. (2010). Heterotextuality and digital foreplay: Cell phones and the culture of teenage romance. *Feminist Media Studies, 10*(1), 1–17.

Danet, B., Ruedenberg-Wright, L., & Rosenbaum-Tamari, Y. (1997). "Hmmm . . . where's that smoke coming from?" Writing, play and performance on Internet Relay Chat. *Journal of Computer-Mediated Communication, 2*(4). Retrieved from http://jcmc.indiana. edu/vol2/issue4/danet.html

Dines, R. (2009, October 23). Why you should care about having a diverse IT ops department. *Forrester Blogs.* Retrieved July 3, 2010, from http://blogs.forrester.com/rachel_ dines/09-10-23-why_you_should_care_about_having_diverse_it_ops_department

Faulkner, W. (2000). Dualisms, hierarchies and gender in engineering. *Social Studies of Science, 30*(5), 759–792. doi:10.1177/030631200030005005

Faulkner, W. (2001). The technology question in feminism: A view from feminist technology studies. *Women's Studies International Forum, 24,* 79–95.

Fausto-Sterling, A. (2000). *Sexing the body: Gender politics and the construction of sexuality.* New York: Basic Books.

Gauntlett, D. (2008). *Media, gender and identity: An introduction.* London: Psychology Press.

Gershon, I. (2010). *The breakup 2.0: Disconnecting over new media.* Ithaca: Cornell University Press.

Gitlin, T. (2000). *Inside prime time: With a new introduction* (1st ed.). Berkeley: University of California Press.

Goffman, E. (1977). The arrangement between the sexes. *Theory and Society, 4*(3), 301–331.

Haraway, D. (1985). A manifesto for cyborgs: Science, technology, and socialist feminism in the 1980's. *Socialist Review, 80,* 65–108.

Henderson, J. M. (2011, July 13). A social media game plan from the internet's self-promotion princess. *The Ground Floor—Forbes.* Retrieved July 14, 2011, from http:// blogs.forbes.com/jmaureenhenderson/2011/07/13/a-social-media-game-plan-from-the-internets-self-promotion-princess/

Herring, S. C. (1993). Men's language: A study of the discourse of the LINGUIST list. *Proceedings of the XVth International Congress of Linguists* (Vol. 3, pp. 347–350).

Herring, S. C. (1996). Posting in a different voice: Gender and ethics in computer-mediated communication. *Philosophical Perspectives on Computer-Mediated Communication, 115,* 45.

Herring, S. C. (1999). The rhetorical dynamics of gender harassment on-line. *The Information Society, 15*(3), 151–167.

Herring, S. C. (2004). Computer-mediated communication and woman's place. In R. T. Lakoff & M. Bucholtz (Eds.), *Language and woman's place: Text and commentaries* (pp. 216–222). New York: Oxford University Press US.

Herring, S. C., Kouper, I., Scheidt, L. A., & Wright, E. L. (2004). Women and children last: The discursive construction of weblogs. In L. J. Gurak, S. Antonijevic, L. Johnson,

C. Ratliff, & J. Reyman (Eds.), *Into the blogosphere: Rhetoric, community, and culture of we-blogs.* Retrieved from http://blog.lib.umn.edu/blogosphere/women_and_children.html

Hindman, M. S. (2009). *The myth of digital democracy.* Princeton, NJ: Princeton University Press.

Hoffman, A. (2009, August). *Oversharing: A critical discourse analysis.* (Master of Library and Information Science Thesis). University of Wisconsin–Milwaukee, Milwaukee, WI.

Hofmann, J. (1999). Writers, texts and writing acts: Gendered user images in word process-ing software. In D. MacKenzie & Judy Wajcman (Eds.), *The social shaping of technology* (pp. 222–243). New York: Open University Press.

Holliger, A. (2007). *The culture of open source computing: An annotated bibliography.* Boulder, CO: National Center for Women and Information Technology.

Hossfeld, K. J. (1990). "Their logic against them": Contradictions in sex, race, and class in Silicon Valley. In K. B. Ward (Ed.), *Women workers and global restructuring* (pp. 149–178). Ithaca, NY: Cornell University Press.

Jacobs, A. (2010, March 29). Fashion democracy: The world of virtual Anna Wintours. *The New Yorker.* Retrieved from http://www.newyorker.com/reporting/2010/03/29/100329fa_fact_jacobs

Jenkins, H. (2006). *Convergence culture.* New York: New York University Press.

Juliaspublicist. (2010, March 22). Apparently we hurt Julia Allison's feelings. *Reblogging NonSociety.* Retrieved April 5, 2010, from http://rebloggingdonk.com/2010/03/22/apparently-we-hurt-julia-allisons-feelings/

Kapidzic, S., & Herring, S. C. (2011). Gender, communication, and self-presentation in teen chatrooms revisited: Have patterns changed? *Journal of Computer-Mediated Communica-tion.* Retrieved from http://ella.slis.indiana.edu/~herring/teenchat.2011.pdf

Kendall, L. (2002). *Hanging out in the virtual pub: Masculinities and relationships online.* Berke-ley: University of California Press.

Kessler, S. J., & McKenna, W. (1978). *Gender: An ethnomethodological approach.* Chicago: Uni-versity of Chicago Press.

Kirkup, G., Janes, L., Woodward, K., & Hovenden, F. (Eds.). (2000). *The gendered cyborg: A reader.* New York: Routledge.

LaVallee, A. (2009, August 31). Only 13% of Wikipedia contributors are women, study says. *The Wall Street Journal.* Retrieved from http://blogs.wsj.com/digits/2009/08/31/only-13-of-wikipedia-contributors-are-women-study-says/

Lawson, R. (2010a, January 8). A reblogger speaks. *Gawker.* Retrieved March 25, 2010, from http://gawker.com/5443842/a-reblogger-speaks

Lawson, R. (2010b, January 7). Into the internet's ninth circle of hell: The rebloggers. *Gawker.* Retrieved from http://gawker.com/5441578/into-the-internets-ninth-circle -of-hell-the-rebloggers

Lenhart, A. (2009). *It's personal: Similarities and differences in online social network use between teens and adults.* Washington, DC: Pew Internet & American Life Project.

Lenhart, A., Purcell, K., Smith, A., & Zickuhr, K. (2010). *Content creation: Sharing, remixing, blogging, and more.* Pew Internet & American Life Project. Retrieved from http://www.pewinternet.org/Reports/2010/Social-Media-and-Young-Adults/Part-3/6-Content-Creation.aspx

Lerman, N. E., Oldenziel, R., & Mohun, A. (2003). *Gender & technology: A reader.* Baltimore: JHU Press.

Lessig, L. (2004). *Free culture.* New York: Penguin Books.

Lorber, J. (1994). Night to his day: The social construction of gender. In *Paradoxes of Gender* (pp. 13–36). New Haven, CT: Yale University Press.

MacKenzie, D., & Wajcman, J. (1985). *The social shaping of technology.* Buckingham, UK: Open University Press.

Marwick, A. (2010). *Status update: Celebrity, publicity and self-branding in Web 2.0.* (Dissertation). New York University, New York.

Meraz, S. (2008). The blogosphere's gender gap: Differences in visibility, popularity, and authority. In P.M. Poindexter, S. Meraz, & A. Schmitz Weiss (Eds.), *Women, men, and news: Divided and disconnected in the news media landscape* (pp. 142–168). New York: Taylor & Francis.

Mowlabocus, S. (2010). *Gaydar culture: Gay men, technology and embodiment in the digital age.* London: Ashgate Publishing.

Nafus, D., Leach, J., & Krieger, B. (2006). *Free/libre and open source software: Policy support (integrated report of findings)* (No. D16). UCAM, University of Cambridge. Retrieved from http://flosspols.org/deliverables/FLOSSPOLS-D16-Gender_Integrated_Report _of_Findings.pdf

National Center for Women and Information Technology. (2007). *NCWIT scorecard 2007: A report on the status of women in information technology.* Boulder, CO: National Center for Women and Information Technology. Retrieved from http://www.ncwit.org/ pdf/2007_Scorecard_Web.pdf

National Center for Women and Information Technology. (2010). *Women and information technology: By the numbers* (No. 012710) (p. 1). Boulder, CO: National Center for Women and Information Technology.

Ness, C. (2010). *Why girls fight: Female youth violence in the inner city.* New York: NYU Press.

O'Neill, J., & Martin, D. (2003). Text chat in action. *Proceedings of the 2003 international ACM SIGGROUP conference on supporting group work* (pp. 40–49). Sanibel Island, FL: ACM. Retrieved from http://portal.acm.org/citation.cfm?id=958167

Partypants. (2010, March 23). YOOHOOOO! Kelly Cutrone!!!!!!! Over here! *Reblogging NonSociety.* Retrieved April 5, 2010, from http://rebloggingdonk.com/2010/03/23/ yoohoooo-kelly-cutrone-over-here/

Paterson, C., & Domingo, D. (2008). *Making online news.* New York: Peter Lang Publishing.

Pinch, T. J., & Bijker, W. E. (1984). The social construction of facts and artefacts: Or how the sociology of science and the sociology of technology might benefit each other. *Social Studies of Science, 14*(3), 399–441.

Plant, S. (1998). *Zeros + ones: Digital women + the new technoculture.* London: Fourth Estate.

Raynes-Goldie, K. (2010). *Privacy, Facebook and the Californian ideology.* Presented at the Internet Research 11, Gothenberg, Sweden.

Robb, A.M., & Coleman, S. (2009). *Sources of financing for new technology firms: A comparison by gender* (No. 5). Fifth in a series of reports using data from the Kauffman Firm Survey. Kansas City, MO: Ewing Marion Kauffman Foundation. Retrieved from http://www. kauffman.org/uploadedFiles/ResearchAndPolicy/Sources%20of%20Financing%20 for%20New%20Technology%20Firms.pdf

Sedgwick, E. K. (2008). *Epistemology of the closet.* Berkeley: University of California Press.

Shapiro, E. (2010). *Gender circuits: Bodies and identities in a technological age.* New York: Routledge.

Stone, A. R. (1996). *The war of desire and technology at the close of the mechanical age.* Cambridge, MA: MIT Press.

Stryker, S. (2006). (De)subjugated knowledges: An introduction to transgender studies. In S. Whittle & S. Stryker (Eds.), *The transgender studies reader.* New York: Routledge.

Terry, J., & Calvert, M. (1997). *Processed lives: Gender and technology in everyday life.* London: Routledge.

Turkle, S. (1995). *Life on the screen: Identity in the age of the internet*. New York: Simon & Schuster.

Van Zoonen, L. (1994). *Feminist media studies*. SAGE: London

Van Zoonen, L. (2001). Feminist internet studies. *Feminist Media Studies, 1*(1), 67–72. doi:10.1080/14680770120042864

Vedantham, A. (2011). *Making Youtube and Facebook videos: Gender differences in online video creation among first-year undergraduate students attending a highly selective research university*. (Doctoral Dissertation). University of Pennsylvania Graduate School of Education. Retrieved from http://repository.upenn.edu/cgi/viewcontent.cgi?article=1083&context=library_papers&sei-redir=1#search=%22vedantham%20dissertation%22

Wajcman, J. (1991). *Feminism confronts technology*. University Park, PA: Penn State Press.

Wajcman, J. (2007). From women and technology to gendered technoscience. *Information, Communication & Society, 10*(3), 287–298. doi:10.1080/13691180701409770

Weber, R. N. (1997). Manufacturing gender in military cockpit design. *Science, Technology & Human Values, 22*(2), 235–253.

West, C., & Zimmerman, D. H. (1987). Doing gender. *Gender & society, 1*(2), 125.

Winner, L. (1993). Upon opening the black box and finding it empty: Social constructivism and the philosophy of technology. *Science, Technology & Human Values, 18*(3), 362–378.

Wolmark, J. (1999). *Cybersexualities: A reader on feminist theory cyborgs and cyberspace*. Edinburgh, Scotland: Edinburgh University Press.

Wynn, E., & Katz, J. E. (1997). Hyperbole over cyberspace: Self-presentation and social boundaries in internet home pages and discourse. *The Information Society, 13*(4), 297–327.

6

POP CULTURE, FANS, AND SOCIAL MEDIA

Francesca Coppa

Organized fandom both antedates and anticipates modern social media; that is, fans have been turning mass cultural events—like reading a story in a magazine, watching a television show, or listening to recorded music—into opportunities for group interaction and creativity long before the advent of today's social networking tools. In the days before commercial services like Facebook, LiveJournal, Twitter, YouTube, and Myspace, fans invented their own tools for communicating and collaborating; in fact, fans built and maintained a vast array of social media tools and networks before there was even an internet. Today, fans continue to develop their own spaces, events, software, practices, rules, and communities within the context of Web 2.0, which, with its focus on "participation" and "interactivity," seems both inspired by fan culture and to want to commodify it. While fans have been early and enthusiastic adopters of almost all forms of social media, adapting and altering them to fit their communities, these tools may also pose a threat to fan culture by standardizing and commercializing it, seeing fans only as "users" and the wonderful history of creative fan activities as mere "user-generated content."

So What Is Fandom, Exactly?

There are many kinds of fans—music fans, sports fans, movie fans, television fans, comic book fans—and many ways people organize into a "fandom." While in common speech, a person can be a fan of almost anything—of Britney Spears or ice cream or Mac computers or Pontiacs or Shakespeare—in this essay I'm going to define "fans" a little more narrowly. While people have always had the kind of enthusiasm and devotion that the word "fan" describes, the modern word "fan"—short for fanatic—dates from the end of the nineteenth century and the emergence of what we now call mass culture. I would argue that our modern idea of fans and fandom arises at the same time as, and in response to, this mass culture.

So what, then, is mass culture? Richard Ohmann's definition in *Selling Culture: Magazines, Markets, and Class at the Turn of the Century*[1] is usefully precise: he defines mass culture as "voluntary cultural experiences produced at a distance by specialists for millions of people to share, in similar or identical form, at the same time or nearly so, with dependable frequency, shaping a habitual audience around common needs or interests, for profit" (Ohmann, 1996, p.14). Ohmann claims that mass culture starts with the nineteenth century rise of the literary magazine,[2] which made literature into a mass media by bringing short stories to a large audience of subscribers on a reliable schedule, creating a habitual audience of fiction readers. Even today, magazines (and comic books) are published on a fixed schedule (weekly, monthly), as are mass media paperbacks; for instance, new Harlequin romance novels come out monthly, or a fantasy series might announce a new sequel each year. Mass media sports like NFL football or thoroughbred racing are played by professional athletes ("specialists") on a fixed schedule and broadcast on radio or television, with the results widely distributed so that everyone hears about them more or less simultaneously; compare this to, say, activities like watching a local football game or actually riding your own horse. Television and movies are made in Hollywood by professionals and delivered to an audience of millions weekly ("Fridays at 9!") or at regular intervals (*Shrek III*).[3] These mass media dramas are very different from the theatrical events of the nineteenth century and before, which include not only local (and therefore not identical) productions of plays, operas, and burlesques,[4] but a whole array of amateur performances, including parades, backyard revues, talent shows, and staged tableaus featuring costumes pulled from the dress-up box. And music didn't used to be a product you purchased and listened to on your Victrola, hi-fi set, or iPod; it was something you made yourself or heard locally.

Ohmann further describes how mass culture was designed to form habitual audiences around common needs or interests. These audiences were constituted primarily as a target for advertising (which was also developed in the nineteenth century to sell a host of newly mass-produced products), but some subset of this habitual audience became a subculture: fans and fandoms. Fans, by this definition, are *those who gather together regularly to experience mass culture but who also respond to its professionalization by creating local, participatory, and amateur group activities for themselves.* Following Henry Jenkins, who contrasted *Dallas* viewers and *Star Trek* fans in *Textual Poachers: Television Fans and Participatory Culture,* I am defining fans as those who move from an isolated enthusiasm for some aspect of mass culture to "participants in a larger social and cultural community"[5]—that is, I am defining fandom not as an individual preference but as a collective identity.

It is because of this collective identity that fans have eagerly adopted all manner of communications technology, including contemporary social media platforms; the mission of fandom, in fact, is *to make mass media social.* Participation in fandom turns the one-way broadcast of mass culture into a two-way street, whether it's music fans creating and sharing mash-ups through SoundCloud,[6] sports fans coming together to play in local fantasy football leagues, television and movie fans posting fan fiction on LiveJournal, fans of celebrities creating picspams on Tumblr,[7] or gamers uploading machinima to YouTube. In each of these cases, a potentially solitary and passive activity (listening to music on an iPod, watching a football game on TV, etc.) has become an opportunity for collaborative discussion, analysis, creativity, and other forms of social engagement.

Analog Fandom: Social Networking before the Internet

Since fandom evolved in tandem with and as a response to the emergence of mass culture in the late nineteenth century, it is not surprising that one of the first modern fandoms formed around Sherlock Holmes, who regularly appeared in a series of detective stories in *The Strand* magazine from 1891 onward. In fact, when Arthur Conan Doyle serialized the Holmes novel *The Hound of the Baskervilles,* fans lined up outside the magazine's headquarters to get the next installment, much like fans today might line up to buy the next Harry Potter book or to see the next *Star Wars* sequel. In the years since, literally hundreds of "Sherlockian" fan groups and clubs—including The Sherlock Holmes Society and The Baker Street Irregulars, both founded in 1934—have been formed all over the world.[8] These societies gather together at dinners and literary weekends to discuss Holmes and his world, and they also create many different kinds of Holmes-related stories and analyses. Some Sherlock fans play what they call "The Grand Game," which is to pretend that Holmes and Watson were historical figures, and thus to write works of "history" explaining the various discrepancies and inconsistencies in the stories. While many of these fan activities have been going on for well over a century (volume one of *The Grand Game: A Celebration of Sherlockian Scholarship* features a number of essays dating from 1902), today Sherlockians have established a presence on almost every conceivable online platform (e.g., the sixty-year-old "Sherlock Holmes Society of London" now tweets at SHSLBakerStweet) and created social networks like The Sherlock Holmes Social Network and the searchable Sherlockian Who's Who.[9]

Similarly, science fiction fandom—which created the template for many modern fan practices—formed around Hugo Gernsback's monthly publication *Amazing Stories* (1926), the first magazine devoted solely to science fiction. More specifically, science fiction fandom was developed on the letters page of that magazine: as Arnie Katz notes in "The Philosophical Theory of Fanhistory," "The large letter column, copied by most of *Amazing*'s competitors, gave readers plenty of space to talk to the editor, and ultimately, to each other."[10] It was this interactive element that sparked the development of modern fandom; fans used the letters column as an analog version of a blog post or forum. Also, by publishing fans' addresses with their letters, *Amazing Stories* gave fans a way to contact each other directly, which led to the formation of the creative and participatory subculture of science fiction fandom.

These science fiction fans invented their own social networks using the common mass communication technologies of the time: for example, carbon paper, mimeography, spirit duplicating or "ditto" machines, and eventually photocopying. With these tools, fans created and distributed fanzines, which published conversation, analysis, gossip, and creative work; the first science fiction zine, *The Comet,* was published in 1930.[11] These zines—sometime called fanzines, letterzines, or APAs (amateur press association zines)—were collaboratively constructed and thus community artifacts: contributors mailed their content (letters, essays, comments, etc.) to a "Central Mailer," who collated and copied everything and sent it back out again through the post. As longtime fan Paula Smith remembers, "We mailed everything—fans went broke on postage—and we had a lot of contact that way."[12] As with today's internet mailing lists, forums, and bulletin boards, the fan network was both the producer and consumer of content; in fact, for many zines, you had to "trib" (or contribute) to get a copy. Zines provided content recognizably similar to today's web-based forums: as science fiction writer Frederick Pohl explains, they "contained comments on the stories in the professional magazines, or news of fan activities, or gossip or debate" (Pohl, 1974, p. 129) as well as stories and art.[13] George Slusser, curator of the Eaton Collection of fanzines at the University of California at Riverside, notes that zines pushed "the limitations of the print medium to its maximum speed and range in terms of its ability to produce interactive dialogue. In this sense, the fanzine is the forerunner of the internet" (Slusser, in Lee, 2011).[14]

When we talk about "media," we often forget text, although printed text was the first mass media and remains, whether printed or online, a significant form of mass media. But text was—and is—also a form of social media: readers and other consumers of writing quickly adopted and adapted a variety of text-based communications technologies in order to foster communication amongst themselves. Moreover, in our rapidly changing media landscape, where social media platforms debut, expand, and fold within a matter of a year or two (remember Friendster? imeem? Pownce?), we should appreciate the durability of text as a medium; as Melissa Conway, now head of Riverside's Special Collections Library, notes, fanzines are "essentially ephemera, produced by the fans for the community, and give incredible insight into what nonpro people in the fandom community were talking and thinking about across more than 70–80 years" (Conway, in Lee, 2011).[15] Because zines were durable, we can still read those communications today; similarly, the textual platforms of early online fandom may in the long run be more stable than the more recent social media platforms of Web 2.0.

Early Internet Fandom: IRC, BBS, Usenet

While the internet has now become home to almost every kind of fan of pop culture, science fiction fans were among the net's earliest users. This is not only because science fiction fans already had a strong analog social network, which they soon extended online, but also because science fiction fans tend to like technology; in fact, many science fiction fans are also scientists, computer programmers, or information specialists—that is, the sort of people who actually *built* the inter-net. As science fiction writer Cory Doctorow put it:

> Science fiction's early adopters defined the social character of the Internet itself. Given the high correlation between technical employment and sci-ence fiction reading, it was inevitable that the first nontechnical discussion on the Internet would be about science fiction. The online norms of idle chatter, fannish organizing, publishing and leisure are descended from SF fandom, and if any literature has a natural home in cyberspace, it's science fiction, the literature that coined the very word "cyberspace."[16]

Consequently, science fiction fans were online before many of the "user-friendly" interfaces most of us now take for granted were developed: for example, in the early 1990s, you had to engage the web through a command-line interface, and know how to write code to put up even the simplest web page. The World Wide Web was not yet standard, and there were no graphical "web browsers" like Internet Explorer or Firefox; rather, you might use a syntax based FTP (File Trans-fer Protocol) search engine called "Archie" or search text files organized with "Gopher" with tools named "Veronica" and "Jughead." While the internet was in many ways a different place, it was already home to what Howard Rheingold calls "virtual communities," which he defines as "social aggregations that emerge from the Net when enough people carry on . . . public discussions long enough, with sufficient human feeling, to form webs of personal relationships in cyberspace."[17] The virtual communities Rheingold documented in his 1993 book, *Virtual Com-munity,* are earlier versions of today's online social networks.[18]

However, at the time Rheingold was writing, most of the internet was still located on government and university servers; there was almost no corporate presence on the net and very few commercial ISPs (internet service providers). Consequently, access to the web was typically controlled by systems administra-tors or librarians at universities, many of whom were, again, science fiction fans. It was on the internet that "geek culture"—a culture associated with computers, science fiction, video games, and "otaku" or obsessive interest esoteric subjects—really took off, and, perhaps unsurprisingly, the "computer geeks" who were early adopters of the internet created communication networks around their favorite forms of pop culture. Among these early forms of online social networking were IRC channels, Usenet groups, Bulletin Board Systems (BBS), mailing lists, and eventually "web rings" of "websites" that used the "http" (hypertext protocol) of the emerging World Wide Web. Each of these were used by science fiction fans almost immediately, and all sorts of fans soon after.

IRC, or *Internet Relay Chat,* allows fans to chat synchronously in the group atmosphere of a "channel," as well as to message each other one-on-one and swap data files. Created in 1988, IRC is still popular, with millions of people gathering to talk in hundreds of thousands of channels. In the early years of its operation, people referred to the "Big Four" IRC networks: EFnet, IRCnet, Undernet, and DALnet;[19] the last of these, DALnet, was founded in 1994 by members of the EFnet #startrek channel (channel names are always marked with a # sign.) The fan known as "MirclMax" describes the founding of DALnet in an essay written in 1999:

> Stardate 7/94. Several users of a laggy, split torn, uncontrollable IRC Network find themselves searching for an extension to their often disrupted activities on the existing #startrek channel and take solace in a lone server made available by a lead operator of the channel named dalvenjah. The server was referred to as "dal's server" . . . to later, after more frequent use, to become "dal's net," and in a more abbreviated form, DALnet. The channel? Of course, DALnet's own, #startrek.[20]

MirclMax notes that the #startrek regulars on DALnet were "those people most active in creating the network. They were the ones running servers, writing policies, creating services." MirclMax goes on to describe the sorts of activities that occurred in the channel, which at that time then included a weekly hour-long discussion on that week's *Star Trek: Voyager* as well as *Star Trek* trivia contests. But it was mainly just a place to hang out and talk with other people who enjoy *Star Trek* in all its forms. Other communities, like manga fans, used IRC to collaborate on and distribute "scanlations," that is, scans and translations of Japanese comics into other languages. This activity, which continues even today, was even more prevalent two decades ago, before mainstream publishing companies realized that there was a market for Japanese comics outside Japan. IRC allowed fans from all over the world to share and discuss material that would not otherwise be available to them.

BBS, or *Bulletin Board Systems,* have been around from the late 1970s but reached their peak in the early 1990s. These were individual servers owned and operated, either from home or on university servers, with BBS software (often hand-coded by the System Operator him/herself) installed on it. While the people who ran BBS servers tended to be avid computer hobbyists, many of those hobbyists were also science fiction fans, and many chose to host fan-related e-mail accounts, mailing lists, and web pages for other fans. The network was localized to that one computer; as Rob O'Hara put it in his book, *Commodork: Sordid Tales from a BBS Junkie,* "During the golden age of bulletin boards (from the early 1980s to the mid-1990s), the modem world was our Internet. It was the way we talked to other computer users, traded programs and met people."[21] One pop culture BBS server was the "FidoNet Star Wars Echo," a message board founded in 1991 for discussing *Star Wars.*

Similarly, *Usenet,* a more distributed computer network also developed at universities in the 1980s, had an architecture that incorporated pop culture fandom almost from the get-go. Information was divided into newsgroups contained within nine categories, each of which had its own designation: alt. (alternative), comp. (computer), humanities., misc., news., rec. (recreation), sci. (science), and soc. (social discussions). These designations were used to name different kinds of newsgroups by subject—for example, rec.games.pinball, alt.politics.libertarian, or sci.physics.relativity. Most of pop culture fandom can be found in the alt.fandom or rec.arts categories of Usenet, and there are still fan groups discussing almost every form of popular culture imaginable. Fanlore, a wiki dedicated to recording and documenting the culture and activities of fandom, lists 145 fannish groups including alt.fan.teen.idols and rec.arts.comics.creative. (Usenet groups that end with ".creative" are for sharing creative work, like fan fiction or fan art.) Fanlore also cites a mention of Usenet in fandom from as early as 1984; that year, the zine *Interstat* published a letter from a fan, saying: "I would like to share my discovery of USENET, a nation-wide computer net accessible from many university mainframe computers and other entry terminals. There is a Star Trek interest group (net.startrek) consisting of people all over the country with computer terminals and some way of getting on the net."[22]

But IRC, BBS, and Usenet groups were not just for science fiction and media fans; other pop cultural fans—like music fans—also used these technologies to connect. For example, in "A Brief History of the Phish.net," Dan Hantman describes how fans of the band Phish used the available social networks in the early 1990s: "One of the early popular 'channels' was called #PHiSH. Ever the early adopters of technology, Phish.netters began to meet online to discuss the band, make friends, or just spend some time, and regular calls were made on 'rec.music.phish' to 'join the Net meeting on EFNet #PHiSH.' "[23] Phish fans also used early mailing lists like phish@world.std.com, and, as with science fiction fandom, well-placed fans at universities actually created new social networking infrastructure for their fellow fans. Phish fan Lee Silverman, in 1994 a Brown University senior, decided to found "a forum for students to learn how to use the Web, and to host their own communities."[24] Silverman got donations from Phish fans and his fellow Brown students and founded Netspace, which hosted mailing lists and websites for all sorts of groups, and particularly music fans. Interestingly, just as science fiction fans drew on the networks and communication strategies of analog fandom as they moved online, Phish fans "took many of their cues from Grateful Dead fans' on- and off-line habits,"[25] just as Phish the band were themselves influenced strongly by the Grateful Dead's music and relation to their fan base. The lesson is that these early online social networks were not inventions; rather, they were evolutions of previous networks created and nurtured by fans, sometimes for decades.

Fan Culture Explodes Online: Mailing Lists, Webrings, Archives, and Forums

As the internet developed, commercial organizations began to create communications platforms and offer social networking services, and, as a result, fans without government or university affiliations (or the technical ability to run their own servers) now able to create fandom infrastructure. In the early years of internet fandom, fans had to have a university account or their own server in order to create a mailing list, but by the late 1990s, companies like OneList, eGroups, and Yahoo!Groups allowed fans to create their own discussion boards on the topic of their choice. Fans tended to see these platforms as contiguous with their old networks, rather than as revolutionary; a writer in a mid-1990s print adzine (a zine that promoted upcoming zines) described the emerging culture of mailing lists as "a convenient way for a group of people to share their input on a given subject. Think of them as online letterzines, only with an instantaneous turnaround."[26]

Despite the cultural continuity, these new forms of online networking invited exponentially greater levels of participation in pop culture fandom. Part of it was that there were simply more entry points. In the early 1990s, a television show might have had one or two mailing lists devoted to it; in fact, the typical organization for media fandom at this time was to have one list for discussion and one for posting creative works like fan fiction (and possibly a third for posting sexually explicit fan fiction). But by the late 1990s, a single fandom could have hundreds of mailing lists, each dedicated to a particular sub-interest. So, for example, in the early 1990s, fans of the television show *Highlander* had two mailing lists: HLFIC-L, for fan fiction, and HIGHLA-L, for discussion (both hosted on university servers at Penn State). But by the late 1990s, a show like *Buffy The Vampire Slayer* had— and still has—literally hundreds of lists, each catering to specific characters, plots, and relationships; not just "buffyandfriends," but also "angelbuffy" (for Angel/ Buffy "shippers"), "xander2" (for the character Xander), "AlysonHannigan," (for discussing the actress who plays Willow), "spikelist," "xander-cordy_fans," "xander_and_oz_lovers," "BetterBuffyFics," "StepAwayFromMyXander," "Buffy-FemSlashers," "sunnydalemagicshop," and on and on.

Similarly, in the 1990s, commercial ISPs (internet service providers) gave fans the option of creating and hosting their own individual fan web pages, and thousands of personal fan sites were created on hosts like AOL, Tripod, and GeoCities. However, the downside of fans having the ability to create their own individual websites was a momentary weakening of fan networks: how were fans supposed to find each other? Fans responded to this challenge with their typical creativity, creating directories of fan web pages and linking individual pages on a common theme together by means of *webrings:* for example, "The Elton John Webring"[27] or "The NFL Fan Ring."[28] Fans also publicized their e-mail addresses, invited site visitors to sign their "guestbooks," and even created mailing lists their visitors could join. They also created centralized hubs like fan fiction archives or conversation forums to maintain community even as the internet began to atomize and more individual fans got the ability to control their own online areas and create their own, personalized content.

On the one hand, this explosion of fannish web pages, mailing lists, forums, archives, and websites in the 1990s was a positive development for popular fan culture, drawing many new participants into existing fandoms and encouraging the creation of thousands of new ones. Fans could now network around every conceivable movie, band, show, team, actor, relationship, or theme. But on the other hand, this proliferation of fan sites and lists was also experienced by some long-term fans as a watering down of fannish culture: with so many entry points and places to gather, fandom was now getting so big that even fans of the same pop culture phenomenon—the same band, the same TV show, the same actor, the same sports team—might never meet. As one television fan put it on a 2010 "fail_fandomanon" anonymous meme on LiveJournal:

> Back in the day, especially on Usenet, there was a larger sense of fandom. Slashers [fans invested in homoerotic subtext on television], shippers, and those who couldn't care less who's banging who all co-existed on the same newsgroup. Oh yeah, there were fights, but fandom was a lot more interesting back then because you were exposed to more opinions. With the advent of OneList and its many evolutions, fandom started to become much more factionalized as each fandom had dozens of lists. Now fandoms have dozens of communities. Slashers never have to be exposed to shippers, and vice versa. It cuts down on shipper wars, sure, but I think it robs of a sense of truly being a fandom.[29]

From Creators to "Users": Fandom's Love/Hate Relationship with Web 2.0

It has never been a better time to be a fan. It has also never been a stranger time to be a fan. Much of fan culture used to be subcultural, taking place at small science fiction conventions or over anime-oriented IRC channels or through Grateful Dead zines. But now, even the people that fans used to call "mundanes" (i.e., ordinary people or nonfans) are using commercial social networks to engage in fan activities: they might have "friended" a band on Myspace or have "liked" an actor on Facebook or be "following" their favorite author on Twitter.[30] Even mundanes might subscribe to Lady Gaga's YouTube channel (or post their own Lady Gaga remixes), add their opinions of their favorite show to the forums at "Television Without Pity," or be members of Major League Gaming, an online community of competitive video game players. In a famous *Saturday Night Live* sketch from 1986, actor William Shatner—who played Captain Kirk on *Star Trek*—berated a group of *Trek* fans at a convention by telling them to "Get a life."[31] But today, a fan not only has a life, but often a Second Life; for example, in her article, "Playing Dress Up: Digital Fashion and Gamic Extensions of Televisual Experience in *Gossip Girl's Second Life*," Louisa Stein describes how the CW network created a virtual version of *Gossip Girl* on Second Life for its young female fans, and how those fans role-play, network, and shop there.[32]

If Web 2.0 is defined by anything, it is defined by the evolution of social networking as a *business model,* which has incentivized the development of new tools. While some have argued that Web 1.0 was characterized by the broadcast of static content while Web 2.0 emphasizes collaboration and interactivity, I believe this is misleading; certainly those definitions don't work for fandom.[33] As I have noted, pop culture fans have always collaborated and interacted—discussing science fiction, writing fan fiction, remixing music, trading bootlegs, scanlating comics, editing anime music videos—using a variety of platforms; fandom is *defined* by its turning of the broadcast of static content into a participatory activity.

What has changed for fandom in the era of Web 2.0 is that a staggering array of for-profit services and interfaces have been (and are still being) created to support fandom's core values of collaboration and interaction. Below are a few examples of how pop culture fandom currently uses these new social networking platforms:

To Share Fan Film and Video. While fans have always made fan film and video—in genres like fan music videos (or "vids"), anime music videos ("amvs"), parody trailers, and fan films—streaming video sites like YouTube have made it radically easier to distribute and discuss this work within the fan community. Before the rise of streaming sites, fans shared video either by mailing videocassettes to each other or by going to centralized conventions (e.g., Anime Expo, Media★West) to attend communal vid shows. The relative difficulty of doing either kept levels of participation relatively low, but with the rise of broadband internet and mainstream streaming sites like YouTube, fan video has grown exponentially. Not only is there more work in established genres like vids and amvs,[34] but new genres like machinima (films made using video games), lipdubs (people lip-synching an entire song in a single shot), autotunes (in which news and other nonmusical footage is made into music by running it through autotune software), wizard rock (amateur bands inspired by Harry Potter), literal videos, and other "do it yourself" forms have emerged.[35]

To Share Interpretations and Information. Fans have always obsessively collected and shared information about stories; as I discussed earlier, Sherlock Holmes fans have been playing "The Grand Game" since the earliest years of the twentieth century. But the rise of easy-to-use wiki engines like MediaWiki and Wikia have resulted in a host of fan wikis: for example, Memory Alpha (*Star Trek*), Wookieepedia (*Star Wars*), the Twilight Saga wiki, Lostapedia (*Lost*), the Battlestar wiki (*Battlestar Galactica*), and separate DC Comics and Marvel Comics wikis, as well as Animepedia, the Filk Discography wiki, and numerous wikis devoted to Harry Potter, including the Unknowable Room and Leakypedia.[36] There are also hundreds of wikis devoted to bands or cataloging sports information. Wiki software has allowed fans to collaboratively catalog facts and interpretations with an ease unknown to previous generations of fans, and most fan wiki sites also have discussion forums, news and spoilers information, and other features.

To Share Visual Art and Music. Fans have always made visual art—line drawings, charcoal sketches, paintings, sculptures, cartoons, digital images, and photoshopped manipulations of photographs and stills—but, until recently, art was either advertised in zines or sold at specially designated "art shows" at conventions. The rise of sites like deviantART (which bills itself as the largest online social network for artists, and hosts a staggering array of different visual genres) and Tumblr (which allows for the easy uploading and sharing of images) has made it much easier for fan artists of all stripes to make and share work. Similarly, fans trade bootlegs of established musical artists and make a staggering variety of their own music: covering their favorite bands, making remixes and mash-ups, and performing "filk" (folk music written and played by science fiction and fantasy fans). No longer are these things traded on battered old audio cassettes; instead, sites like SoundCloud and Myspace allow fans to distribute music to a likeminded network.

These new tools—by broadening the modes and increasing the speed of fan communication—have radically improved many aspects of fan culture. But they are not without their downsides; in fact, arguably, what we see in Web 2.0 *is the mass-acculturation of the internet itself:* that is, the actual code used to construct the platforms and systems of the internet is now being made at a distance, by specialists, for millions, to shape habitual audiences (e.g., the Facebook audience, the Twitter user), for profit. Most fans and other users of the internet no longer "roll their own" code or websites. But if professionals are now providing the code, individuals are still providing the content. Contemporary social networks aim to turn interactions between individuals and the sharing of amateur content into the stuff of mass culture, regularizing and commodifying it the way magazines and television changed reading and drama. However, unlike in other mass media, here the content providers don't profit. Rather, these individuals (now labeled "users," "subscribers," or "customers," rather than creators or members) are seen as resources to be harnessed; as John Battelle and Tim O'Reilly told the crowd in their opening remarks at the first Web 2.0 conference in 2003: "Customers are building your business for you."[37]

But the priorities of these new businesses may or may not be the priorities of fans. Take, for instance, the case of imeem. Relaunched in 2006 as a site for sharing photos, video, and music, imeem was adopted by fan vidders due to its superior visual quality and audio-visual synchronization. imeem also had strong social networking features, allowing fans to friend each other and to create discussion forums, technical-support groups, and thematic video playlists. However, over the next three years imeem's service worsened as the site struggled. Banner ads were splashed over the videos, taking up a full third of the screen: a situation intolerable to artistically minded vidders. Finally, imeem announced, with no warning, that it was eliminating all of its users' works and would focus on hosting professional content instead, having decided that "simply put, there's no ROI [return on investment] for us in UGV [user generated video]."[38] But with that one stroke, an entire fan network was disrupted and an archive of fan vids was destroyed; vidders were not even allowed to back up their own videos before they were eliminated. (imeem didn't survive either; it was bought out and closed down in 2009 by Myspace, itself now struggling.)

Similarly, in her article, "A Fannish Field of Value: Online Fan Gift Culture," Karen Hellekson describes the culture clashes that can happen when corporate-minded social networks encounter media fandom's "gift economy." She analyzes

"The Case of FanLib," an attempt by "(male) venture capitalists to profit financially from (female-generated) fan fiction."[39] FanLib advertised itself as "an amazing fan-powered media event" but promised media corporations that they, not fans, would have power over and control of fan activities:

MANAGED & MODERATED TO THE MAX

All the FANLIB action takes place in a highly customized environment that YOU control.

- As with a coloring book, players must "stay within the lines"
- Restrictive players' terms of service protects your rights and property
- Moderated "scene missions" keep the story under your control
- Full monitoring & management of submissions and players
- Automatic "profanity filter"
- Completed work is just 1st draft to be polished by the pros[40]

As one might imagine, the longstanding community of fan fiction writers were furious at what they saw as exploitation and infantilization. Hellekson quotes an open letter from one fan to the FanLib founders saying, "You do not understand us and our communities, nor do you respect us. . . . You cannot build a new community at your site all nicely regimented and controlled because the community already exists and we will not be controlled by the likes of you" (Hellekson 2009, p. 118). After being rejected and vilified by the fan community, FanLib folded in 2008.

From Myspace to Our Space: Fan-Owned Social Networks

The growing commercialization of the internet, and of social networks in particular, has galvanized fandom in many ways. Some fans have gotten politicized around issues such as net neutrality, online privacy, and intellectual property reform, including a strengthening of fair use rights and the public domain. Others have called for fans to take control back from corporations by creating their own social networks. As fan Versaphile notes, "The fandom community cannot depend upon the kindness of corporations to maintain our platforms and tools. We must serve ourselves, and rely on each other, because we share the same collective values and goals."[41] Buttressed by larger cultural trends like the open source movement (which promotes the making of collaborative, free software code) and the free culture movement (which advocates the creation and distribution of free content), many fans have created their own online social spaces and networks.

This has led to the development of a series of alternative sites for fans, many of which are nonprofit, or, at least, fan owned and operated. Some of today's most notable fan-owned social networks include:

AnimeMusicVideos.org. This site is one of the earliest fan-run video-sharing networks and was designed as a guide to finding and making anime music videos (amvs): that is, fan-made videos made by setting anime to music, often with literally spectacular results. Originally open only to members, the site was announced as open to the public by creator Kris McCormic (aka Phade) on the AMV mailing list on December 19, 2000. As Mimi Ito notes, the site quickly became "a central clearinghouse for editors to upload their videos and to communicate with one another and their audiences."[42] AnimeMusicVideos.org currently lists over a hundred-thousand amvs; the site also hosts user forums, technical guides to making amvs, and critical essays like "Phade's Guide to Good Anime Music Videos."

The Archive of Our Own. (Disclosure: I am one of the founders of the Organization for Transformative Works, which created the Archive of Our Own.) In the wake of the FanLib debacle, some fans decided to push back against the commercialization of fandom. As a fan known as Wickedwords noted, "We have to do something before some commercial entity comes in and homesteads our territory, relegating us a tiny piece of our land as long as we pony up content and eyeballs that can be sold to some advertiser."[43] There was a call among fans for "an archive of our own"—a fan fiction archive designed, built, and owned by fans—and in 2007, a group of fans (myself included) created a nonprofit company charged with building this archive. The Organization for Transformative Works (OTW)—so named in order to emphasize the transformative nature of fan fiction, art, and vids—launched several projects, including *Transformative Works and Cultures,* a peer-reviewed, open-access academic journal; Fanlore, a fan wiki to preserve the history of fandom; and a legal advocacy team, to proactively protect fanworks from exploitation and legal challenge.

The OTW's flagship project, however, is the Archive of Our Own (AO3): a fan-designed-and-built, free, nonprofit, open-source fan fiction archive hosted on servers bought through member donations. The AO3 is also currently the largest female-dominated open-source coding project on the web; the OTW's team of volunteer coders has invited any fan interested in learning to code to join the project. The AO3 entered open beta at the end of 2009 and continues to add features like subscriptions, customizable skins, and .epub downloads. As we go to press, the AO3 has over two hundred thousand members and hosts over eight hundred thousand stories; it will also eventually host art and video.

Dreamwidth.org. While not a nonprofit venture, Dreamwidth was conceived as an ethical, fan-run alternative to popular fan blogging platforms like LiveJournal. Dreamwidth's founders, Denise Paolucci and Mark Smith, wanted to create a social networking site around community needs rather than commercial imperatives. As Paolucci wrote:

> I believe there's a way to sustain an online community, a community made
> up of smart, intelligent, and creative people, that functions *as* a community,

not as a cash cow. I believe that it's possible to build a site that serves its community, not its board of directors or its venture capitalists or its investors or its advertisers.

I believe it's possible for smart people, *creative* people, to build a service and *understand* the people using that service, because they're part of the userbase too. I believe it's possible for a small group of highly motivated, highly experienced people to build a service that accepts it's always going to be a niche market, and I believe it's possible to *rock the everliving hell* out of that niche.[44]

Dreamwidth's desired niche is creative types or, as they put it, people who make things. This group explicitly includes fandom as a longstanding community of makers: as creators of commentary, culture, and community. While Dreamwidth is not a nonprofit organization, its founders are "personally and ideologically against displaying advertising on a community-based service" and so have adopted a subscription model: basic service is free, advanced features are fee based.

All these projects, in their attempt to keep the making of online community a local, participatory, hands-on activity, embody the fannish ethos of participation and interaction. Fans are refusing to let even the making of software and social networks become a purely mass media activity. Just as fan fiction lets amateurs write their own version of *Doctor Who* and fan forums allow amateurs to show that their knowledge of baseball rivals any sports commentator on television, fan-owned-and-operated social networks let technologically and community-minded fans collaborate on their own terms of service.

Conclusion: Pottermore and More and More . . .

In the time between my writing this essay and its going to press, fandom has moved *en masse* onto two networks I haven't discussed: Twitter and Tumblr. Fans are creating new works based on the strengths of these platforms: we are seeing the emergence of the tweet and the animated .gif set as fannish art forms. Fandom has also seen the debut of Pottermore, a new site for Harry Potter fans that is part online store and part social network. In her video introduction to the site, Rowling claims that "Pottermore will be the place where fans of any age can share, participate in, and rediscover the stories."[45] But despite being the author of the Harry Potter stories, Rowling is late to this party. While Pottemore might well be a success—if there's one thing fans want, it's "more"—fans have already created literally thousands of spaces where they can share and participate in the Harry Potter stories. In recent years, fans have created huge for-profit networks (e.g., Mugglenet.com, founded by then twelve-year-old fan Emerson Spartz) as well as nonprofit companies (like FictionAlley, the largest fan fiction site for Harry Potter fandom and an important community hub). There are already thousands of ways for Harry Potter fans to connect: by fighting for real human rights through the Harry Potter Alliance, by discussing the books in The Sugar Quill's forums, or by surfing the Floo Network of Harry Potter–related websites. As Henry Jenkins observed, by offering fans a place of participation and community in Pottermore, J. K. Rowling is merely "offering fans what they already have on their own terms."[46] Pottermore may also end up being the test case for a new generation of authorized (and commodified) fandom; if it's successful, other mass media franchises may try to draw their fans into authorized networks where their social interactions are regulated and profitable. One can only hope that this new generation of authorized fan sites will be able coexist happily alongside fan-run social networks in the complicated ecosystem of the modern internet.

Notes

1. Ohmann, Richard. 1996. *The Origins of Mass Culture. Selling Culture: Magazines, Markets, and Class at the Turn of the Century.* London: Verso, p. 14.
2. Arguably, novels became mass culture even before this; Jane Austen's *Northanger Abbey* (1817) depicts a recognizable form of fan culture as many of its characters have read (and want to talk about) the same group of contemporary gothic novels.
3. Moviemakers are using sequels to create habitual audiences now that fewer people go to the movies regularly; in cinema's heyday, new films came out weekly.
4. Some forms of live theater are being turned into mass culture, too: consider the simultaneous, franchised, and therefore nearly identical productions of shows like *The Phantom of the Opera* or *Les Misérables* or *The Lion King* in cities all over the world.
5. Henry Jenkins, *Textual Poachers: Television Fans and Participatory Culture* (London: Routledge, 1992), p. 23.
6. Sample mash-ups can be found at SoundCloud at http://soundcloud.com/tags/mashup.
7. Picspam is an annotated collection of screen captures or other photographs of a celebrity posted online, generally as an affectionate tribute.
8. A list of hundreds of Sherlock Holmes societies from all over the world as of May 24, 2013 can be found at http://www.sherlocktron.com/two.pdf.
9. The Sherlock Holmes Social Network can be found at http://sherlockholmes.ning.com/ and The Sherlockian Who's Who is at http://www.sh-whoswho.com.
10. Arnie Katz, "The Philosophical Theory of Fanhistory," http://web.archive.org/web/20080820020954/http://www.smithway.org/fstuff/theory/phil4.html, accessed July 22, 2013.
11. Stephen Perkins, "Science Fiction Fanzines," http://www.zinebook.com/resource/perkins/perkins2.html, accessed October 22, 2005.
12. Cynthia W. Walker, "A Conversation with Paula Smith," *Transformative Works and Cultures,* no. 6 (2011): para. 3.12, http://journal.transformativeworks.org/index.php/twc/article/view/243/205.
13. Pohl, Frederick. 1974. "The Publishing of Science Fiction," in *Science Fiction, Today and Tomorrow,* ed. Reginald Bretnor. New York: Harper & Row, p. 23.
14. Slusser is quoted in Lee, Regina Yung. 2011. "Textual Evidence of Fandom Activities: The Fanzine Holdings at UC Riverside's Eaton Collection." *Transformative Works and Cultures,* no. 6. Doi: 10.3983/twc.2011.0271.paragraph 4.1
15. Conway is quoted in Lee, Regina Yung. 2011. "Textual Evidence of Fandom Activities: The Fanzine Holdings at UC Riverside's Eaton Collection." *Transformative Works and Cultures,* no. 6. Doi: 10.3983/twc.2011.0271.paragraph 4.1

16. Cory Doctorow, "Giving It Away," *Forbes.com*, December 1, 2006, http://www.forbes.com/2006/11/30/cory-doctorow-copyright-tech-media_cz_cd_books06_1201doctorow.html.

17. Howard Rheingold, *Virtual Community* (Cambridge: The MIT Press, 2000), p. xx.

18. For additional discussion of fans on the early internet, see Rheingold, *Virtual Community*, chapter five.

19. Alex Charalabidis, "IRCing on the Macintosh: Ircle," *The Book of IRC: The Ultimate Guide to Internet Relay Chat* (San Francisco: No Starch Press), p. 61.

20. MirclMax, "The Birthplace of a Network," via the Wayback Machine, http://web.archive.org/web/20110723073240/http://zine.dal.net/previousissues/issue8/startrek.html, accessed July 22, 2013.

21. Rob O'Hara, *Commodork: Sordid Tales from a BBS Junkie* (Lulu.com, 2006), p. 12.

22. "Usenet," Fanlore, http://fanlore.org/wiki/Usenet, accessed July 14, 2011.

23. The Mockingbird Foundation, *The Phish Companion: A Guide to the Band and Their Music* (San Francisco: Miller Freeman Books, 2000) distributed in the U.S. by. Backbeat/Hal Leonard Publishing, p. 813.

24. Farhad Manjoo, "Netspace Moves Its Net Space," *Wired*, May 17, 2001, http://www.wired.com/culture/lifestyle/news/2001/05/43801.

25. The Mockingbird Foundation, *Phish Companion*, p. 813.

26. "Mailing List," Fanlore, http://fanlore.org/wiki/Mailing_List, accessed July 14, 2011.

27. Latitude's Homepage, http://www.oocities.org/sunsetstrip/1004/, accessed July 14, 2011.

28. "The NFL Fan Ring," http://mcmillenandwife.tripod.com/nfl_fanring_home.html, accessed July 14, 2011.

29. "OneList," Fanlore, http://fanlore.org/wiki/OneList, accessed July 14, 2011.

30. "Mundane," *Wikipedia*, http://en.wikipedia.org/wiki/Mundane, accessed July 14, 2011.

31. "Get a Life," Saturday Night Live Transcripts, http://snltranscripts.jt.org/86/86hgetalife.phtml, accessed July 14, 2011.

32. Louisa Stein, "Playing Dress-Up: Digital Fashion and Gamic Extensions of Televisual Experience in *Gossip Girl*'s *Second Life*," *Cinema Journal* 48, no. 3 (Spring 2009): p. 116–122.

33. Similarly, World Wide Web inventor Tim Berners-Lee called the phrase Web 2.0 "jargon" because "Web 1.0 was all about connecting people. It was an interactive space." See "developerWorks Interviews: Tim Berners-Lee," August 22, 2006, http://www.ibm.com/developerworks/podcast/dwi/cm-int082206txt.html.

34. For more about fan vids, see Francesca Coppa, "Women, 'Star Trek,' and the Early Development of Fannish Vidding," *Transformative Works and Cultures*, no.1 (2008), http://journal.transformativeworks.org/index.php/twc/article/view/44. For more about anime music videos, see Mizuko Ito, "The Rewards of Non-commercial Production: Distinctions and Status in the Anime Music Video Scene," *First Monday* 15, no. 5 (2010).

35. You can see more examples of DIY video in the "24/7 DIY 2010: Collective Action" video show produced by the University of Southern California, now available online at https://vimeo.com/15782168.

36. For more about wikis and science fiction fandom, in particular, see Karen Hellekson, "SF Fan Wikis: Source, Reference, World," July 20, 2008, http://khellekson.wordpress.com/2008/07/20/sf-fan-wikis.

37. "Web 2.0," *Wikipedia*, http://en.wikipedia.org/wiki/Web_2.0, accessed July 14, 2011.

38. Elisa Kreisinger, "Imeem Removes Fan Vids Along with All UGV," July 6, 2009, http://www.politicalremixvideo.com/2009/07/06/imeem-removes-all-fan-vids-along-with-all-other-ugv/.

39. Karen Hellekson, "A Fannish Field of Value: Online Fan Gift Culture," *Cinema Journal* 48, no. 4 (Summer 2009): p. 118.

40. FanLib promotional .pdf, 2007. Available at http://fanlore.org./w/images/4/42/FanLib _info.pdf.
41. Versaphile, "Silence in the Library: Archives and the Preservation of Fannish History," *Transformative Works and Cultures*, no. 6, doi:10.3983/twc.2011.0277.
42. Ito, "Rewards of Non-commercial Production."
43. OTW Annual Report 2007 is available at http://transformativeworks.org/about/ reports.
44. "Announcing Dreamwidth Studios. Coming Summer 2008," Synecdochic LiveJournal, June 11, 2008, http://synecdochic.dreamwidth.org/221888.html.
45. "J. K. Rowling Announces Pottermore," YouTube video, 1:49, posted by pottermore, June 23, 2011, http://www.youtube.com/watch?v=oYs1d3jAdG0.
46. Henry Jenkins, "Three Reasons Why Pottermore Matters . . .," Confessions of An Acafan, June 24, 2011, http://www.henryjenkins.org/2011/06/three_reasons_why_ pottermore_m.html.

7

TEACHING AND LEARNING WITH SOCIAL MEDIA

Alexander Halavais

During a large undergraduate course I was teaching in 2005, a group of students approached me and asked that I remove their blogs from the course list. It was easy enough in this case: the blogs were not required. Blogging had been provided as an opportunity to replace one of the exams in the course. But I was curious as to the reasons. Was it because the topic of the course—online pornography—was too risqué? Was it because it made them uncomfortable to share their discussions with a public audience? No, it was just that these students thought of their blogs as somehow separate from their academic lives, and wanted to maintain that separation. They had not realized this until several weeks into the course. They remained active in discussions, and in fact continued to talk about the topics we covered on their now independent blogs, but had no interest in having those discussions graded or count for course credit.

Something similar has happened on other occasions as well, particularly in attempts to use Facebook as a home for a course. Some of the students complained that this struck too close to home: Blackboard (a widely used commercial Learning Management System) was for school, Facebook was for fun. Other faculty members have heard something similar from their own students (Sreenivasan, 2010). However, in recent years, this expectation of separation seems to have diminished, or even reversed. Young people are often heavily engaged in informal learning in multichannel online and offline learning ecologies and are frustrated when classroom instruction seems closed and backwards by comparison (Greenhow, Robelia, & Hughes, 2009).

These examples indicate one of the ways in which new social media seem to change the boundaries of the classroom and redefine ideas about the appropriate time and place for learning (Halavais, 2006a). Centuries of slowly evolving educational institutions have created a set of expectations of the school and the university as places separate from society, divided from it. As Ivan Illich (1971) had it, the modern school and university represent a "magic womb" (p. 47) in which the student is kept segregated until she is eventually born into adult life. Social media test boundaries in all areas of social life, and no less so in learning and teaching. New technologies are allowing the process of learning to be unbundled from traditional institutions of education. The results are disruptive and challenge our conceptions of what it means to educate and to be educated.

These days, few would argue in favor of learning being confined to the school day or the campus. Social media represent technologies that can, when applied appropriately, break down barriers of time, space, and authority. But in so doing, they also represent a significant challenge to the structures of formal education and how we define, measure, and communicate about learning within society. To better understand what these challenges are, it is worthwhile to examine some of the practices of learning with social media and their implications.

Educational Technology and Social Media

The most common approach to defining the catchall term "social media" is simply to indicate the sorts of web applications that exemplify it. These often include popular social networking sites like Facebook or Google+, media hosting sites like YouTube or SlideShare, and blogging and micro-blogging platforms like Word-Press and Twitter. They generally also include web applications like blogs and wikis, no matter where they are hosted. By this definition, as of 2011, more than 90 percent of university faculty made use of social media for teaching or professional activities (Moran, Seaman, & Tinti-Kane, 2011).

The difficulty with such a definition by example is that networked communication is a swiftly moving target, and it is all too easy to define social media as "every networked application that has arrived recently." Instead, these tools suggest some characteristics of social media and some of the implications of these characteristics for learning environments. The most common understanding of social media is that it appears in networked communication systems, and particularly on the internet. As Ithiel de Sola Pool (1984) notes, networked technical architecture alone does not necessitate less centralized and authoritarian control of content, but it allows for it. Social media emerges under conditions that permit and encourage everyone to act as authors as well as consumers of content.

We might profitably suggest some characteristics that help to define applications that are more "social" than earlier web applications. A number of people have attempted to provide such a catalog—including some indication of what this means for educational spaces—with varying degrees of agreement. An application that provides for easy creation of media, that can be freely and openly accessed, is easily re-created in other contexts, and leads to greater conversation and collaboration among the creators and consumers of the content is likely to be considered a part of the sphere identified as "social media."

Pushbutton Publishing

For a system to be considered part of the social media environment, the barriers to entry for those wishing to create media must be as low as possible. Although creating a website may be far easier and less expensive than creating a printed pamphlet, and result in a much larger potential audience, it traditionally required the author to learn a number of technical details, from the scripting languages of the web to design processes. A platform like a wiki or a blog makes it simple to add textual and multimedia content by clicking "edit," just as Facebook and YouTube provide similar "drag-and-drop" interfaces to publishing for the web. Blogger's original tagline was "Pushbutton Publishing for the People." Many of the technologies that make up "Web 2.0" are really ways of easily making content available on the web to audiences large and small.

Because these tools make creation and dissemination easy, they have in many cases become a staple in the classroom. Teachers have always needed to create texts, as have students. Just as word processors made a rapid transition from industry to the university and school classroom, other tools that allow untrained users to produce texts of high quality have been embraced by teachers and by students alike. Blogs and wikis, in particular, have now had a long history of use in the classroom and produce both intended and unintended consequences.

At one level, simply making available a new tool for document creation and sharing should not represent a revolution in the classroom. But putting publication and editing tools in the hands of students runs contrary to expectations long held among teachers and students about authorship and the creation of knowledge, and it forces them to think more critically about their media worlds (Hemmi, Bayne, & Land, 2009). Moreover, because most of these systems default to open access, in many cases teachers who have adopted them are pushed toward more open and transparent engagement.

The division between course management systems and tools used on the social web has gradually closed. By making use of technologies that are not specific to educational institutions, teachers and students benefit from a much wider, more demanding user base and reap the benefits of a shared need. They also do not spend time learning systems that cease to be used upon graduation. Even as a few large course management systems have come to increasingly dominate higher education, many teachers are choosing to use learning management systems that are assembled from platforms students are already familiar with.

Free Access

As the development of open software often reminds us, "free" has two associated meanings, relating not just to price but to liberty. There is a growing feeling that social media and sociable texts should be accessible without restriction of either payment or authority. National governments or large corporations should have little or no control over what can be accessed and how. At times, this becomes less a characteristic and more an ideology. The opening up of educational resources is a movement that extends across higher education, but social media plays a particularly important role in its development as it further enforces the idea that "users" are also creators, not just of the content, but of the way that content is linked together (Alexander, 2006).

This does not mean that everything in social media has to be open. As debates over privacy settings on Facebook demonstrate, there remains a significant amount of interest in shaping public exposure to various audiences. However, there does seem to be a tendency to default to open access, with an understanding that the knowledge commons serves everyone who contributes to it. This dedication to access and openness goes hand in hand with many traditional values of scholars and librarians, but particularly because it tends to conflict with issues of intellectual property rights and administrative control, it can lead to organizational disruption.

Conversation and Community

Many identify "interactivity" as a hallmark of social media, but that term is itself vague. What is meant is that while social media allows for storytelling, it also assumes that there is a mechanism for conversation, for feedback. While there are a number of formal elements that make a blog a blog, it is difficult to think of a blog without the ability to comment. In fact, more and more sites around the web provide the ability to comment on the material provided, and even those that do not may be annotated and commented on via Twitter, StumbleUpon, Digg, Diigo, or any number of other services that make use of the hypertextual nature of the web to extend conversation.

This conversation leads to new forms of community, new kinds of friendship, and ad hoc association. Perhaps "social" is too inactive a description of such uses: Donath (2004) refers to "sociable" media and Illich (1973) to "convivial" communication technologies. The new social media seem in some ways to be the culmination of many centuries of media technologies that allow for communities to form at a distance. In particular, work on "communities of practice" (Wenger & Lave, 1991)—in which situated, informal learning is a key process—can readily emerge in many online environments. Even when the groupings are too loosely joined to be considered communities, many of the learning pathways common to communities of practice can also be found in these networks (Brown & Duguid, 2000).

Adoption and Co-option

If we accept the above elements as indicators of social media in learning environments, it becomes clear that social media has played a role in learning for a period longer than might be suggested by focusing on YouTube or Facebook. In fact, the ancestor of many of the social and community uses of the internet today is to be found in an education computing system of the 1970s called PLATO. While PLATO was designed to deliver lessons and quiz students, it also could be used to support communication among the users (Smith & Sherwood, 1976). This began with "letters" being exchanged between users, evolved into the first multiplayer online games, and represented a new way to think about learning with machines.

Many uses of modern social media in educational settings are simply analogues for existing technologies. They may be more efficient or less expensive, but they replace a practice that is already well established in the classroom. Among the 90 percent of social media users noted above, the most frequent use was showing online videos. Teachers recognize the attraction of these platforms, as well as the advantage of some of their functionality, and attempt to make use of social media without ceding control. Some educational technologies adopt certain formal characteristics of social media without fully embracing the more challenging affordances of the platforms. When Blackboard introduced blogging to their popular course management system, for example, they included the ease of publishing and many of the visual cues of existing blogging systems, but made it difficult to open the discussion to the wider world beyond the university or to alter the way the blog looked. As one college noted, doing so violated student privacy and potentially the law (College of DuPage, 2010).

Many see wide-open social media—and particularly social networking platforms like Facebook—to be a real danger to students. By lowering the boundaries between school, home, and the public, students are open to discussion both among themselves and with strangers. In the name of reducing harm from sexual predators or bullies, many social media sites are blocked by filters on school computers, and mobile phones—which make such filters superfluous—are often outlawed from the campus. If social media are not dangerous, they are at least seen as a distraction. An article that discussed the use of Facebook by British high school students noted in passing that "no educator would knowingly allow such a distraction in their classroom" (Warner, 2008).

As a result, most schools and universities tend to walk a fine line between full adoption and banning the social media. There is a parallel here to the ways in which authoritarian governments have tried to establish boundaries on the use of networked media. An official in Singapore explained the desire to create a semi-porous membrane around the country, allowing beneficial uses of the internet while protecting its citizens from the more salacious or disturbing material that might be found there (Yeo, 1995). Certainly the filters regularly installed on school computers hope to serve such a function, but rather than just filtering violent or pornographic sites, many schools add common social media sites to their black lists. Likewise, the banning of mobile devices in schools has remained a hotly debated issue in many communities. In universities, the question is whether networked laptops are helpful or distracting (Zenilman, 2005), and some professors have demanded that wireless internet be blocked from their classrooms (Jan, 2011).

In recent years, there have been more vociferous claims that social media is not just something that should be available to students at school, but that it can benefit the learning process. Some of that comes of the ubiquity of social media; as one teacher notes: "The fact that we as educators even have to have discussions on whether or not social media is good for schools is sad. Social media just IS . . . it's life" (Johnson, 2010). But the incursion of everyday life on the institutionalized spaces of education acts as a kind of solvent, making us question why school is put together the way it is.

The Great Unbundling

Naturally, schools and universities have never been the only place where people learn, but there has long been an artificial boundary between learning in school and what happens in "real life." The latter often gets termed "lifelong learning" or "informal learning." Formal and informal education have never been completely separated. Those who have succeeded most readily in formal settings often arrived there and were motivated to study by their more informal experiences (Falk & Dierking, 2000). As the walls between school and informal learning are eroded, the organization of education is moving from one centered on teachers to one centered on learners.

Learning Networks

One of the problems with institutionalized learning practices is that they tend to create a one-size-fits-all model of education. New efforts at making schools accountable employ exams and other forms of assessment that encourage superficial learning and educate students for an industrial working world that has mostly ceased to exist (Davidson, 2011). Certainly, in recent decades teachers have shifted to recognize different styles of learning, encouraged by a range of researchers' models (Kolb, 1984; Honey & Mumford, 1982), and generally an emphasis on constructivism in teaching (Bruner, 1966). And teachers have for many years attempted to provide for instruction that is customized to an individual learner (e.g., Connor et al., 2007). Since everyone learns at home and in their communities in addition to inside their classrooms, everyone has a somewhat different overall learning environment.

Shaping those learning environments and making them more effective is accomplished in part by being purposeful in planning a "learning network." In examining education that stretches beyond the school, both in space and in time, it becomes clear that the focus should not be on the teacher, but on the learner. Lifelong learning is self-directed (Brockett & Hiemstra, 1991), and so it is important to understand how such self-directed learners construct information environments to support their learning. Koper and Tattersall (2004) describe four essential elements of an effective learning network: they must put the learner in a position of control over the environment, draw from a variety of different institutions over time, make allowances for different stages of learning, and provide the means for recording and reflecting on the process of learning.

These four elements are readily found in most social media platforms and technologies. Blogs provide an illustrative example, and one that has now been well tested in and out of educational settings. In most cases, the blog provides the user with control over not just content, but how that content is presented and how it is connected to other content out on the web. Particularly through hyperlinking and drawing feeds from a variety of sources, the blog can be used to curate connections to materials and to other people (Efimova & Fiedler, 2004). Finally, the blog presents a public notebook that can encourage reflection and assessment (Halavais, 2006b). These characteristics apply not just to the blogosphere, but to the spectrum of social media (Berlanga et al., 2007).

The combination of informal and formal learning environments can lead to deeper learning. Many of the assessment processes that are common in formal educational settings reward short-term retentions of large quantities of information, resulting in a surface-level understanding. Deeper understanding requires actively engaging in dialog and experiential activities that are difficult to accomplish in the university (Bowdon & Marton, 1998; Marton & Säljö, 1976). Open learning networks are in many ways ideally suited to promote deeper learning, promoting "divergent thinking," valuing multiple perspectives on a problem, and encouraging the kinds of fuzzy real-world solutions that are rarely found in textbooks (Hannafin, Land, & Oliver, 1999). A multitude of independent learners leads to a diversity of paths through a field and a variety of ways of thinking (Downes, 2007). Social media provides students an opportunity to engage in discussions and activities outside the classroom, to "learn in public" (Walker, 2005), and makes transparent some of the processes of informal learning that otherwise might be too latent to easily observe, so that others may follow along the same path.

Peer-to-Peer Learning

These learning networks may be centered on the autonomous individual, but learning is never exactly personal. Individual choice is inherent to the learning process, but learning happens best in dialog, embedded in a learning community (Vygotsky, 1978). As more open educational materials are made available, the open learner has an embarrassment of riches within easy reach, but open learning is most effective when it is peer learning. Social media foster new kinds of flexible communities of learning that help individuals to shape their own learning within a supportive social structure.

The key technology that allows this to happen online is the forum or bulletin board, a technology that has been used to communicate on computer networks before the web and before internet. Asking and answering questions leads to an ability to articulate knowledge and to learning for both the person who poses the question and for the respondent (Barak & Rafaeli, 2004). Recently, improvements to this structure have been created on sites like Stack Overflow, which allows users to discuss and rank answers to problems and to connect them with other problems on the system. These formal structures enhance the informal interaction that happens on the site, providing a framework for learning for neophytes and experts alike.

Peer-to-Peer University, along with several similar efforts, provides a site and framework for organizing study around various topics. Part of what it provides is a set of community expectations about learning and interacting, moving learning networks into more communal and shared environments (Bateson, Paharia, & Kumar, 2008). Certainly, you can learn in wide-open networks, mixing the professional and personal short messages found on Twitter into your own learning network, for example (Richardson, 2010). But sites like Peer-to-Peer University provide some semblance of the scaffolding that might be found in more formal educational environments. Included in this framework are connections to assessment and external recognition.

Assessment

The process of assessment is essential to learning. Just as individuals think more directly about shaping their learning environment, they must think about how to assess their learning. The term "assessment" is often tied up with "grading": you create something, turn it over to a teacher, and that teacher then assigns a grade to it, generally based on some openly available rubric. This common structure often fails to help learning in two ways. First, the assessment is disconnected from the sort of work that is being done: how well can filling in bubbles represent the sort of complex, analytics, deeper learning discussed above? Second, the assessment is top-down from a single authority, rather than representing multiple perspectives or the assessment of those who may be better contextually situated to improve a learning outcome. As students become more aware of collaborative forms of assessment in social spaces, the problems with popular assessment regimes become clearer.

Assessments should be, as much as is possible, directly related to the learning outcomes. When we study outside of a school or university, this seems very much the norm. If you take a driving class, you expect that you will be able to both demonstrate your driving ability during a driving exam and drive safely on the road. Determining success or failure in social media is multidimensional: not everyone is seeking the same outcome. Some may choose to assess their success based on the number of followers they attain; others may assess their success based on what they see as their own improvement in drawings shared in a community. Although these kinds of evaluations are not often called "assessments," they reflect what Biggs and Tang (2007) call "constructive alignment"—that is, a clear relationship between the learning objective and the means for deciding whether it has been met. These more authentic forms of assessment are intended primarily as formative learning instruments rather than a way of classifying students by ability, though they can be used to serve these functions of certification as well.

At the same time as we hear talk of authentic assessment, embedded in the context of learning and drawing students deeply into the process, there are also calls for "stealth assessment" (Shute, 2011). These are what might in other contexts be called unobtrusive measures—ways of determining how well students (or their learning environment) have done without having the assessment intrude directly on their consciousness. It would be difficult and expensive to instrument a traditional classroom, but drawing on analytics tools for the web allows us to gather "learning analytics" when students engage in social media (Romero & Ventura, 2010). By examining the actions and interactions of a large number of independent learners, it is possible to classify their learning behaviors and discover ways of improving learning resources.

When humans are doing the assessing, it should not be restricted to teachers. The student and her peers should also actively engage in the assessment process. What is the commonality between any sort of expert? The accomplished director, skilled auto mechanic, and brain surgeon all share the ability to assess their work and the work of others—"evaluative skill is the basic cognitive ability that characterizes all these areas" (Weiss & Shanteau, 2003). When a court calls on an "expert witness," it is usually seeking just such an assessment: how well was something done? People can only improve their work if they are aware of where it might be deficient, and developing the ability to see this in their own work is an important part of becoming an autonomous learner. Across higher education there is a press to move toward "authentic" assessment that provides some indication that deeper learning has occurred.

In the traditional school and university model, it is the teacher who normally performs an assessment, and this contributes to the control structures of education. Of course, peer assessment has long been used by researchers to review scholarly writings for publication, so it is not an entirely foreign way of thinking about assessment. Nonetheless, ceding control of the assessment process to students or to others marks a significant change. Even the process of allowing other experts to engage in assessing student outcomes—as has happened at Western Governors University, for example—represents a significant unraveling of authority (Paulson, 2002).

Credentialing and Reputation

The university's monopoly on postsecondary education has been assailed on many fronts, many of them associated with social media (Wiley & Hilton, 2009). The physical library is being replaced by an electronic library, and with an open access movement afoot, many of the materials we would need to learn in any area are just a few clicks away. Informal and nonformal venues for learning abound. There are new spaces for finding peer learners, asking questions, and getting expert feedback. The last piece that universities are holding on to is the act of credentialing. You may know all there is to know about a topic, but that is not the same as having a recognized diploma in hand. Universities continue to offer a wide range of services relating to learning, but they make sure that they remain vertically integrated by making the diploma dependent on students engaging in the traditional university experience.

University and school diplomas and their transcripts are particularly important because there are fewer formal markers of expertise outside of the school setting. Certainly, there may be informal recognitions of the gurus within a particular organization, or someone within an informal network may be vested with "geek cred" (Horst, Herr-Stephenson, & Robison, 2010). And in certain technical areas, one may have explicit licenses: say, to pilot a dirigible or to train others to use SCUBA equipment. But largely, informal learning results in informal credentials, perhaps with some form of evidence of experience that is provided as a line on the résumé.

Just as other forms of informal learning have begun to bleed over into more formal settings, informal credentials have started to gain some purchase, particularly around the reputation invested in online badges. There is some discussion, for example, of whether indicators of reputation earned as a member of the Stack Overflow site should appear on someone's professional résumé (Davis, 2009). There is some indication that a measure of influence on social networking sites—Klout, for example—may also be used for employment recruiting (Chulik, 2011). Mozilla is developing a "badge infrastructure," intended in part to provide a way of demonstrating informal learning in places like Peer-to-Peer University (Mozilla-Wiki, 2011). As badges and similar formal indicators of credentials make their way through social media platforms, we begin to see universities and schools remaining important issuers of valuable certifications of learning, but not the only game in town. Some may dig in, insisting that they are the only acceptable source of knowledge and that they provide a unitary college experience. Others will issue and accept credentials that demonstrate knowledge learned in other contexts and take a position in the wider learning ecosystem.

Education without Walls

Social media, then, does to education what each successive new medium has done. Meyrowitz (1985), in the introduction to his *No Sense of Place,* suggests that the "walls of the mightiest fortress no longer define a truly segregated social setting if a camera, a microphone, or even a telephone is present" (p. viii). Earlier, McLuhan (1964) noted that electronic communication technologies brought down walls, including those of schools, and turned us all into nomads. Schools and universities can no longer remain isolated from our everyday existence, nor should they.

Unbundling of the processes of learning is encouraged by the modular technologies of the internet, but the results of this unbundling reach far beyond the technology. If the printing press helped to usher in an era of universality in knowledge, thanks to the wide availability of comparable and citable libraries (Eisenstein, 1980), perhaps the unbundling of the learning process will erode that universality. Naturally, such universal claims have already been under assault in modern scholarship (Barnett, 2005), but the breakdown of authoritative sources of knowledge and practice may accelerate this process.

The rhetoric surrounding disintermediation of the web was largely left aside as new intermediaries have stepped into the breach. Today new ways of learning on the web are arising daily, from Khan Academy to Peer-to-Peer University to Stack Overflow to social sites that may not be focused on learning but provide it nonetheless. The space for this occurs as universities and schools disintegrate, providing space for others to take up new roles. That disintegration can be dangerous, particularly for students who are not prepared to take on the task of constructing their own learning networks. It can also be liberating, allowing for innovation in institutions that have remained among our most conservative and resistant to change. During this period of rapid change, it is important to measure the ways in which students learn in both formal and informal contexts, and to critically assess the role of institutions in that process. This is not the end of institutionalized forms of learning environments, but institutions must be responsive to students who have found a new way to write their own futures.

Recommended Readings

Brown, J. S., & Duguid, P. (2000). *Social life of information*. Cambridge, MA: Harvard Business Press.

Digital Media and Learning Hub (2011). *DMLCentral*. Retrieved from http://dmlcentral.net

Downes, S. (2007). Learning networks in practice. In D. Ley (Ed.), *Emerging technologies for learning* (Vol. 2) (pp. 19–27). Coventry, UK: British Educational Communications and Technology Agency.

Greenhow, C., Robelia, B., & Hughes, J. E. (2009). Web 2.0 and classroom research: What path should we take now? *Educational Researcher, 38*(4), 246–259.

Iiyoshi, T., & Kumar, M. S.V. (2008). *Opening up education: The collective advancement of education through open technology, open content, and open knowledge*. Cambridge, MA: MIT Press.

Ito, M., Baumer, S., Bittanti, M., boyd, d., Cody, R., Herr-Stephenson, B., Horst, H. A., Lang, P.A., Mahendran, D., Martinez, K. Z., Pascoe, C. J., Perkel, D., Robinson, L., Sims, C., & Tripp, L. (2010). *Hanging out, messing around, and geeking out: Kids living and learning with new media*. Cambridge, MA: MIT Press.

Richardson, W. (2010). *Blogs, wikis, podcasts, and other powerful web tools for classrooms*. Thousand Oaks, CA: Sage.

Scholz, T. (2011). *Learning through digital media: Experiments in technology and pedagogy*. Retrieved from http://learningthroughdigitalmedia.net/

Shute, V. J. (2011). Stealth assessment in computer games to support learning. In S. Tobias & J. D. Fletcher (Eds.), *Computer games and instruction*. Charlotte, NC: Information Age Publishers.

Webb, E. (2009). Engaging students with engaging tools. *Educause Quarterly, 32*(4). Retrieved from http://www.educause.edu/EDUCAUSE+Quarterly/EDUCAUSEQuarterlyMagazineVolum/EngagingStudentswithEngagingTo/192954

Bibliography

Alexander, B. (2006). Web 2.0: A new wave of innovation for teaching and learning. *Educause Review* (March/April), 32–44.

Barak, M., & Rafaeli, S. (2004). On-line question-posing and peer-assessment as a means for web-based knowledge sharing in learning. *International Journal of Human-Computer Studies, 61*(1), 84–103.

Barnett, R. (2005). Recapturing the universal in the university. *Educational Philosophy and Theory, 37*(6), 785–797.

Bateson, T., Paharia, N., & Kumar, M. S. V. (2008). A harvest too large? A framework for educational abundance. In T. Iiyoshi & M. S.V. Kumar, *Opening up education: The collective advancement of education through open technology, open content, and open knowledge*. Cambridge, MA: MIT Press.

Berlanga, A. J., Sloep, P. B., Brouns, F., Van Rosmalen, P., Bitter, M., & Koper, R. (2007). *Functionality for learning networks: Lessons learned from social web applications*. Presented at ePortfolio, October 17–19, Maastricht, Netherlands.

Biggs, J., & Tang, C. (2007). *Teaching for quality learning at university*. New York: Open University Press.

Bowden, J., & Marton, F. (1998). *The university of learning*. London: RoutledgeFalmer.

Brockett, R. G., & Hiemstra, R. (1991). *Self-direction in adult learning: Perspectives on theory, research and practice*. London: Routledge.

Brown, J. S., & Duguid, P. (2000). *Social life of information*. Cambridge, MA: Harvard Business Press.

Bruner, J. (1966). *Toward a theory of instruction*. Cambridge, MA: Harvard University Press.

Chulik, A. (2011). Klout and recruitment: Passing trend or permanent hiring tool? *The Hiring Site*. Retrieved from http://thehiringsite.careerbuilder.com/2011/08/04/klout-and-recruitment/

College of DuPage. (2010*). Blackboard release 9: What's NEW?* Retrieved from http://www.cod.edu/it/blackboard/bb9_new/Blogs.htm

Connor, C. M., Morrison, F. J., Fishman, B. J., Schatschneider, C., & Underwood, P. (2007). Algorithm-guided individualized reading instruction. *Science, 315,* 464–465.

Davidson, C. N. (2011). *Now you see it: How the brain science of attention will transform the way we live, work, and learn*. New York: Viking.

Davis, A. (2009). At what point do you put your SO reputation in your resume? *Meta Stack Overflow*. Retrieved from http://meta.stackoverflow.com/questions/58947/at-what-point-do-you-put-your-so-reputation-in-your-resume

Donath, J. (2004). Sociable media. In W. S. Bainbridge (Ed.), *Berkshire encyclopedia of human-computer interaction* (pp. 627–637). Great Barrington, MA: Berkshire Publishing Group.

Downes, S. (2007). Learning networks in practice. In D. Ley (Ed.), *Emerging technologies for learning* (Vol. 2) (pp. 19–27). Coventry, UK: British Educational Communications and Technology Agency.

Efimova, L., & Fiedler, S. (2004). *Learning webs: Learning in weblog networks*. Paper presented at the Web-based Communities Conference, March 24–26, Lisbon, Portugal.

Eisenstein, E. L. (1980). *The printing press as an agent of change*. Cambridge: Cambridge University Press.

Falk, J. H., & Dierking, L. D. (2000). *Learning from museums: Visitor experiences and the making of meaning*. Lanham, MD: AltaMira Press.

Greenhow, C., Robelia, B., & Hughes, J. E. (2009). Web 2.0 and classroom research: What path should we take now? *Educational Researcher, 38*(4), 246–259.

Halavais, A. (2006a). Weblogs and collaborative web publishing as learning spaces. In J. Weiss, J. Nolan, & P. Trifonas (Eds.), *International handbook of virtual learning environments*. Dordrecht, Netherlands: Springer.

Halavais, A. (2006b). Scholarly blogging: Moving toward the visible college. In A. Bruns & J. Jacobs (Eds.), *Uses of blogs*. New York: Peter Lang.

Hannafin, M., Land, S., & Oliver, K. (1999). Open learning environments: Foundations, methods, and models. In Reigeluth, C. M. (Ed.), *Instructional-design theories and models* (Vol. 2). Mahwah, NJ: Lawrence Erlbaum Associates.

Hemmi, A., Bayne, S., & Land, R. (2009). The appropriation and repurposing of social technologies in higher education. *Journal of Computer Assisted Learning, 25*(1), 19–30.

Honey, P., & Mumford, A. (1982). *The manual of learning styles*. Maidenhead, UK: Peter Honey Publications.

Horst, H. A., Herr-Stephenson, B., & Robinson, L. (2010). Media ecologies. In M. Ito et al. (Eds.), *Hanging out, messing around, and geeking out: Kids living and learning with new media*. Cambridge, MA: MIT Press.

Illich, I. (1971). *Deschooling society*. New York: Harper & Row.

Illich, I. (1973). *Tools for conviviality*. New York: Harper & Row.

Jan, T. (2011). Tangled in an endless web of distractions. *Boston.com*. Retrieved from http://articles.boston.com/2011–04–24/news/29469460_1_mit-social-networking-laptops

Johnson, S. (2010, March 11). Guest blog: Making the case for social media in education. *Edutopia*. Retrieved from http://www.edutopia.org/social-media-case-education-edchat-steve-johnson

Kolb, D. (1984). *Experiential learning: Experience as the source of learning and development*. Englewood Cliffs, NJ: Prentice-Hall.

Koper, R., & Tattersall, C. (2004). New directions for lifelong learning using network technologies. *British Journal of Educational Technology, 35*(6), 589–700.

Marton, F., & Säljö, R. (1976). On qualitative differences in learning I: Outcome and processes. *British Journal of Educational Psychology, 46*, 4–11.

McLuhan, M. (1964). *Understanding media*. New York: McGraw-Hill.

Meyrowitz, J. (1985). *No sense of place: The impact of electronic media on social behaviour*. New York: Oxford University Press.

Moran, M., Seaman, J., & Tinti-Kane, H. (2011). *Teaching, learning, and sharing: How today's higher education faculty use social media*. Boston: Pearson Learning Solutions.

MozillaWiki. (2011). *Badges*. Retrieved from https://wiki.mozilla.org/Badges

Paulson, K. W. (2002). Reconfiguring faculty roles for virtual settings. *Journal of Higher Education, 73*(1), 123–140.

Pool, I. de S. (1984). *Technologies of freedom*. Cambridge, MA: Belknap Press of Harvard University Press.

Richardson, W. (2010). *Blogs, wikis, podcasts, and other powerful web tools for classrooms*. Thousand Oaks, CA: Sage.

Romero, C., & Ventura, S. (2010). Educational data mining: A review of the state of the art. *IEEE Transactions on Systems, Man, and Cybernetics—Part C, 40*(6), 601–618.

Shute, V. J. (2011). Stealth assessment in computer games to support learning. In S. Tobias & J. D. Fletcher (Eds.), *Computer games and instruction*. Charlotte, NC: Information Age Publishers.

Smith, S. G., & Sherwood, B. A. (1976). Educational uses of the PLATO computer system. *Science, 192*, 344–352.

Sreenivasan, S. (2010, December 16). What we learned teaching social media. *blogtalkradio*. Retrieved from http://www.blogtalkradio.com/columbiajournalism/2010/12/16/social-media-what-we-learned-teaching-social-media

Vygotsky, L. S. (1978). *Mind and society: The development of higher mental processes.* Cambridge, MA: Harvard University Press.

Walker, J. (2005). Weblogs: Learning in public. *On the Horizon, 13*(2), 112–118.

Warner, B. (2008, March 12). Is social networking a waste of time? *The Sunday Times.* Retrieved from http://technology.timesonline.co.uk/tol/news/tech_and_web/article3536749.ece

Weiss, D. J., & Shanteau, J. (2003). Empirical assessment of expertise. *Human Factors, 45*(1), 104–116.

Wenger, E., & Lave, J. (1991). *Situated Learning: Legitimate peripheral participation.* Cambridge: Cambridge University Press.

Wiley, D., & Hilton, J., III. (2009). Openness, dynamic specialization, and the disaggregated future of higher education. *The International Review of Research in Open and Distance Learning, 10*(5). Retrieved from http://www.irrodl.org/index.php/irrodl/article/viewArticle/768/1414

Yeo, G. (1995). The soul of cyberspace. *New Perspectives Quarterly, 12*(4).

Zenilman, A. (2005, November 18). The rules of distraction. *Slate.* Retrieved from http://www.slate.com/articles/news_and_politics/college_week/2005/11/the_rules_of_distraction.html

8

RACE AND SOCIAL MEDIA

Theresa Senft and Safiya Umoja Noble

Introduction

Discussing race and social media can be touchy business. "Usually, the only way people talk about race in their lives is when they're feeling defensive about it," points out W. Kamau Bell (in King, 2012). Or, we might add, when laughter is involved.

Recently, online dating source OKCupid released data demonstrating that, as they put it, "racism is alive and well" (Rudder, 2009) on the site, despite its having a demographic that tends to be younger and more educated than most. Although OKCupid is designed to match people based on common interests and values, the site notes that most White men and women responded almost exclusively to messages from Whites. This was in spite of the fact that most White users claimed to have no preferences regarding a potential partner's ethnicity. White women in particular "only reply well to guys who look like them," and according to OKCupid data, Hispanic and Asian women sought out White men as partners as well (Rudder, 2009).

The OKCupid findings are significant both because they complicate fantasies of a new "post-racial" era of romance, and because they underscore just how far things have changed since the text-based beginnings of the internet where, as an old *New Yorker* cartoon opined, "nobody knows you're a dog." Today's social media includes text, image, sound, and video, allowing the transmission of bodily cues heretofore unavailable; it's delivered through devices designed to merge our online and offline social selves, moving us from personal fantasies to social and political realities. For White social media users, these realities are often voiced through anxiety. For instance, at the OKCupid Research Blog, there was "a huge fear on the part of most of the commenters about being labeled a racist" (Chang,

2009). This reaction was consistent with White teens who claimed they had left Myspace because it had become "too ghetto," yet insisted that they didn't mean that in a racist way (Watkins, 2009).

Like most social media sites, OKCupid and Myspace don't present themselves as explicitly political sites of discussion of race, gender, and class, but rather as locales where users can relax and have fun. It was in the vein of fun that the 2012 video "Sh★t Girls Say" went viral on YouTube, garnering eleven million viewers.[1] The video—featuring two gay White men in drag repeatedly ransacking their purses and saying things like, "Can you fix my computer?"—inspired a slew of copycats that year: women making videos about what men say; gay southern men making videos about what they say; New Yorkers making videos; and so forth. Of all these, the most popular videos focused on race.

The first race-related video was comedian Billy Sorrell's "Sh★t Black Girls Say," featuring his "ghetto" character named Peaches saying things like "My computer got an apple bit out of it" and "Ooo, *Basketball Wives* is on."[2] Although there were a few attempts by women of color to invert the formula by dragging men, the most popular videos featured men as women, as in "Sh★t Asian Girls Say"[3] and "Sh★t Spanish Girls Say."[4]

To scholars of race and gender, the most popular videos coming out of this meme seemed predictable enough, until African American comedian Franchesca Ramsey's, "Sh★t White Girls Say to Black Girls."[5] Posted on January 4, 2012, this video featured Ramsey in an ill-fitting blonde wig, using the vocal tone of a White California "Valley Girl," addressing what we presume is her offscreen Black friend. In addition to repeatedly trying to touch her friend's hair, her monologue is peppered with racist phrases ("Not to sound racist, but . . ."), questions ("Is blackface still, like, a thing?"), and pronouncements ("Jews were slaves too, and you don't hear us complaining about it all the time.").

Ramsey's video received 1.5 million hits in the days after its release, boosting her comedy career and spawning a follow-up video.[6] "Just by adding 'to' and a second group, the meme found new life," observed Latoya Peterson (2012) on the blog *Racialicious*. Most critics agreed, pointing out that "of the dozens of videos that took up the . . . meme, Ramsey's was the first one to offer a popular and critical examination of race" (King, 2012). As might be expected, the video's success paved the way for similar projects focused on things White girls say to Brown/Desi/Indian Girls,[7] Latinas,[8] Arab Girls,[9] and others.

Race, Racialization, Racism: Some Background and History

For those seeking to understand the political significance of "Sh★t White Girls Say to Black Girls" and videos of its ilk, it is important to grasp the persistent impact of race and racism in the lives of social media users, both online and off.

Many contemporary theorists argue that race is best understood as a verb, pointing out that it is through the process of *racialization* that we "race" others in our mind's eye, giving them a label that corresponds or contrasts with the one we give ourselves. The Marxist psychoanalyst Louis Althusser developed a concept called *interpellation* that is useful when trying to understand the mechanics of racialization. According to Althusser (1971), we derive our sense of identity from how we respond to the ways in which others implicitly categorize us through public speech and gestures each day.

Although we can experience interpellation positively (for instance, when being hailed as alumni of a school, or a fan of our favorite performer) we can also feel otherwise. As Ghassan Hage (2010) explains, we might experience *non-interpellation,* in which we feel "ignored or non-existent" (p. 121) . We may experience *negative interpellation,* where we feel uncomfortably noticed and made visible. Althusser's famous example of negative interpellation is the person who turns when a police officer yells, "Hey you!"

Most important for our purpose in this essay is Hage's notion of *mis-interpellation,* which results when we understand ourselves to be included in a definition of "everybody" and are later addressed in a way that makes it clear that we are not. In *Black Skin, White Masks,* Frantz Fanon (1967) describes riding a train in silence when suddenly White child points to him, exclaiming, "Look. A Negro!" In that moment Fanon, an Algerian intellectual, ceases to be part of "everyone" on the train, interpellated as "Negro" through the public exclamation of the child.

As Charlton McIlwain notes, racialization through interpellation requires both vision and blindness. First, "we unconsciously 'notice' racially marked features, like skin color or eye shape, while ignoring other visible traits" (Caliendo & McIlwain, 2011, p. 206) And while these responses are culturally specific and constantly shifting—in the eighteenth century, the English were describing Irish as "black" and the Hottentots of Africa as "tawny"—they gain their power from the belief that they are eternal, unchanging, and essential.

If race is an invention, why was invented? Stephen Spencer (2009) argues that "the use of racial divisions emerged as a way of resolving the conflict between, on the one hand, the ideology of equality for all and universal reason and, on the other, facts of social inequality" (p. 44). Spencer's argument may feel counterintuitive, until we remember that the Enlightenment value of social equality for all emerged near simultaneously with the new systematic brutalities of modern chattel slavery. In a world where nearly all were unfree to one degree or another, enslavement required no justification—it was only after freedom emerged as a birthright that withholding it from some needed explanation.

More than one scholar has argued that, as a concept, race should be "confined to the dustbin of analytically useless terms" (Miles, 1989, p. 72). And yet it persists: race has been used to refer not just to physical features, but also to differences in "nationality, religion, ancestry, class and biological sub-categories" (Caliendo & McIlwain, 2011, p. 203). The belief in race as scientific truth started in the 1700s, with European colonialism, the slave trade, and pronouncements that Whites were the highest "race" of humans. By the twentieth century, advances in evolutionary theory and genetics utterly refuted "racial science," as scholars came to regard race not as biological fact, but as an ideological system for "thinking about, categorizing, and treating human beings" (Caliendo & McIlwain, 2011, p. 206).

One of the upshots of colonial history is that while each of us has been ascribed race, Whites are reminded of it far less frequently than others. This phenomenon has been described as *white invisibility*. Here, we refer not to the number of Whites visible in literature, film, and television; for surely, Whites are everywhere in this sense. Instead, we mean the *privilege* Whites have to render themselves raceless: to "tacitly assume that they are race neutral and that only those who are members of racial (power) minority groups have a race" (Caliendo & McIlwain, 2011, p. 6).

For minority groups, then, visibility is a double-edged sword. At one level, the experience of non-interpellation creates an understandable desire for more and better representation in all forms of the public sphere: history books, public office, universities, businesses, media, and so forth. Yet while increased visibility for ethnic minorities remains high on the agenda of multiculturalism, it is important to understand that *invisibility* has offered distinct advantages for Whites. By defining themselves as raceless, they deny the advantages their Whiteness brings, laying the foundation for a new form of racism more "covert, coded, and cultural" than older forms, which tended to depend on biological explanations and legal segregation for their power (Ferber, 2007, p. 14).

In this "colorblind" racist ideology, economic and social inequalities between Whites and people of color are seen primarily as a result of differences in culture rather than as heritage of supremacist laws and policies (Bonilla-Silva 2006). Black and brown failures to secure or maintain home mortgages are attributed to "laziness," where White failures are seen as representative of the failure of the banking system. Black and brown successes in sports are attributed to natural talent, while White athletes are described as focused and hardworking. Barack Obama and Oprah Winfrey are celebrated as role models, while the huge and growing White-Black wealth gap is ignored (McGreal, 2010).

Race and Racialization on the Internet

There are three ways to tell the story of race and social media. In the first, we would speak of race as a static property and of racial "inclusiveness" as an unalloyed good. An internet history of this type in the United States would begin by detailing the paucity in non-Whites online in the early days of cyberspace and move to a discussion of remedies undertaken from 1995–2010 to address the "digital divide" in African American and Latino computer ownership (Leggon, 2006; NTIA, 1995, 1999; Warschauer, 2003). This history might then chart how "smart phones" have changed the demographics of internet access, noting that, in the United States at least, "over the last decade, the internet population has come to much more closely resemble the racial composition of the population as a whole" (Smith, 2010, July 7).

A history of this sort might end on a celebratory note, pointing out that in the United States, social network use by people of color is now higher than that of Whites: in 2010, 70 percent of African Americans and English-speaking Latinos reported using social networks (higher than Whites at 60 percent), with half of Black users saying they logged into social networking sites at least once a day compared to 30 percent of White users (Smith, 2010, Sept. 17).

In a second version of this story, we might remind readers that even when they were few in number, people of color have gathered in online communities from the internet's earliest days. They could be found on mailing lists like the South Asian Women's Network (SAWNET); on websites like MiGente.com, Asian-Avenue.com, and BlackPlanet.com; as creators of early pre-smartphone mobile web apps like Afronet.com; and on personal home pages like Mimi Nygun's now defunct Worse Than Queer—which began as a zine for women of color in the punk rock scene.[10]

In our preferred and third version of this story, we would understand race not as a fixed property, but rather as an ideological system that classifies and stratifies through the process of racialization. It is with this understanding that we discuss two Pew Reports about the fastest growing racial group in America: Asians.

The first report, written in 2001 at the height of American efforts to remedy its digital divide, declared Asian Americans the "most wired" people in the United States (Spooner, 2001). From the original publication of the study, scholars questioned Pew's definition of "Asian American," noting that Pew surveys "routinely exclude[d] the 69% of Asian-Americans who speak little or no English" (Daniels, 2012, p. 14).

A second Pew report, written in 2012, pronounced Asians as America's most educated and successful minority (Pew Research Center, 2012). Once again, scholars contested Pew's definition of "Asian" as Chinese, Filipino, Indian, Vietnamese, Korean, or Japanese, noting that while those communities do make up 85 percent of Asian Americans, they don't include those most at risk, such as Cambodians or Laotians (Hing, 2012). More disturbingly, the study took no notice of the one million undocumented Asians in the United States, many of whom arrive as refugees with "levels of educational attainment similar to Latinos and African Americans" (AACAJ, 2011).

Like every other racial category, "Asian American" is socially constructed; Pew's construction was one that buttressed preexisting narratives of Asian American achievement, even at the cost of non-interpellating many of the poorest and most socially marginal members of that community. Rejecting the notion that Asian Americans are "naturally" inclined toward education, Hing (2012) argues, "The far less exciting explanation . . . has more to do with immigration policy, which has driven selectivity about who gets to come to the U.S. and who doesn't."

The problem is not confined to Pew, which actually has a history of soliciting and responding to critiques of their methodology. In their 2010 study of Latinos online, they took care to distinguish between English-dominant Latinos

(87 percent), bilingual Latinos (77 percent), and Spanish-dominant Latinos (35 percent). Pew also pointed out that 76 percent of US-born Latinos went online, compared to 43 percent born outside the United States (Fox & Livingston, 2007), which echoes Andre Brock's (2011) suggestion that at least some of the digital divide might be explained by lack of perceived relevant content.

Examples like those above demonstrate how researchers, governments, members of the press, and even advocates for underserved populations still struggle to come to terms with the way *globalization* creates categories of people who "fit in" and "fall out" of discussions of the digital divide. Yet in spite of (or perhaps because of) the complicating effects of globalization, the desire remains to locate, define, measure, and evaluate minority groups against Whites, and one another.

Anna Everett (2004) refers to this as a "master narrative" (p. 1282) in which "undereducated, undermotivated and underemployed minorities are competing against technologically sophisticated Whites" (Jenkins, 1994). Or, we might add, as "model minority" Asians, who, as Nakamura (2008) reminds us, stand in as "honorary or approximate whites" (p. 179). As Luyt (2004) points out, the primary beneficiaries of digital-divide competition rhetoric tend to be multinational communications companies, who expand their global consumer base while presenting themselves as neutrally delivering essential services to warring parties in need.

Racism, "Neutrality," and Cybertypes

Racism is part of life on the internet; in a networked world, it is now a global reality. Sometimes racism is impossible to ignore, as when one looks at websites filled with White supremacist "hate speech" (Daniels, 2009) or reads about how Australians used mobile phones to organize an attack against "foreign looking" men on their beaches (Goggin, 2008). Other times, it manifests in more subtle ways, as when a young girl who types a term like "black woman" on a search engine is often led immediately to pornography sites (Noble, 2012), or when internet discussions break over anxiety over "terrorists among us."

Earlier, we argued that racism requires the presence of a group who perceive itself as "neutral" or unraced. Arguably, the history of racism online began in earnest during the mid-1990s, when text-only environments were celebrated as unchartered, yet inherently democratic territories (Barlow, 1996; Pavlik, 1996). Lisa Nakamura (2002) has long argued that since the net's earliest days, the declaration that one could "be anyone" online was translated by many as permission to engage fantasies of "identity tourism," with heterosexual White men trying to pass online as females, engaging in online sex scenarios that they would eschew offline, and opting for stereotypical roles like ninjas and samurais in games.

Importantly, when these same users were called to speak in public forums online "as themselves," their views reflected dominant neoliberal notions of individualism in which freedom from gender, race, socioeconomics, and any sexuality other than heterosexuality is idealized (Kolko, Nakamura, & Rodman, 2000). Of course, given that the internet began as a project funded by the US military, extended through efforts of universities and delivered to the masses through private businesses (all historically White male-dominated institutions), the dream that it might portend an inherently democratic future has always been somewhat unrealistic.

As early as 1997, critics were observing that net users tended to reproduce hegemonic discourses unintentionally, even as they described themselves as "apolitical" (Warf & Grimes, 1997, p. 260). In her recent ethnographic work on twentysomething White male programmers at social media technology start-ups in Silicon Valley, Alice Marwick (2013) notes that things haven't changed much: when asked, many described race and gender as relative "non-issues" in their lives, as they perceived themselves as dwelling in the "value free" realms of engineering and software coding.

As a number of critical race theorists have observed, the default assumption the internet is non-raced (i.e., White) mirrors the history of software coding itself, where contributions of people of color have been all but erased and obscured (Everett, 2008; Taborn, 2008). The fact that many Whites coding for Silicon Valley unconsciously associate their racial identity with neutrality explains why DOS commands such as "master and slave disk" existed without protest (Everett, 2004). It also explains why nearly all early social media systems involved pull-down menus and other architectural features that began with the default assumptions that users were White (Brock, 2011; Daniels, 2009; Kolko, Nakamura, & Rodman, 2000; Nakamura, 2002, 2008; Noble, 2012; Roberts, 2013).

Indeed, ideologies of whiteness are now so ingrained into users' perception of "normal" internet use that programmers who design for non-White default users (for instance, the developers of Blackbird, a Mozilla Firefox browser designed to help turn up content of greater relevance to African Americans) find themselves explaining why their efforts are not "reverse racist" (Brock, 2011).

In addition to being subjected to hate speech, default assumptions of whiteness, digital-divide rhetoric that encourages "model minority" competition, and accusations of "reverse racism" when they design systems to reflect their own interests, people of color have also had to navigate a range of digitally circulated stereotypes or "cybertypes" (Nakamura, 2002) in social media environments. To see the pervasive and historically consistent nature of cybertyping, one need only compare studies of behavior of White males in online "pubs" from the internet's glory days (Kendall, 2002) to currently popular networked games like *Grand Theft Auto* or *America's Army*—featuring multiple opportunities to kill "gangstas" and "America's enemies" (Dyer-Witheford & De Peuter, 2009; Leonard, 2009)—to online fan boards for television shows like *The Wire* where the term "thug" is both lionized and fetishized as a way to avoid actual conversations about race and urban politics (Brock, 2009).

Race and Performed Communities: The Case of Black Twitter

A paradox of our age is that even as we have come to recognize race as a synthetic, problematic, ideologically toxic concept, and as we fight against supremacist language and demeaning stereotypes, many of us still feel—and, are uninterested in abandoning—our races as social realities. Charlton McIlwain explains why: "Not only is racism a pervasive social construction, race is also a powerful way of orga-nizing community, both as a technique of oppression and as a strategy of resistance and community among people of color" (Caliendo & McIlwain, 2011, p 101).

As we noted earlier, people of color have long used the internet to gather together (Byrne, 2008a, 2008b; Everett, 2004, 2008; Nakamura & Chow-White, 2011). Whites, too, have created spaces devoted to racial identity (McPherson, 2003), although as Jesse Daniels (2013) notes, these sites tend to come with overtly racist political agendas. These days, our increasingly overlapped social net-works make it difficult to say for sure where one online community begins and another ends. That said, there have been discussions (in the United States at least) about how Asian Americans appear to "own" YouTube's "favorites" section (Bal-ance, 2012), as well as explorations of the phenomenon known as "Black Twitter."

The phrase "Black Twitter" refers to a Pew Study that found 25 percent of online Blacks use Twitter, as opposed to 9 percent of online Whites (Smith, 2011). Just as important, it refers to the popular belief that Black users dominate Twit-ter's "trending topics" feature by generating multiple back and forth responses via hashtags (Brock, 2012). Historically, explains Andre Brock, Black Twitter behavior would have been considered niche, "like other Black online activities," but the hashtag/trending topic features brought "the activities of tech literate Blacks to mainstream attention, contravening popular conceptions of Black capitulation to the digital divide" (2012, p. 545).

Brock emphasizes that it is important to understand that Black Twitter repre-sents a "public group of specific Twitter users" rather than a "Black online public" (2012, p. 545). Sarah Florini (2013) draws the distinction still further, noting that just as there is no monolithic "White Twitter," Black Twitter does not exist in any unified way. Still, she points out, "What *does* exist are millions of Black users on Twitter networking, connecting, and engaging with others who have similar concerns, experiences, tastes, and cultural practices" (2013, p. 3). She adds that although these users could easily "pass" in a medium like Twitter, they choose not to, instead "prioritizing the performance of their racial identity" (2013, p.12).

In their analyses of performance styles on Black Twitter, both Brock (2012) and Florini reference the African American practice known as signifyin', "a genre of linguistic performance that allows for the communication of multiple levels of meaning simultaneously, most frequently involving wordplay and misdirection" (Florini, 2013, p. 2). For example, consider this tweet:

#NextonNightline Tyler Perry discusses black feminist theory.

As Florini (2013) argues, to find this tweet funny, the reader needs to know two things: first, that the television show *Nightline* purports to tackle "tough" (often race-related) social issues, and second, that Black filmmaker Tyler Perry has been critiqued by Black feminists for his problematic portrayal of Black women. For Black users, signifyin' on Twitter allows not only opportunities to reject "colorblindness" but the chance to connect with others to "create and reify a social space for the 'Blackness' " (Florini, 2013, p.13).

"Sh*t White Girls Say to Black Girls" and the Politics of Micro-Aggression

Bearing in mind the political terrain mapped above, we now return to our discussion of "Sh★t White Girls Say to Black Girls" (hereafter, SWGSBG). Before SWGSBG, most successful "Sh★t People Say" videos featured male comics demeaning (sometimes playfully, other times cruelly) women of color. After SWGSBG, women from a range of global locales had a formula to "use humor to say something smart and discomforting about race" (King, 2012). In the pages that follow, we ask: what was racially "smart" about Ramsey's message? What made these videos both funny and politically progressive?

For many of us working on race and gender issues at universities, SWGSBG was exciting because it struck us as a clear "real world" response to academic calls to correct the demeaning portrayals of non-White women on social media platforms (Brock, 2009; Brock et al., 2010; Everett, 2008 Nakamura, 2002, 2008; Nakamura & Chow-White, 2011; Noble, 2012). As Ramsey makes clear on her YouTube page, her inspiration for SWGSBG came from her personal objection to Billy Sorrell's video "Sh★t Black Girls Say," which featured a range of unpleasant stereotypes in the form of his "ghetto girl" character, Peaches.

In most formal respects, Ramsey stays close to the established "Sh★t People Say" formula: cast a comedic protagonist who cross-dresses or otherwise "drags" a member of a group being lampooned, create a script that features this protagonist in one-way conversations with an offscreen presence who does not (or cannot) speak back, and edit using quick cuts that repeat phrases deemed the most annoying, upsetting, or problematic (presumably, to the unseen listener).

The presence of the invisible interlocutor is especially significant, since the conventions of film encourage the viewer to identify not with the characters being watched, but with the point of view of the person doing the filming. In cinema, the viewer understands themselves as watching the action, not participating in it. Here, it helps to remember Toni Morrison's admonition: "Definitions belong to the definers, not the defined." The bodies displayed on screen are the defined, while the viewer (invited to identify with the gaze of the filmmaker) is the definer.

In a typical "Sh★t People Say" video, characters address one another or an invisible offscreen presence. In the latter scenario, audiences are left to answer the question, "Say to whom?" The ambiguity of the enterprise is reflected in comments left on YouTube sites, which tended to range from "Hilarious—my girlfriend is just like this" to "Spanish girls don't speak like this" (coming from a poster in Madrid, unaware that in the United States, many Latinos describe themselves as "Spanish"). By contrast, the very title "Sh★t White Girls Say to Black

Girls" answers the question "To whom?" and replaces it with "How do you feel about the behavior transpiring in this video?"

One of the biggest barriers to discussing White privilege is the fact that in press accounts, literature, and the law, racist acts are generally described as somewhat singular exceptions to general rules of civil society: even while such narratives concede that some people suffer from racism, they reinforce the belief that most do not. By contrast, many critical race theorists hold that particularly for people of color, "racism is ordinary . . . an everyday occurrence, pedestrian rather than spectacular" (Holland 2012, p. 86). One of the most powerful ways in which this transpires is through *mis-interpellation:* the experience of being encouraged to believe we are part of "everybody" (i.e., dominant culture) and then being addressed in a way that makes it clear that we are not.

In his observations of behavior directed at Black Americans, Chester Pierce et al. (1977) gave the name "racial micro-aggression" to the automatic and often unconsciously uttered insults and dismissals routinely directed toward people of color. One example of racial micro-aggression is when someone places the phrase "not to be racist" in front of a patently racist statement. A slightly murkier example is when someone substitutes the word "ghetto" for "unpleasant." Heard once, this phrase might be shrugged off as ignorant or annoying. Heard multiple times in a week it becomes part of what Sharon Patricia Holland (2012) describes as the "everyday system of terror and pleasure" of living as a person of color (p. 86).

It is precisely because acts of micro-aggression are so complex that they are so difficult to discuss: to some extent, the smartness of SWGSBG comes from the fact that it was created as a vehicle by which the discussion of micro-aggressive behaviors could be broached in a non-accusatory way, simply by retweeting a link, or "liking" it on a Facebook page. As is the case with many YouTube micro-celebrities, Ramsey began responding to viewers' comments on her video the moment she posted SWGSBG, and her engagement has continued long after the video went viral. On February 25, 2013, more than a year after she first uploaded the video, she responded to the comment, "Ghetto loud black girls give us a bad name," by writing:

> No they don't. That would require black people to be one monolithic group, which we are not. If you subscribe to the idea that one black person's bad behavior reflects negatively on all of us, then you're giving racists justification to continue seeing us as one entity rather than individuals. (Ramsey, 2012).

Pointing out a friend's racism is never easy, especially in this ostensibly "post-racial" moment, where it is often perceived as an aggressive, even racist act. After a number of comments appeared on her site alleging she was "racist against Whites," Ramsey posted an extensive set of links on her YouTube page, telling viewers, "If you think this video is 'racist,' please read the video description box. Cuz it's not" (Ramsey, 2012).

Yo, Is This Funny? Race and the Politics of Laughter

Even when they objected to SWGSBG as an exercise in "reverse racism," for many, the video's saving grace seemed to be Ramsey's humor. Philosopher Joshua Shaw (2010) offers three major reasons why things make us laugh: because they help us feel superior to others; because they display incongruity, unexpectedness, or weirdness of some sort; and/or because they provide relief in socially tense environments. Clearly, superiority theory explains why some people laugh at a character like Billy Sorrell's "Peaches," but according to Shaw, it can also be used to explain why we might laugh at lampoons of ourselves.

By way of example, Shaw (2010) discusses his own laughter as a White male reading *Stuff White People Like,* a blog designed to expose clichéd behaviors of White people. After confessing that he has perused *Stuff White People Like* "while sipping coffee at a breakfast spot in Portland and listening to indie music," (p. 115) he argues that reading helps him feel superior not to others, but to a more naïve version of his prior self. Importantly, he notes, the effect is cumulative, as "each week the author manages to expose yet another way in which I resemble . . . clichés" (ibid).

Despite the fact that Shaw uses the term "superiority" to describe the pleasure he takes reading *Stuff White People Like,* it is clear he perceives his enjoyment as harmless, if not somehow politically progressive. In their analysis of the way some "gleefully" identify with *Stuff White People Like,* Patrick Grzanka and Justin Maher (2012) suggest otherwise. After acknowledging how *Stuff White People Like* began as a well-intentioned critique of White privilege, they argue the problem with the site is that ultimately it fails to address the fact that all stereotypes are not equal: while some are simply reductive, others are deployed to marginalize and stigmatize entire groups. In the strict sociological sense, *Stuff White People Like* doesn't reveal stereotypes so much as it pokes fun at Whites' "idiosyncratic and non-stigmatizing consumption choices" (p. 373). In truth, argue Grzanka and Maher, "being the proverbial butt of the joke in Stuff White People Like is the consequence of power and privilege, not socioeconomic disadvantage, unfair identity-based labels or stigma" (p. 373).

To understand why the tenor of the humor delivered in Ramsey's video differs from *Stuff White People Like,* it helps to think about how she deploys the principles of incongruity: that addition of unpredictable features or twists in a video that causes it to go "viral" on the internet (Shifman, 2011). In the original "Sh★t Girls Say" video, viewers experienced incongruity at two junctures: when they realized they were watching men in drag and again when a famous "real" actress showed up for a cameo appearance. Ramsey decided to do away with men entirely and instead used her own body, to which she added a ridiculous blonde wig, dragging a high femme version of White power and privilege.

In the viral parody video "Ching Chong! Asians in the Library Song,"[11] Asian American performer Jimmy Wong likewise surprises his audiences by adopting an R & B musical persona and dedicating a "love" ballad to Alexandra Wallace, the White undergraduate who posted a racist video complaining about Asians

American students in the library at UCLA.[12] Inverting Wallace's narration in which she describes Asian American students speaking "all ching chong ling long" on their phones, Wong croons:

> Don't think I didn't see you watching me talking on my phone yesterday
> All sexy . . . All Ching Chong Ling Long . . .
> Baby, it's just code . . .
> It's just the way that I tell the ladies that it's time for me to get funky.

Christine Bacareza Balance (2012) argues that viral media depends not just on circulation through networks, but on creators who "craft emotional hooks, key signifiers that touch upon a shared set of affective investments and affiliations" (p. 145). She notes that Wong's announcement in comically broken "Engrish" at the start of his video that he's "not the most politically correct person" resonates with his target audience, who will recall that Wallace made a similar proclamation at the start her infamous video. Wallace prefaces her rant by explaining that she isn't directing her anger at her friends, but at "people I don't even know." In SWGSBG, Ramsey's character tells her offscreen Black friend, "What I like the most about them is that they aren't stereotypical Black people. You know what I mean?" Shortly thereafter, she asks, "You can say the N word but I can't? How is that okay?"

Videos like Ramsey's and Wong's are important because they give voice to those feeling confusion, frustration, and rage in a "post-racial" moment, inviting expressions of *affective solidarity* with those suffering. Consider this exchange about hair, in which Ramsey's character delivers the following lines in rapid succession to her offscreen Black friend:

Can I touch it? Oh, I'm already touching it a little . . .
Is this real? It's all yours?
It's not real? It is. It is. Okay, sorry.
It's so nappy! Kind of feels like a Brillo Pad.
(*Extends hand into hair*) Did that hurt? Sorry.
You guys can do so much with your hair!
It kind of feels like Cheetos . . .

Because both Ramsey and Wong's videos were smart and funny in unexpected ways, they wound up redistributed through a range of social media, delivering a message that might otherwise be derided or shrugged off. Yet for those of us engaged in antiracist politics, should "delivering the message" be the final objective?

Antiracism and the Limits of Laughter

Perhaps in addition to asking whether something is funny enough to go viral and raise awareness, it is worth asking, as Erin Hurley and Sara Warner (2012) do, "Which emotions are likely to marshal and mobilize spectators into collectives and communities?" (p. 99).

In their analysis of White responses to *Stuff White People Like,* Patrick Grzanka and Justin Maher (2012) worry over what they see as "White people talk[ing] about antiracism without actually doing anything to catalyze structural change to combat racism" (p. 386). Similar worries have been voiced over use of the hashtag #firstworldproblems on Twitter, as well as the exceedingly enthusiastic response to a recent *Saturday Night Live* skit that featured Chinese "peasant" workers (played by White actors) railing at American reporters whining about their iPhone 5.[13] As Asia Society's Liz Flora (2012) wrote, "While no one really expects SNL parodies to be heavy on accuracy, another issue for critics is the use of workers' mistreatment for a joke meant only to poke light fun at the attitudes of the privileged." Sarah Ahmed (2006) has dubbed this phenomenon the "nonperformativity of antiracism."

Certainly, the argument that humor has the power to defuse anger is as old as Sigmund Freud. More troubling still for antiracist feminists is the fact that only specific combinations of race and gender create laughter, rather than derision, fear, or anger.

It is worth underscoring that although Ramsey originally conceived her project as a response to male-produced sexualized stereotypes of women of color, in reality, it critiques two females. Watching Billy Sorrel's character Peaches yell, "Hit me again and Imma call my brother," it becomes clear that although watching White female privilege might be "discomforting," watching masculine privilege over women can be downright frightening.

As the debate of the hashtag #firstworldproblems makes clear, humor isn't simply constructed along axes of race and gender. For something to be considered funny, it must also correspond to a sense of place and history. There are reasons American audiences find it funny rather than threatening when Asian American Jimmy Wong overtly sexualizes a White female in an R & B song—reasons that begin with a slavery-born "myth of the Black rapist," and end with the image of Asian men as inherently sexless, an image largely remnant of early US immigration policies that made it impossible for Asian laborers to bring their wives over or for them to intermarry with Whites (Feng, 1996). There are likewise historical reasons the ending of a video like "Sh★t White Guys Say to Asian Girls"[14]—in which the White male character (played by an Asian woman) says, "This was a great beginning; now let's have a happy ending," and then forces the camera into his crotch—isn't funny. That doesn't mean it shouldn't be made, shown, or circulated, but it does mean that massive popularity on the order of virality probably won't figure in its future.

Addressing the Problem

"Rather than asking non-white people how it feels to be a problem," argues Charlton McIlwain, "it is long past time for white people to ask ourselves: How does it feel to be a problem? What will we do about it?" (Caliendo & McIlwain, 2011, p. 28)

In addition to laughing at videos that strike us as politically on the mark, we might make a point to seek out social media projects designed to highlight and combat racist behaviors in our own neighborhoods. In the United States, one particularly successful example of this was the "Jenna 6" campaign, designed to pressure police in Louisiana to release a group of African American high school students arrested for fighting, while the White students fighting only received school punishment (Greenlea, 2011; Brock et. al, 2010).

Another powerful example of an antiracist campaign waged via social media involved the Florida shooting death of unarmed Black teenager Trayvon Martin. Frustrated with the delay in charging suspect George Zimmerman in the shooting, activists urged Twitter users to post with the hashtag #Trayvon Martin. Between March 10 and March 20 of 2012, the hashtag had appeared more than 150,00 times. Shortly thereafter, the Department of Justice initiated an independent investigation of Zimmerman's involvement (Ardoin, 2013, p. 139).

After a Florida jury acquitted Zimmerman in July of 2013, antiracist activists again turned to social media to organize street demonstrations, claiming "We are all Trayvon Martin." A powerful inversion of this message appeared on the blog "We are Not Trayvon Martin" (Phelan, 2013). Started by Joseph Phelan, who is White, the site "has morphed into a roster of mostly white Americans acknowledging their undeserved white privilege, how it protects them in every facet of their lives, and just how wrong it is that black people are treated differently" (Lucas, 2013) .

If we take seriously the notion that racism is global, it seems critical that we expand our focus beyond our domestic sphere and begin to learn more about "others" in information economies: young men and women assembling computer and phone components in "free trade zone" sweatshops set up to "outsource" business from the First World (Chan & Pun, 2010); young Asian men working in cramped quarters as "gold farmers" for companies that sell their labor to online game players in places like the United States (Nakamura, 2009); nannies and gardeners surveyed by their employers via webcams; young people of color who face greater dangers of police racial profiling as a result of DNA database adoption (Duster, 2012).

Finally, those interested in antiracist politics would be well served by following the following blogs, where critical race analysis abounds: Racialicious, The Root, Colorlines, The Asia Society, Ill Doctrine, NewBlackMan, and MuslimahMedia-Watch. The Microaggressions Project is a particularly powerful site, as it allows people to share thoughts about race anonymously that are difficult to articulate in public.[15] These recommendations could easily be expanded, and should be thought of as ways to start conversations, not end them.

At the very least, we can all pledge to keep our hands off one another's hair.

Notes

1. "Sh*t Girls Say" can be watched at http://www.youtube.com/watch?v=u-yLGIH 7W9Y.
2. "Sh*t Black Girls Say" can be watched at http://www.youtube.com/watch?v= fXDpfhehb6I.

3. "Sh★t Asian Girls Say" can be watched at http://www.youtube.com/watch?v=Xkaa Oei6oZ8.
4. "Sh★t Spanish Girls Say" can be watched at http://www.youtube.com/watch? v=LpaDBD84ET0.
5. "Sh★t White Girls Say to Black Girls" can be watched at http://www.youtube.com/ watch?v=ylPUzxpIBe0.
6. The second installment of "Sh★t White Girls Say ... to Black Girls" can be watched at http://www.youtube.com/watch?v=YnwqECbNm4Y.
7. "Sh★t White Girls Say to Brown (Desi/Indian) Girls" can be watched at http://www .youtube.com/watch?v=EQXboElx_V8.
8. "Sh★t White Girls Say to Latinas" can be watched at http://www.youtube.com/ watch?v=ZcQSLJHpwCA.
9. "Sh★t White Girls Say to Arab girls" can be watched at http://www.youtube.com/ watch?v=vXpIR1qxBpM.
10. For more on the history of "Worse than Queer," see the Fales Library Statement at http://threadandcircuits.wordpress.com/.
11. This video can be watched at http://www.youtube.com/watch?v=zulEMWj3sVA.
12. "Asians in the Library" can be watched at http://www.youtube.com/watch?v= NeHjx4TQyxw.
13. This skit can be watched at http://www.youtube.com/watch?v=ybDKfGEw4aU.
14. "Sh★t White Guys Say to Asian Girls" can be watched at http://www.youtube.com/ watch?v=2TK02tMOp_g.
15 URLs for the sites listed in this section are as follows:
    Racialicious (http://www.racialicious.com)
    Colorlines (http://www.colorlines.com)
    The Root (http://www.theroot.com)
    The Asia Society (http://www.asiasociety.org)
    Ill Doctrine (http://www.illdoctrine.com)
    NewBlackMan (http://www.newblackman.blogspot.com)
    MuslimahMediaWatch (http://www.patheos.com/blogs/mmw)
    The Microaggressions Project (http://www.microaggressions.com)

Bibliography

Ahmed, S. (2006). The Nonperformativity of Antiracism. *Meridians: Feminism, Race, Trans-nationalism, 7*(1), 104–126.

Althusser, L. (1971). *Lenin and Philosophy, and Other Essays* (B. Brewster, Trans.). London: New Left Books.

Ardoin, P. (2013). Why Don't you Tweet? The Congressional Black Caucus' Social Media Gap. *Race, Gender & Class, 20*(1–2), 130–140.

Asian American Center for Advancing Justice (AACAJ). (2011). *Community of Contrast: Asian Americans in the United States.* Retrieved from http://mn.gov/capm/pdf/A-Community-of-Contrast.pdf

Balance, C. B. (2012). How It Feels to Be Viral Me: Affective Labor and Asian American YouTube Performance. *WSQ: Women's Studies Quarterly, 40*(1–2), 138–152.

Barlow, J.P. (1996). *A Declaration of the Independence of Cyberspace.* Retrieved May 10, 2011, from https://projects.eff.org/~barlow/Declaration-Final.html

Bonilla-Silva, E. (2006). *Racism without Racists: Color-Blind Racism and the Persistence of Racial Inequality in the United States* (2nd ed.). Lanham, MD: Rowman & Littlefield.

Brock, A. (2009). Life on the Wire. *Information, Communication and Society, 12*(3), 344–363.

Brock, A. (2011). Beyond the Pale: The Blackbird Web Browser's Critical Reception. *New Media and Society, 13*(7), 1085–1103.

Brock, A. (2012). From the Blackhand Side: Twitter as a Cultural Conversation. *Journal of Broadcasting & Electronic Media, 56*(4), 529–549.

Brock, A., Kvasny, L., & Hales, K. (2010). Cultural Appropriations of Technical Capital. *Information, Communication and Society, 13*(7), 1040–1059.

Byrne, D.N. (2008a). Public Discourse, Community Concerns, and Civic Engagement: Exploring Black Social Networking Traditions on BlackPlanet.com. *Journal of Computer-Mediated Communication, 13*(1), 319–340.

Byrne, D.N. (2008b). The Future of (the) "Race": Identity, Discourse, and the Rise of Computer-Mediated Public Spheres. In A. Everett (Ed.), *Learning Race and Ethnicity* (pp. 15–38). Cambridge, MA: MIT Press.

Caliendo, S. & McIlwain, C. (2011). *The Routledge Companion to Race and Ethnicity*. New York: Routledge.

Chan, J. and Pun, N. (2010). Suicide as Protest for the New Generation of Chinese Migrant Workers: Foxconn, Global Capital, and the State. *The Asia-Pacific Journal, 37*, 2–10.

Chang, J. (2009, October 9). Of OKCupid and Denials of Racism. *Racialicious*. Retrieved from http://www.racialicious.com/2009/10/09/of-okcupid-and-denials-of-racism/

Daniels, J. (2009). *Cyber Racism: White Supremacy Online and the New Attack on Civil Rights*. Lanham, MD: Rowman & Littlefield.

Daniels, J. (2012). Race and Racism in Internet Studies: A Review and Critique. *New Media & Society*. Released December 10, 2012, at http://nms.sagepub.com/content/early/2012/12/06/1461444812462849.full

Duster, T. (2012). The Combustible Intersection of Forensic Science, Genomics and Race. In L. Nakamura & P. Chow-White (Eds.), *Race after the Internet* (pp. 310–332). New York: Routledge.

Dyer-Witheford, N., & De Peuter, G. (2009). *Games of Empire: Global Capitalism and Video Games*. Minneapolis: University of Minnesota Press.

Everett, A. (2004). On Cyberfeminism and Cyberwomanism: High-Tech Mediations of Feminism's Discontents. *Signs, 30*(1), 1278–1286.

Everett, A. (2008). Introduction. In A. Everett (Ed.), *Learning Race and Ethnicity: Youth and Digital Media* (pp. 1–14). Cambridge, MA: The MIT Press.

Fanon, F. (1967). *Black Skin, White Mask* (C. L. Markmann, Trans.). New York: Grove Press.

Feng, P. (1996). Being Chinese American, Becoming Asian American: "Chan Is Missing." *Cinema Journal, 35*(4), 88–118.

Ferber, A.L. (2007). The Construction of Black Masculinity and White Supremacy, Now and Then. *Journal of Sport & Social Issues, 31*, 11–24.

Flora, L. (2012, October 17). What the Web is Saying about SNL's Chinese "Peasant Laborers." *Asia Society*. Retrieved from http://asiasociety.org/blog/asia/what-web-saying-about-snls-chinese-peasant-laborers

Florini, S. (2013). Tweets, Tweeps, and Signifyin': Communication and Cultural Performance on Black Twitter. *Television and New Media, March*, 1–15.

Fox, S., & Livingston, G. (2007, March 14). *Latinos Online*. Pew Research Hispanic Center. Retrieved from http://www.pewhispanic.org/2007/03/14/latinos-online/

Freud, S. (1960). *Jokes and Their Relation to the Unconscious* (J. Strachey, Trans. & Ed.). Harmondsworth, UK: Penguin Books.

Goggin, G. (2008). Reorienting the Mobile: Australasian Imaginaries. *Information Society, 24*, 171–181.

Greenlea, S. (2011) *Free the Jena Six! Black Technospiritual Practices and Racial Justice in the Digital Age.* Presented at the SSRC Conference on Spirituality, Political Engagement, and Public Life, June 3–4, 2011.

Grzanka, P. R., & Maher, J. (2012). Different, Like Everyone Else: Stuff White People Like and the Marketplace of Diversity. *Symbolic Interaction, 35*(3).

Hage, G. (2010). The Affective Politics of Racial Mis-interpellation. *Theory Culture Society, 27*(7–8), 112–129.

Hing, J. (2012). Asian Americans Respond to Pew: We're Not Your Model Minority. *Colorlines.* Retrieved from http://colorlines.com/archives/2012/06/pew_asian_american_study.html

Holland, S. (2012). *The Erotic Life of Racism.* Durham, NC: Duke University Press.

Hurley, E., & Warner, S. (2012). Affect/Performance/Politics. *Journal of Dramatic Theory and Criticism, 26*(2), 99–107.

Jenkins, R. (1994). Rethinking Ethnicity: Identity, Categorization and Power. *Ethnic and Racial Studies, 17*(2), 197–223.

Kendall, L. (2002). *Hanging Out in the Virtual Pub: Masculinities and Relationships Online.* Berkeley: University of California Press.

King, J. (2012, January 6). How "Sh*t White Girls Say to Black Girls" Blew Up the Internet. *Colorlines.* Retrieved from http://colorlines.com/archives/2012/01/sht_white_girls_say_to_black_girls_viral_video.html

Kolko, B., Nakamura, L., & Rodman, G. (2000). *Race in Cyberspace.* New York: Routledge.

Leggon, C. (2006). Gender, Race/Ethnicity, and the Digital Divide. In M. F. Fox, D. G. Johnson, & S. V. Rosser (Eds.), *Women, Gender, and Technology.* Urbana: University of Illinois.

Leonard, D. (2009). Young, Black (or Brown), and Don't Give a Fuck: Virtual Gangstas in the Era of State Violence. *Cultural Studies Critical Methodologies, 9*(2), 248–272.

Leonard, D.J. (2006). Not a Hater, Just Keepin' It Real: The Importance of Race- and Gender-Based Game Studies. *Games and Culture, 1*(1), 83–88.

Lucas, D. (2013, July 22). 'We Are Not Trayvon Martin' Tumblr springs up as space for whites to share sympathy with Martin supporters. *The Grio.* Retrieved from http://thegrio.com/2013/07/22/we-are-not-trayvon-martin-tumblr-springs-up-as-space-for-whites-to-share-sympathy-with-martin-supporters/

Luyt, B. (2004). Who Benefits from the Digital Divide? *First Monday, 8*(9). Retrieved from http://firstmonday.org/htbin/cgiwrap/bin/ojs/index.php/fm/article/viewArticle/1796

Marwick, A. (2013). *Status Update: Celebrity & Attention in Web 2.0.* New Haven, CT: Yale University Press.

McGreal, C. (2010, Sept. 15). A $95,000 Question: Why are Whites Five Times Richer than Blacks in the US? *Guardian UK.* Retrieved from http://www.guardian.co.uk/world/2010/may/17/white-people-95000-richer-black

McPherson, T. (2003). *Reconstructing Dixie: Race, Gender and Nostalgia in the Imagined South.* Durham, NC: Duke University Press Books.

Miles, R. (1989). *Racism.* London: Routledge

Nakamura, L. (2002). *Cybertypes: Race, Ethnicity, and Identity on the Internet.* New York: Routledge.

Nakamura, L. (2008). *Digitizing Race: Visual Cultures of the Internet.* Minneapolis: University of Minnesota Press.

Nakamura, L. (2009). Don't Hate the Player, Hate the Game: The Racialization of Labor in World of Warcraft. *Critical Studies in Media Communication, 26*(2), 128–144.

Nakamura, L., & Chow-White, P. (Eds.). (2012). *Race after the Internet.* New York: Routledge.

National Telecommunication and Information Administration (NTIA). (1995, July). *Falling through the Net: A Survey of the "Have Nots" in Rural and Urban America* [Report]. Washington, DC: National Telecommunication and Information Administration. Retrieved from http://www.ntia.doc.gov/ntiahome/fallingthru.html

National Telecommunication and Information Administration (NTIA). (1999, July). *Falling through the Net: Defining the Digital Divide* [Report]. Washington, DC: National Telecommunication and Information Administration. Retrieved from http://www.ntia.doc.gov/legacy/ntiahome/fttn99/contents.html

Noble, S.U. (2012). Missed Connections: What Search Engines Say about Women. *Bitch, 12*(54), 37–41.

Pavlik, J.V. (1996). *New Media Technology: Cultural and Commercial Perspectives.* Boston: Allyn and Bacon.

Peterson, L. (2012, January 19). Exploring the Problematic and Subversive Sh*t People Say [Meme-ology]. *Racialicious.* Retrieved from http://www.racialicious.com/2012/01/19/exploring-the-problematic-and-subversive-shit-people-say-meme-ology/

Pew Research Center. (2012). *The Rise of Asian Americans.* Retrieved http://www.pewsocialtrends.org/2012/06/19/the-rise-of-asian-americans/

Phelan, P. (2013). *We are Not Trayvon Martin.* Retrieved from http://wearenottrayvonmartin.com/

Pierce, C.M., Carew, J.V., Pierce-Gonzalez, M., & Wills, D. (1977). An Experiment in Racism: TV Commercials. *Education and Urban Society, 10*(1), 61–87.

Ramsey, F. (2012, Jan. 4). *Sh*t White Girls Say to Black Girls.* Retrieved from http://www.youtube.com/watch?v=ylPUzxpIBe0

Roberts, S. (2013). *Behind the Screen: Unveiling the Digital Labor of Online Content Moderation.* (Dissertation). University of Illinois at Urbana-Champaign, Urbana, IL.

Rudder, J. (2009). How Your Race Affects the Messages You Get. *OKTrends: The OKCupid Blog.* Retrieved from http://blog.okcupid.com/index.php/your-race-affects-whether-people-write-you-back/

Shaw, J. (2010). Philosophy of Humor. *Philosophy Compass, 5*(2), 112–126.

Shifman, L. (2011). An Anatomy of a YouTube Meme. *New Media and Society, 14*(2).

Smith, A. (2010, July 7). *Mobile Access 2010.* Pew Internet and American Life Project. Retrieved from http://pewinternet.org/Reports/2010/Mobile-Access-2010.aspx

Smith, A. (2010, Sept 17). *Technology Trends Among People of Color.* Pew Internet Life Project. Retrieved from http://www.pewinternet.org/Commentary/2010/September/Technology-Trends-Among-People-of-Color.aspx

Smith, A. (2011, June 1). *Twitter Update 2011.* Pew Internet and American Life Project. Retrieved from http://pewinternet.org/Reports/2011/Twitter-Update-2011.aspx

Spencer, S. (2009). *Race and Ethnicity: Culture, Identity and Representation.* New York: Taylor & Francis.

Spooner, T. (2001, December 12). *Asian Americans and the Internet.* Pew Internet and American Life Project. Retrieved from http://www.pewinternet.org/Reports/2001/Asian-Americans-and-the-Internet.aspx

Taborn, T.D. (2008). Separating Race from Technology: Finding Tomorrow's IT Progress in the Past. In A. Everett (Ed.), *The John D. and Catherine T. MacArthur Foundation Series on Digital Media and Learning* (pp. 39–59). Cambridge, MA: MIT Press.

Warf, B., & Grimes, J. (1997). Counterhegemonic Discourses and the Internet. *Geographical Review, 87*(2).

Warschauer, M. (2003). *Technology and Social Inclusion: Rethinking the Digital Divide.* Boston: MIT Press.

Watkins, S.C. (2009). *The Young and the Digital: What the Migration to Social-Network Sites, Games, and Anytime, Anywhere Media Means for Our Future.* Boston: Beacon.

9

DISABILITY AND SOCIAL MEDIA

Katie Ellis and Gerard Goggin

Social media is social. It is important for us all and it should be open to all. . . . It is not necessarily about living a life on the Internet. It is about bypassing distance in the real world, making new friends, and participating in all the conversations between our family members and the communities we live in. . . . Social media can break down barriers and change lives. For example, a hearing impaired child can now share stories with their friends via Skype, and a vision impaired user can read about his brother's trip to the Far East via a blog site. . . . Social media is truly social. It connects the dots. (Cahill & Hollier, 2009)

Introduction

Media have long been social. The social nature, functions, and implications of media are something that have been widely debated, especially with the new kinds of convergent, digital media centering on the internet that have emerged since the early 1990s. As discussed in this book, the term social media is now widely used to indicate particular qualities of digital media. Central to social media are social networks; interactivity; the role of users in generating media content; participatory cultures; sharing; reliance on personal information; locational technologies, mapping and navigation; mobile media; and new kinds of closed versus open platforms. The implication of social media in the reshaping of media cultures, social relations, and everyday life is something that is being avidly researched and debated. As yet, there is little work on disability and social media—a fascinating and important topic. Critical theories over the past two decades have contributed much to our understanding that disability is as much a social phenomenon as it is a bodily, material, economic, technological, spiritual, and philosophical matter. Disability, then, has much to tell us about what the *social* in social media means.

For people with disabilities, social media is seen as a "social lifeline" (Morrison, 2010). Take the case of Edsel Odom. Edsel has a disability and is an avid user of social media. His favorite platform is Myspace because "you really get a chance to know people [on Myspace] as opposed to the glimpse you get from looking at Facebook" (Morrison, 2010). Eclipsed in recent years by Facebook and many other social networking applications, Myspace was the most popular social networking site in the United States between 2006 and 2008 (Ostrow, 2009) and was widely used elsewhere. What is interesting about Myspace is that members design their own page to reflect their interests and personalities. As a result, Myspace pages tend to be cluttered and often do not follow accessibility guidelines. The hundreds of links that can appear on a page make navigation with a screen reader problematic (Cahill & Hollier, 2009). In the case of Odom, while Myspace is compatible with the adaptive technology he uses, many other users with disabilities, particularly those with vision impairments, experience accessibility problems:

> Users of MySpace are encouraged to "pimp their page" by adding features unique to their identity. For example users select music to automatically load when other people navigate to their page. Automatic loading of audio disrupts screen readers when they attempt to navigate a page and breaks one of the simplest rules of creating an accessible page. While users are creating the inaccessibility, MySpace has a responsibility in establishing tool kits because the skill required to "pimp" a page is minimal. (Ellis & Kent, 2011)

Although the opportunity for unstructured user-generated content on Myspace alleviates the social isolation experienced by many people with disabilities, it also illustrates an inherent problem of access regarding social media participation for people with other disabilities. Myspace has been aware of their accessibility issues since at least 2006, when the American Federation for the Blind first alerted them. In 2010 Myspace continued to be inaccessible (Cahill & Hollier, 2009). While there are various reasons for Myspace's declining popularity, its failure to address accessibility issues and embrace users with disabilities certainly plays a part (Ellis & Kent, 2011).

In recent years the dominance Facebook and Myspace have exhibited over social media has been challenged by the micro-blogging site Twitter. Users of Twitter communicate tweets using 140 characters or less. Barbara, profiled on BBC disability blog *Ouch!*, believes Twitter is popular amongst people with disabilities, and vision impairment in particular, because it is text based:

> Twitter does away with the eye-contact element of a conversation. We're all equal and I think that's why people like it so much. (Tracey, 2011)

She accesses it using Qwitter for PC, Tweets60 for smart phones running the Symbian series 60 operating system, and Tweetlist for iPhone, which she describes as accessible. However, Twitter does not have an explicit accessibility policy. Unlike Myspace, Twitter is largely text based and does not rely on video or images. Nor are users encouraged to "pimp" their pages; in fact, the text size cannot be changed. The site is also heavily reliant on the use of a mouse. Although Twitter has a reputation of being simple to use, this is not the case for a significant number of users. This is a problem that cuts across the understood dynamics of social media: namely, that social media is valued for encouraging innovation and collaboration and so is felt to get better as more people use it more often.

A third vignette is the case of Apple's iPhone, the acclaimed technology that has galvanized the smartphone market. Many users with disabilities have adopted the iPhone with alacrity, quite a number praising its accessibility features. One prominent such user is famous singer Stevie Wonder, who in the middle of a concert in a Los Angeles nightclub in September 2011 praised Steve Jobs and Apple for making the iPhone accessible, saying: "There is nothing that you can do on the iPhone or iPad that I can't do" (The Next Web, 2011). The iPhone and other smartphones (such as those operating on Google's Android operating system) have instigated the "apps culture," a new force in mobile social media. However, the iPhone did not have accessibility features when first launched in mid-2007. It took until mid-2009 for Apple to make available on its iPhone (and then iPad) the VoiceOver accessible features for users with vision and mobility impairments, similar to those available on its operating system on its computers. For this reason, New Zealand–based Blind technology expert and blogger Jonathon Mosen (2009) has been alternately frustrated and impressed by Apple's much vaunted iPhone:

> Apple should be congratulated for taking a device that clearly breached Section 255 of the US Telecommunications Act [regarding accessibility] and having a go and making it compliant. . . . Whether it can compete with well established offerings in terms of productive, efficient access, I am not convinced. . . . Are arrow keys and a keyboard or number pad really so bad? It would appear to me to be an optimal interface for a blind person to use.

For its part, Google has been steadily rendering its Android phones accessible. Amazon.com has also finally been tackling the accessibility issues with its Kindle devices. Despite this, there remain accessibility problems with smartphones, e-readers, and tablet computers compared to the existing accessibility features on preexisting second- and third-generation mobile phones.

These three brief case studies illustrate the central issues in disability across leading social media—whether social networking systems (Myspace, Facebook, and a multitude of other applications around the world); micro-blogging (Twitter and many other applications, especially in emerging markets such as China); internet-based video and audio sharing sites such as YouTube; immersive worlds (such as Second Life); or mobile media (smartphones, tablets, locative media, and other media). Yet inaccessible design remains a central and constant problem across many social media platforms, including those designed exclusively for use by people with disabilities (AbilityNet, 2008; Ellis & Kent, 2011). This prevents many people with disabilities from participating in social media. This has serious implications not just for how people with disabilities figure in contemporary digital media, but for their wider participation in culture and society.

A further difficulty is that where disabled users of digital technology do surface in cultures of social media, their public discussion, and analysis, tends mostly still to be in uncritical celebration of how social media magically overcome discrimination and social rejection. However, this is only one part of the picture, as many with disability are prevented from initial and continuing access while some become effectively disabled by the online environment. For example, in many social media, people with mobility impairment will no longer need to disclose their disability, while people with dyslexia, who in traditional face-to-face interaction would have an invisible disability, find themselves "outed" by the affordances and norms of many applications and emergent online social norms. Significantly, inaccessible interfaces may prevent people with vision impairments from participating at all. In this light, we offer an overview and analysis of social media and disability, highlighting the two contradictory but linked aspects that characterize it.

Despite such inaccessibility, we can still point to a great deal of innovation amongst users with disabilities, their advocates, and those interacting with them on sites including Facebook, Twitter, YouTube, and Second Life—as our vignettes reveal. Disabled people form a sizable proportion of users of social media. Many people with disabilities have taken avidly to the full range of social media. Their use and consumption of (and, quite often, innovations with) social media are not well recognized—compared to other uses and users of social media. Thus, the innovative uses of the technology and cultures of social media by people with disabilities not only form an important part of the overall picture—such uses offer important insights into the nature of social media themselves.

Against this backdrop, our first aim in this chapter is to bring to readers' attention the important variety of uses of social media by people with disability. Secondly, when it does surface, use of social media by people with disabilities is still too often talked about in ways that stereotype, discriminate, and "disable." So our second aim is to describe, analyze, and critique the ways of talking about ("discourses") disability in social media. This leads us to our third aim in this chapter: to highlight accessibility issues. The way people with disabilities are talked about—and imagined—as using social media are often out of kilter, as we have suggested, with their actual uses. This is a problem related to how disability exists and is created in society. These power relations of disability shape technology too. So here we identify and discuss the very serious problems with inaccessibility of social media technology, which forms barriers to participation in social media by people with disabilities (and indeed many other people as well) (Craven, 2008).

The Paradox of Disability and Social Media

Before we proceed, it is important to understand a little about contemporary approaches to disability. Many view disability as an undesirable tragedy that should be cured. An alternative approach called the "social media" sees disability as located in social structures and inaccessible environments (Barnes & Mercer, 2004). Other approaches have followed that explore the cultural, political, economic, psychological, and bodily dimensions of how disability is shaped and how we can understand its distinctive power relations (Campbell, 2009; Sieber, 2008). Despite these new ideas, popular definitions of disability are still often premised on a discourse of deficit. That is, disability is a problem that particular individuals have, which makes them less able to cope with society or, worse still, inferior or less than human. Whereas, the impairments that definitions of disability revolve around can instead be seen as an integral part of being human and mortal (Goggin & Newell, 2005; Shakespeare, 2006). This model of disability is based on principles of empowerment and argues that able-bodied mainstream society disables people that have impairments through an inaccessibly built environment and the perpetuation of stereotypes and prejudicial attitudes. For example, digital media creates disability when its designers build inaccessibility into their interfaces, devices, programs, and assumptions. Thus people are "disabled" by such technological environments. Despite work into creating enabling environments, the examples with which we begin this chapter underscore the fact that some aspects of social media—such as the increasing use of graphics and user-generated content and a rejection of web standards—are having a detrimental effect on the inclusion of people with disability (Craven, 2008). As the importance of social media proliferates in all our lives, the potential cost of being excluded escalates.

Thus the new critical approaches to disability (Goodley, 2010; Pothier & Devlin, 2005) emphasize the importance of acknowledging, analyzing, and debating the ways in which new technologies—such as social media—shape disability and its relations (Ellis & Kent, 2011; Goggin & Newell, 2003). An obvious, yet unrealized, implication of this is that it is vitally important to create accessible environments—especially in online, mobile, social media. The increasing use of social media and other digital technologies is advancing this model, as adaptive technologies can be used to enable a fuller participation of people with disability—and there are many excellent examples of this occurring (Soderstrom, 2009). Moreover, the advent of the internet has coincided with a greater awareness of disability and accessible environments (Craven, 2008).

Having briefly established the key dimensions of disability, let us now turn to the antecedents of today's social media. In 1997, Sir Tim Berners-Lee (1997), inventor of the World Wide Web and director of the World Wide Web Consortium, described his vision for the web:

> The dream . . . is of a common information space in which we communicate by sharing information. . . . Once the state of our interactions was online, we could then use computers to help us analyze it, make sense of what we are doing, where we individually fit in, and how we can better work together.

As we can see, the kinds of social communication, interaction, and networking that characterize social media go further back into the histories of the internet than merely emerging with the notion of Web 2.0. What is significant about Berners-Lee's (1997) vision, and the origins of the web, is that he presciently foregrounded the inclusion of people with disabilities:

> As we move towards a highly connected world, it is critical that the Web be useable by anyone, regardless of individual capabilities and disabilities. . . . The W3C is committed to removing accessibility barriers for all people with disabilities—including the deaf, blind, physically challenged, and cognitively or visually impaired.

Of course, Berners-Lee's vision has distinct shortcomings and thus has received significant criticism. For instance, video bloggers have raised questions about Berners-Lee's accessible web ideas, suggesting that they do not give sufficient consideration to the importance of interactive video communication (Out-Law News, 2006). Despite these weaknesses, access to the internet for everyone regardless of disability was essential for Berners-Lee relatively early in the inception of the web—as it has been more recently in his efforts to inaugurate a truly accessible mobile Web 2.0.

Despite accessibility problems, people with disabilities have used the internet very widely indeed. We have already alluded to the importance of online technologies for social and cultural participation. A central reason why the internet has been important for people with disabilities is something shared by many other groups: namely, the internet provides new opportunities for communication, information, and media. Consider, for instance, the long-standing problem with how people with disabilities are represented in the media. While social attitudes are changing and media representations becoming more diverse, disability is typically represented in very stereotypical ways. The internet has provided a multitude of ways in which people with disabilities and disability media organizations and advocates can broadcast themselves (to borrow the famous YouTube motto)—and in so doing offer a wide range of representations of disability. E-mail was an early way that Blind people, for instance, were able to distribute information—using mail lists not only as a form of communication with people around the world, but also as a form of alternative media to mainstream media and even well-established minority options (the long-standing Radio for the Print Handicapped, for instance). Web pages, especially with accessibility measures, were a way that individual users wishing to share information, news, and views about disability could do so relatively easily. Alejandro Martínez-Cabrera (2010) describes the web as life changing for people with disabilities, allowing them a greater range of inclusion:

> The Internet has brought enormous benefits to people with disabilities, allowing them to become more competitive when applying for jobs, lessen their dependence on others, engage more actively in public debates and connect with their peers in ways that were impossible before.

With the advent of blogs, disability culture on the internet developed in fertile ways (Kuusisto, 2007). For many disabled users, blogs offered a platform for distributing news, critique, and commentary, as well as personal stories and information. Notable innovations included widespread use of audio blogs by Blind users (building on internet radio and podcasting) and video blogs by Deaf users (as, especially with broadband networks, video supports the visual medium of sign language). These cultures of use of the internet by people with disabilities prefigure—and overlap with—what we regard as the full-blown platforms of social media.

As our case studies suggest, there are many ways in which people with disabilities are using social media—most of these remaining relatively uncharted and unresearched. YouTube has offered a new platform for people with disabilities to produce their own content about their lives, perspectives, and narratives—and circulate it to others. Whereas, previously, video, film, and televisual content and programming representing disability in non-stereotypical ways was difficult to find, YouTube has made available a wide selection of amateur, professional, and, of course, "pro-am" accounts of disability, mixing the everyday, banal representation of disability (the quotidian, quirky, and tedious being YouTube's strong suit) with documentaries, entertainment, and other kinds of video. To take but one example, Marty Sheedy, in April 2007, uploaded a three-minute video to YouTube, entitled "Living and Overcoming Life with a Disability," aiming to explain "what it's like to be me"—which four years later had approximately fifty thousand views (Sheedy, 2007). Sheedy's video also attracted a wide range of comment, ranging from enthusiastic support and identification, to cruel jokes and abuse. As with many other social media, highlighted in hate sites and offensive humor groups on Facebook widely covered by other media, we find discrimination, violence, and disavowal of people with disabilities openly brandished (as it still exists in everyday life), whereas in other media such attitudes now require censorship, euphemism, sublimation, or use of code words to convey the same point. There has been little discussion of this continuing, oppressive discursive construction of disability in social media, or indeed other digital technologies; however, we can look to the important work on race on, and after, the internet as a very suggestive example, with striking parallels and echoes (Nakamura & Chow-White, 2012).

Immersive worlds have had a long history, dating back to the text-based MUDs and MOOs of the relatively early internet (Goggin & Newell, 2003). Disabled users, and disability, have also long figured in such online communities and now have received considerable attention and debate, especially with Second Life (Hickey-Moody & Wood, 2008). While a distinctive media form in its own right, Second Life is now closely bound up with the alliance of different kinds of media under the social media banner. Within the context of their use by people with disability, virtual worlds are often celebrated for their potential to allow people with disability an opportunity to "pass" as nondisabled. However, for some people, disability is an identity that cannot be left behind. Take for example Simon Stevens (aka Simon Walsh) who founded the Wheelies nightclub for people with disabilities in *Second Life*. Stevens suggests we all have impairments and describes Wheelies as inclusive (Hickey-Moody & Wood, 2009). Initially unable to find a wheelchair for his avatar, Stevens began creating his own (fig. 9.1, fig. 9.2). Thus he was the first to use a wheelchair full time in Second Life. As Stevens shows, virtual worlds such as Second Life offer unlimited potential for participation, social

FIGURE 9.1

FIGURE 9.2

engagement, and political activism. When everything about the construction of an avatar is mediated and usually highly stylized, people with disability can choose whether or not to reveal their impairment.

Social networking systems have become very important to users with disabilities, especially as these applications now predominate among populations around the world. In the Anglophone world, much attention has been paid to the salience of Facebook, with which disability communities and disabled users have experimented widely. Such applications and user cultures build on the histories of online communities important to early disability internet use, such as bulletin boards. Glenda Watson Hyatt (aka the Left Thumb Blogger), accessibility expert and person with a disability, describes the importance of accessible social media to people with disabilities:

> For someone who has always struggled to communicate verbally and who has often felt isolated and alone when in group gatherings, social networking has opened a world to me. (Glenda Watson Hyatt, in Ellis & Kent, 2011, p. 15)

Social media facilitates the creation of communities as people can quickly and easily mobilize online around a common interest. Facebook provided the opportunity for people with disabilities to form a community and through feedback provide more people with disabilities the opportunity to participate on Facebook. Thus many users with disabilities and many advocates also see social media as bringing great changes for people with disabilities. For instance, Australian Human Rights Commissioner Graeme Innes (2009) describes social networking, when made accessible, as opening a new world for people with disabilities. This is also the view of leading media and disability scholar Beth Haller, whose blog, website, and Twitter feed have been significant in charting the migration of, and take-up by, users with disabilities of social media. We would note here that while there is some discussion of disability users and Facebook, there is little discussion—in English language at least—of how users with disability are taking to the multitude of other social networking systems around the world, especially in the Asia-Pacific region, in countries such as Korea, Japan, and China (Ability-Net, 2008; Berners-Lee, 1997; Ellis & Kent, 2011; Goggin & Newell, 2003; Foley & Voithofer, 2008).

Disability Innovations and Challenges in Social Media

From this discussion of the many uses and innovations in social media by people with disabilities, let us now return to the vexed issue of accessibility. An interesting contrast can be drawn between disability and accessibility in the first decade of the web and the situation obtaining currently with social media. Take, for example, the respective visions of Berners-Lee and Mark Zuckerberg, founder of Facebook. In many ways, Zuckerberg's descriptions of his motivations for creating the social networking site Facebook resonate with that of Berners-Lee (and, further back, to other pre-web internet pioneers):

> People being able to share the information they wanted and having access to the information they wanted is just a better world: People can connect better with the people around them, understand more of what's going on with the people around them, and understand more in general. Also, openness fundamentally affects a lot of the core institutions in society—the media, the economy, how people relate to the government and just their leadership. We thought that stuff was really interesting to pursue. (Quoted in Vogelstein, 2009)

Zuckerberg too speaks of creating social connections online, but where Berners-Lee saw the inclusion of people with disabilities as vital, Zuckerberg did not—and, to our knowledge, has not done so elsewhere. This is a crucial difference that goes to the heart of disability and social media. Unless the expectations, habits, and uses of people with disabilities are explicitly acknowledged and explored, and accessible design ardently pursued, much of the social media landscape can be disabling. Thus critiques of disability and accessibility form a significant additional agenda to add to current work highlighting the problems with social media as open platforms. Many important, if not ubiquitous, social media are owned by entrepreneurs, by commercial interests, and, increasingly, by the very large horizontally and vertically integrated corporations that dominate communications and media (Castells, 2009; Goggin, 2011). As yet, however, few of those many researchers and commentators drawing attention to the enclosure of digital media incorporate disability and accessibility in their accounts. Yet the same forces and patterns that are shaping social networking systems, such as Facebook, for instance, to deal in a preemptive way with user data and information also are likely involved in the reluctance to take accessibility seriously.

Much discourse on disability and social media, of which mainstream media coverage is a useful index, is underpinned by a long-standing assumption (or myth) that technology brings salvation for people with disability—allowing us to transcend the limitations of our impairments. Here the way that social media and disability is represented has strong echoes in how such technology is presented in general (Goggin & Newell, 2003). Social media is either something magical and transformative, or it is an evil and contributes to a dystopian society. The reality, of course, is that social media has been involved in very significant transformations for people with disabilities. However, in doing so, social media does not "end" or "transcend" disability. Further, the threshold issue for so many people with disabilities when it comes to social media remains accessibility.

As we have noted, Tim Berners-Lee (1997) envisioned the World Wide Web as a common information space where people could benefit from collaboration. Ease of access was vital to his vision, and he argued that "access regardless of disability" was particularly important. The well-known work of the World Wide Web Consortium Web Accessibility Initiative (W3C WAI) has sought to put these into practice, providing technical standards and guidance for accessible websites followed by many governments, businesses, organizations, and users around the world—with mixed results (Asakawa, 2005; Ellcessor, 2010). The Web Accessibility Initiative is perhaps the best known of a welter of accessibility initiatives undertaken by various disability and technology specialist organizations around the world. Such organizations often work with social media and other technology companies and organizations, implementing social and online media to encourage and pursue accessible technology. What is clear is that digital information can potentially be accessed in many different formats (such as text, image, sound, multimedia) using a range of adaptive technology (whether screen readers, Braille outputs, or keyboard and/or mouse).

The importance of the Web Accessibility Initiative was bound up with the public internet—a commonly available platform that would also be accessible for people with disabilities. As the internet has developed—especially via the complex, interdependent technological systems that social media represents—it has proven difficult to implement such a vision. And there has been surprisingly little commitment to making accessibility a "natural" feature of social media by the multitude of specific software, hardware, and network providers and other technology companies that make up the social media landscape. This is evident in the case of social networking systems, notably Facebook.

As we have mentioned, the accessibility of social networking sites and the implications this has for the exclusion of people with disabilities has been of concern for some time. In 2008, UK charity AbilityNet (2008) noted:

> Social networking websites are an increasingly important part of the internet and have become vitally important both for work and leisure activities. For many disabled people, social networking websites offer huge opportunities to conduct business and to socialise without physical barriers.

However, AbilityNet was critical of accessibility across social media. Their analysis covered Myspace, Facebook, YouTube, Yahoo!, and Bebo and found five accessibility and usability issues common to the five sites: no help section or accessibility page for people with disabilities; sites were impossible to access using keyboard only; graphics lacked alternative text; use of CAPTCHA (a text-based method of authenticating user identification); and little support for or encouragement for including captions in online videos, with only Yahoo! providing an option to do so.

These issues combine to make navigation of the social networking sites using assistive technology difficult or impossible. Valuable opportunities for social networking are prevented by an inaccessible interface (AbilityNet, 2008). Foley and Voithofer (2008) target the disabling use of CAPTCHA at the login stage of Facebook as proof that exclusion is built into social technologies in such a way that reflects certain discourses of power. By design, the visual verification system of CAPTCHA requires "human" and not machine translation. This reflects an assumption that all humans can see or—in the case of audio CAPTCHA—hear, and it can block those using adaptive technologies such as a screen reader (Ellis & Kent, 2011). CAPTCHA is a concrete example of the way technology is designed to limit our use with it and exclude people with disability. Unfortunately, since 2007 there has been limited progress with accessibility in social networking systems. In 2009 the Australian disability technology organization Media Access Australia analyzed Skype, Facebook, YouTube, Flickr, Twitter, and Myspace and significantly found Facebook to be a good choice for people with disabilities, although issues with CAPTCHA remained (Cahill & Hollier, 2009). This was because Facebook overhauled its site in consultation with the America Foundation for the Blind in 2008. Key to this achievement was the political mobilization of groups of people with disabilities, fittingly via Facebook.

The decision to make a social networking site inaccessible is inherently political, not least because there are many more different options available digitally than there usually are in the offline world. In suggesting that inaccessibility of social media implies a politics is to take away from the complexity of both technology design and implementation, on the one hand, and the reconfiguration of the social relations of disability currently underway, on the other hand. Take, for instance, the range of social media applications used by a typical user. This would likely include Facebook (or another social networking system, such as LinkedIn); Twitter (available via many different forms, including mobile apps); YouTube; photo-sharing sites (such as Flickr); locative media (such as Foursquare and Facebook Places); navigation, maps, and way-finding software (such as Google Maps and Google Earth); web browsers; social bookmarking; Second Life or other immersive worlds; and blogs. Add to this, for many disabled users, particular adaptive or favored interfaces such as screen readers. The obvious issue is that making social media accessible requires each of these particular applications to take seriously accessible design, and for each to work together with each other—upping the ante with compatibility and interoperability issues among social media applications with which technology developers and investors are already struggling (Annable, Goggin, & Stienstra, 2007).

Yet despite the obvious difficulties posed by accessible design, there are also real commercial benefits to be gained. Accessible design ensures that technology is available to a greater range of users—those who are not disabled (or do not identify with a disability), as well as people with disability. There exist many business, government, social, and citizenship benefits for accessibility. These possibilities underscore the importance of ensuring that social media technologies do not remain inaccessible, thus following a trajectory by which they perpetuate ableist assumptions of normativity (Goggin & Newell, 2003). Given the expanding possibilities of technology for opening up accessibility, there remains little rationale for building in inaccessibility—unnecessary limitations of technology that reflect a disabling world view (Foley & Voithofer, 2008).

By definition, social media refers to platforms that encourage input from its community of users. This dynamic feedback blurs the line between media and audience and provides the opportunity for improvement in the site's functioning. People with disabilities have been integral in improving Facebook's accessibility for people with disabilities and usability for the entire community. Shortly after Facebook was launched, the Facebook group The Official Petition for a More Accessible Facebook was created by a student with a vision impairment in order to highlight issues of access experienced by people with vision impairment and learning disabilities. The group quickly attracted the attention of Facebook administration, who eventually improved the site in consultation with The American Association for the Blind the following year.

Skeptical approaches to digital technology and disability recognize that as we develop technology we can choose to enable or disable users, and that superficial approaches to universal design and disability can again reproduce narrowly defined notions of normality. As Goggin and Newell (2003) recognize, accessibility for a person with a certain type of impairment can have disastrous consequences for a person with a different impairment:

> There is no doubt that [universal design] offers a great deal in reorienting thinking and design to factor in a variety of functional needs. Yet a

challenge for universal design is found in the very diversity of situations and human circumstances. (Goggin & Newell, 2003, p. 149)

The implications of this is the need for incorporation of difference into cultural and policy formations and consultation of disability groups in the design phase of digital technologies. The result, they argue, will be the inclusion of not just people with disability but all people who exist on the margins. (It is worth noting that Goggin and Newell are wary of the discourse of "inclusion" throughout digital disability, believing it can sometimes function as an excuse to perpetuate disablism.) Ellis and Kent (2011) extend Goggin and Newell's digital disability argument in *Disability and New Media* in light of both user-generated content and the possibility for user-generated output and accessibility 2.0, which accompanies social media. Accessibility 2.0 is a user-centric approach that assumes technological innovation and that users will access the same information in different ways. Such openness and ease of access is vital to the success of social media.

Conclusion and Future Avenues for Research

Social media continue their rise in media, culture, and society. As other contributions to this *Handbook* illustrate, social media offer extraordinary opportunities for new ways to communicate, gain information, tell stories, offer cultural expressions and representation, conduct business, do politics, and, above all, connect and participate. Social media also heighten existing problems and debates about the role of media—and lead to the formulation of new problems. In this chapter, we have sought to provide an overview and analysis of the important area of disability in social media. What we have highlighted are the great variety and innovation in uses of social media by people with disabilities and the kinds of issues and conversations that are underway regarding this—and that perhaps should be fostered. Approaching disability in this way remains an unfamiliar approach for students, teachers, and researchers of media—as indeed it does for policymakers and publics.

A much more familiar way of framing disability and new media, which we now see in relation to social media, is accessibility. When disability is discussed at an academic conference or public event about social media, it is more often than not about accessibility. Accessibility is extremely important, and we too have continually drawn attention to it as an issue in this chapter. As we have sought to illustrate, social media platforms are characterized by networks that get stronger the more people are in and contributing to them. Excluding an entire group of people makes little sense when success is achieved through collaboration with as many people as possible. So accessibility is unfinished business—indeed business that many technology companies, organizations, and institutions have not yet even begun to embark upon. However, there are many reasons now for grasping the nettle of accessibility and design—from international and national legal compliance, through economic, social, and cultural benefits, to the imperatives of ethics and justice. Accessibility is actually no simple matter. So some of the most promising approaches to accessibility seek to open it up as a concept and set of practices, something in which the vibrant experimentation, emerging practices, and research concerning social media can play an important part. Work on disability and accessible technology in the humanities and social sciences is relatively recent; however, there is important research emerging that seeks to understand the social and cultural underpinnings of digital technology, including social media—yet there remains much to do.

There are some obvious directions for future work, then, in disability and social media. Firstly, we need to know much more about how people with disabilities are actually using social media. Other than discussions (including those using social media) by individuals and groups of people with disabilities and work by disability technology specialist organizations, there is almost no scholarly research into disability and social media. Actually there is little critical research on disability and the internet, disability and mobile media, and disability and media either. While there now exists recognition of the importance of disability in communication, culture, and media studies, there is very little work. So we lack baseline statistics and demographic information on how many people with disabilities are using social media, which applications they use, how often, where, why, and for what purposes: the fundamental data of any communications and media research. Building on this, we have very few qualitative studies of any sort—whether sociological, critical, or cultural or using interdisciplinary methods and frameworks, such as those in disability studies or internet studies—of different communities, groups, audiences, or publics of social media users with disabilities. We have even less—we can safely say "no"—international comparative studies of the cultures of use of social media by people with disabilities across different cultural, linguistic, economic, gender, or national settings.

Secondly, a central problem for research and practice is understanding why designing, framing, and implementing technology for people with disabilities—including the achievement of accessibility—proves so difficult to bring about. The stakes in these struggles over accessibility and social media have been heightened with the advent of the 2008 United Nations Convention on the Rights of Persons with Disability, which, if fully implemented, include many provisions dealing with the importance of accessibility of digital technology as a human right.

Recommending Readings

AbilityNet. (2008). *State of the eNation web accessibility reports: Social networking websites.* State of the eNation Reports. Retrieved June 19, 2010, from http://www.abilitynet.org.uk/docs/enation/2008SocialNetworkingSites.pdf

Cahill, M., & Hollier, S. (2009). Social media accessibility review—version 1.0. *Media Access Australia.* Retrieved from http://www.mediaaccess.org.au

Ellis, K., & Kent, M. (2010). Community accessibility: Tweeters take responsibility for an accessible Web 2.0. *Fast Capitalism,* 7(1). Retrieved from http://www.fastcapitalism.com/

Ellis, K., & Kent, M. (2011). *Disability and new media*. New York: Routledge.

Goggin, G., & Hollier, S. (2014, forthcoming). Disability and affordable online, mobile media: Social inclusion in new global media markets.

Goggin, G., & Newell, C. (2003). *Digital disability: The social construction of disability in new media*. Lanham, MD: Rowman & Littlefield.

Haller, B. (2010). *Representing disability in an ableist world: Essays on mass media*. Louisville, KY: Avocado Press.

Kelly, B., Lewthwaite, S., & Sloan, D. (2010). Developing countries; developing experiences: Approaches to accessibility for the real world. W4A2010, April 26–27, 2010, Raleigh, USA, co-located with the 19th International World Wide Web Conference. Retrieved from http://portal.acm.org/citation.cfm?doid=1805986.1805992; also available at http://www.ukoln.ac.uk/web-focus/papers/w4a-2010/

Lewthwaite, S., & Swan, H. (2013, forthcoming). Disability, web standards and the majority world. In N. L. Meloncon (Ed.), *Rhetorical accessAbility: At the intersection of technical communications and disability studies*. Amityville, NY: Baywood.

Wood, D. (2010). Communicating in virtual worlds through an accessible Web 2.0 solution. *Telecommunications Journal of Australia, 60*(2), 19.11–19.16.

Bibliography

AbilityNet. (2008). *State of the eNation web accessibility reports: Social Networking Websites*. State of the eNation Reports. Retrieved June 19, 2010, from http://www.abilitynet.org.uk/docs/enation/2008SocialNetworkingSites.pdf

American Foundation for the Blind. (2006). *Are social networking sites accessible to people with vision loss?* American Foundation for the Blind. Retrieved from http://www.afb.org/Section.asp?SectionID=57&TopicID=167&DocumentID=3153

Annable, G., Goggin, G., & Stienstra, D. (2007). Accessibility, disability, and inclusion in information technologies. *The Information Society, 23*(3), 145–147.

Asakawa, C. (2005). *What's the web like if you can't see it?* W4A '05 Proceedings of the 2005 International Cross-Disciplinary Workshop on Web Accessibility (W4A), Chiba, Japan, May 10-14, 2005, 1-8.

Barnes, C., & Mercer, G. (Eds.). (2004). *Implementing the social model of disability: Theory and research*. Leeds, UK: The Disability Press.

Berners-Lee, T. (1997, April 7). *World Wide Web Consortium (W3C) launches international Web Accessibility Initiative*. Web Accessibility Initiative (WAI). Retrieved from http://www.w3.org/Press/WAI-Launch.html

Campbell, F. (2009). *Contours of ableism: The production of disability and abledness*. New York: Palgrave Macmillan.

Castells, M. (2009). *Communication power*. Oxford; New York: Oxford University Press.

Craven, J. (2008, August). *Web accessibility: What we have achieved and challenges ahead*. Paper presented at the World Library and Information Congress, 74th IFLA General Conference and Council, August 10–14, Québec, Canada.

Ellcessor, E. (2010). Bridging disability divides: A critical history of web content accessibility through 2001. *Information, Communication & Society, 13*(3), 289–308.

Ellis, K., & Kent, M. (2011). *Disability and new media*. New York: Routledge.

Foley, A., & Voithofer, R. (2008, March). *Social networking technology, NetGen learners, and emerging technology: Democratic claims and the mythology of equality*. Paper presented at the American Educational Research Association (AERA) National conference, March

24–28, New York. Retrieved from http://flynnfoley.typepad.com/alan_foley/2008/04/social-networki.html

Goggin, G. (2011). *Global mobile media.* London; New York: Routledge.

Goggin, G., & Newell, C. (2003). *Digital disability: The social construction of disability in new media.* Lanham, MD: Rowman & Littlefield.

Goggin, G., & Newell, C. (2005). *Disability in Australia: Exposing a social apartheid.* Sydney: University of New South Wales.

Goggin, G., & Noonan, T. (2006). Blogging disability: The interface between new cultural movements and internet technology. In A. Bruns & J. Jacobs (Eds.), *The uses of blogs* (pp. 161–172). New York: Peter Lang.

Goodley, D. (2010). *Disability studies: An interdisciplinary introduction.* Los Angeles; London: Sage.

Haller, B. (2010). *Representing disability in an ableist world: Essays on mass media.* Louisville, KY: Avocado Press.

Hickey-Moody, A., & Wood, D. (2008). Virtually sustainable: Deleuze and desiring differenciation in Second Life. *Continuum, 22*(6), 805–816.

Hickey-Moody, A., & Wood, D. (2009). Ethics in Second Life: Difference, desire and the production of subjectivity. In C. Wankel & S. Malleck (Eds.), *Emerging ethical issues of life in virtual worlds* (pp. 153–175). Charlotte, NC: Information Age Publishing.

Innes, G. (2009, April). *Creating welcoming school communities.* Paper presented at the More Than Gadgets Conference, April 3. Fremantle, Western Australia. Retrieved from http://www.hreoc.gov.au/disability_rights/speeches/2009/welcoming.htm

Kuusisto, S. (2007). A roundtable on disability blogging. *Disability Studies Quarterly, 27*(1/2). Retrieved from http://www.dsq-sds.org/article/view/1/1

Martínez-Cabrera, A. (2010, January 1). Web more accessible to those with disabilities. *San Francisco Chronicle.* Retrieved from http://www.sfgate.com/news/article/Web-more-accessible-to-those-with-disabilities-3205623.php

McKay, A. (2007). *The official petition for a more accessible Facebook.* Retrieved May 17, 2010, from http://www.facebook.com/?ref=home#!/group.php?gid=2384051749&ref=ts

Morrison, D. (2010, Jan. 26). Social Media opens social world to elderly, disabled. *Star News Online.* Retrieved from *http://www.starnewsonline.com/article/20100126/ARTICLES/100129756*

Mosen, J. (2009, June 9). Email post. Retrieved from http://mark.candleshoreblog.com/2009/06/11/the-accessible-iphone-3g-s-for-the-blind-and-low-vision-a-reality-check/

Nakamura, L., & Chow-White, P. (Eds.). (2012). *Race after the internet.* London; New York: Routledge.

Ostrow, A. (2009, February 19). Facebook overtakes MySpace (again). *Mashable.* Retrieved from http://mashable.com/2009/02/19/facebook-bigger-than-myspace-in-us/

Out-Law News. (2006). Berners-Lee applies Web 2.0 to improve accessibility. *Out-Law News.* Retrieved June 25, 2010, from http://www.out-law.com/page-6946

Pothier, D., & Devlin, R. (Eds.). (2005). *Critical disability theory: Essays in philosophy, politics, policy, and law.* Vancouver: University of British Columbia Press.

Roulstone, A. (1998). *Enabling technology: Disabled people, work, and new technology.* Buckingham, UK; Philadelphia: Open University Press.

Shakespeare, T. (2006). *Disability rights and wrongs.* London; New York: Routledge.

Sheedy, M. [wingsmanh1]. (2007, April 17). *Living and overcoming life with a disability* [Video File]. Retrieved from http://www.youtube.com/watch?v=_TbWcdN-W8o

Sieber, T. (2008). *Disability theory.* Ann Arbor: University of Michigan Press.

Soderstrom, S. (2009). Offline social ties and online use of computers: A study of disabled youth and their use of ICT advances. *New Media & Society, 11*(5), 709–727.

The Next Web. (2011, September 15). *Stevie Wonder sings Steve Jobs' praises for iOS accessibility.* Retrieved from http://thenextweb.com/apple/2011/09/15/stevie-wonder-sings-steve -jobs-praises-for-ios-accessibility/

Tracey, E. (2011, April 5). Social networking, the disabled view. *Ouch!* Retrieved from http://www.bbc.co.uk/ouch/features/social_network_savvie.shtml

Vogelstein, F. (2009, June 29). The Wired interview: Facebook's Mark Zuckerberg. *Wired.* Retrieved from http://www.wired.com/epicenter/2009/06/mark-zuckerberg-speaks/

10

ON NETWORKED PUBLICS AND PRIVATE SPHERES IN SOCIAL MEDIA

Zizi Papacharissi

In early 2011, a wave of political unrest swept through North Africa and the Middle East. Beginning late in December of 2010, Mohammed Bouazizi, a twenty-six-year-old Tunisian college-educated fruit vendor, set himself on fire in protest to corruption, bureaucracy, and pronounced income inequalities. Bouazizi had been publicly humiliated by a municipal officer who confiscated his apples and weighing equipment, while her aids subsequently beat him up. It has been reported that Bouazizi had repeatedly refused to bribe municipal officers and the police and that the governor's office had turned a deaf ear to Bouazizi's attempts to file a complaint. On January 4, 2011, Bouazizi died from burns covering 90 percent of his body, but by then, his act had triggered mass protests throughout the country, leading to Tunisian President Ben Ali's resignation ten days later. Inspired by the fall of Tunisia's prime minister, Egyptian protestors took to the streets on January 25 to protest the thirty-year rule of then President Hosni Mubarak, who was forced to resign after eighteen days of antigovernment demonstrations. Heartened by these results, thousands of Algerians rallied on February 12, demanding democratic reforms. On February 14—the anniversary of Bahrain's 2002 Constitution, which ushered in an elected parliament and other democratic reforms—demonstrators engaged in protests that escalated to violence and would continue for the next few months with as of yet uncertain outcomes. On February 16, small demonstrations in Benghazi, Libya, quickly escalated to mass protests throughout the country over the next few days. As these protests turned violent, government forces began to fight with rebels for control of the country, leading to United Nations involvement to protect civilians. The outcomes of the Libyan uprising are uncertain as I write this, as are the outcomes of other protests that erupted, and some of which continue in Jordan (January 28), Syria (February 4),

Kuwait (February 6), Yemen (February 11), Iran (February 14), Iraq (February 16), Morocco (February 20), Oman (February 27), and Lebanon (February 28).

Much has been written about the role of social media in these uprisings. Some dismiss, or downplay, the existence of a causal relationship between use of social media and subsequent protests; they argue that people protested and brought down governments long before social media existed and that Facebook and Twitter are simply places where revolutionaries congregate online (Gladwell, 2011; Morozov, 2011). Others maintain that use of social media accelerated the development of social movements in those countries, in ways similar to those in which the printing press, and other media, facilitated revolutions in the past (Ingram, 2011; Tufekci, 2011). At the same time, it is important to not lose sight of the fact that these are *human* revolutions, ultimately enabled by human cost and sacrifice (York, 2011; Zuckerman, 2011). As the chronology of the recent wave of political unrest reveals, demonstrations that make use of social media lead to a variety of outcomes, some of which include government upheavals, democratic reforms, violence, or further suppression of political freedoms, and some of which that are yet to be determined. Demonstrations protesting the outcome of the 2009 Iranian elections were accelerated by social media use but did not result in regime reform. Social media use in the Tulip Revolution facilitated information dissemination that, along with other factors, led to the overthrow of the Kyrgyz government. Without a doubt, context matters. Moreover, whether these reprises will historically be claimed as revolutions can only be determined by long-term democratic outcomes. In the meantime, asking the question of whether social media *caused* these uprisings misses the point. It also mischaracterizes the nature of the media employed in the context of these upheavals.

If one were to look for the cause of the unrest, one need not look beyond the case of Bouazizi, the Tunisian fruit vendor who set himself on fire in response to decades of exploitation, corruption, and bureaucracy. It is these three factors, and the ways in which they reinforce and reproduce income inequalities, that summarize the sentiment behind these demonstrations. Despite putting up with decades of repression, however, it was the specific affront to the dignity of Bouazizi, as an autonomous individual, that incited his own act of protest and inspired the millions that followed. Perhaps internet-based platforms had little place in Bouazizi's ecosystem, but they were important in affording the act of a *private* individual *public* exposure that got around the hierarchies of government-censored media and global mainstream news. Concurrently, they were important in interrupting the private-to-public/public-to-private flow of information in ways that helped emancipate the collective imaginations. If we are to understand the role social media play in connecting individuals, publics, and societies, we must realize that they present a path, a digital one and certainly not the only one, via which the private becomes public—but, more to this case, the personal can become political.

In this chapter, I discuss how this path is activated within and outside democratic forms of government. Social platforms like Facebook and Twitter are brands; they represent a specific interpretation and application of the networked infrastructure of the internet. It is that networked premise, as implemented by specific social media brands, that is utilized in activating what Arendt termed the "in-between" (1970, p. 4)-bond among individual actors and networks. I begin by discussing how the premise of democracy intersects with the logic of networked technologies.

The Mythologies of Technology and Democracy

There is a complex relationship between technology and democracy. This relationship is informed by the mythology of the new: a vernacular that suggests new(er) media could revive old democracy. It is also sustained by the connection between technology and space: the belief that newer media can rearrange space, in ways that are empowering and restrictive at the same time. Finally, the relationship between technology and democracy is shaped by the balance between public and private: a socioculturally sensitive balance that produces modalities of citizenship across different eras. These evolving modalities of citizenship sustain personal and collective fantasies of autonomy and control.

Yet, it should be emphasized that autonomy and control are effected reflexively, through simultaneous processes of liberation and discipline connoted by the architectures of newer technologies. Thus, technological architectures that provide empowering options do so by multiplying layers of controlled choices people select from. Deleuze (1998) uses the metaphor of the highway, a metaphor popular in narratives of technological empowerment, to explain the process of controlled autonomy: "A control is not a discipline. In making highways, for example, you don't enclose people but instead multiply the means of control. I am not saying that this is the highway's exclusive purpose, but that people can drive infinitely and 'freely' without being confined yet while still being perfectly controlled. This is our future" (p. 18). Similarly, new technologies suggest worlds upon which autonomy and power can be claimed. These worlds, however, are shaped by the following tendencies, prominent in contemporary democracies:

- Nostalgia for past forms of political engagement, frequently wrapped in rhetoric that idealizes past iterations of a public sphere (e.g., Calhoun, 1992; Schudson, 1998)
- Limitations to civic involvement imposed by the representative democracy model as it functions in a mass society fueled by a capitalist economy (e.g., Coleman, 2005; Habermas, 2004; Mouffe, 2000)
- The aggregation of public opinion within representative democracy models through polling (e.g., Herbst, 1993)
- Declining civic participation through formal channels of political involvement (e.g., Carey, 1995; Hart, 1994; Putnam, 1996)

- The growth of public cynicism and disillusionment towards politics and the mass media (e.g., Cappella & Jamieson, 1996, 1997; Fallows, 1996; Patterson, 1993, 1996)

These five tendencies shape both the civic expectations we form and the civic options we provide ourselves. They present circumstances that we simultaneously seek to escape and recreate in some form through our civic uses of social media.

In nondemocratic regimes, or societies that are undergoing transition, these circumstances shift shape, subject to local context. Howard (2010) compared the digital origins of democracy and dictatorship across Islamic political regimes and identified the following causal conditions that map the path to democratization and individual autonomy:

- A comparatively active online civil society
- A relatively small population
- A relatively well-educated population
- A state with a comparatively well-developed information infrastructure
- An economy not dominated by fuel exports

Different combinations of these causal conditions may yield specific democratizing outcomes and may permit "banal tools for wasting time, like Twitter and YouTube, [to] become the supporting infrastructure of social movements" (Howard, 2010, p. 12).

Technology, then, presents a way to counter powerlessness by allowing individuals to propose new spaces, upon which newer, potentially more empowering, habits and relations may be cultivated. These social spaces present the sum of experiences past with interpretations present and potential of the future. They capture nostalgia and dissatisfaction with the past along with anticipation of the future through a mix of practices that are both actual/given and potential, thus reflecting "a locus of possibilities" (Lefebvre, 1991, p. 191). Representing "at once a collection of materials (objects, things) and an ensemble of matériel (tools—and the procedures necessary to make efficient use of tools and of things in general)" (ibid), these technologically enabled social spaces host civic activities marked by both convention and innovation.

These civic activities develop around the praxis of the actual and the promise of the potential, combining internalized perceptions of the political with thoughts of what that which is political might signify in the future. In other words, they liberate the personal and collective imaginations. Depending on the sociopolitical context within which they are put to use, uses, patterns of mobilization, and outcomes will vary. They will all, however, seek some renegotiation of hierarchy and power and, thus, all be connected by autonomy as a constant. Autonomy, personal and collective, is defined by the way in which the private is balanced against the public, and vice versa. The following section explains how the specific balance of public/private that a regime affords will then inform the uses, patterns, and out-comes that might be associated with online technologies.

Public and Private Imaginaries

Political governance is defined by the ways in which it allows public and private entities to interact. The economic, sociocultural, and political texture of systems is woven as public and private concerns intersect to form distinctions between what is termed private and what is commonly understood to be public. More than organizing categories, public and private serve to qualify and distinguish mani-fested choices in everyday life. Much like all constructs characterized by bipolarity, what is important is not just the territory marked by public and private, but the distance and potential disparity between how public and private are situated in societal groupings. It is the tension between these two that sets the stage for political interaction. "Public and private, sic et non," Jean Bethke Elshtain (1997) remarks, and continues: "Only in the space opened up by the ongoing choreogra-phy of these categories can politics exist—or at least any politics that deserves to be called democratic" (p. 180).

The distinction between public and private is elusive, as it is culturally formed and sensitive to historical context (e.g., Sennett, 1974; Weintraub & Kumar, 1997). Public and private may be defined, on the simplest level, on the basis of mutual exclusivity. Thus, public is that which does not remain private and thus can be shared in common; is associated with the greater public good; can serve as a mask or fiction for private desires for power and position; can suggest a way for mem-bers of a public to become associated and effect action; and can exist within or outside the realm of the state. Conversely, private is that which does not become public and thus remains under private ownership, in the realm of the personal or domestic, possibly considered unofficial, and involving actions and consequences structured around the self. Most discourses, whether theoretical or applied, evoke these terms in identifying the boundaries around which perceptions of public and private are formed. Weintraub (1997) describes the public/private distinction as "not unitary, but protean, [comprising] not a single opposition, but a complex family of them, neither mutually reducible nor wholly unrelated" (p. 2). Thus, separating the two terms, even if just for definitional purposes, conjures a variety of constructs, which may overlap in both theory and practice.

Weintraub (1997) puts forth two criteria for discerning private and public that capture the etymological denotations of the terms with adequate, yet not distracting, focus on their connoted meanings. Employing the criteria of visibility and collectivity, private is defined in contrast to public as (a) what is hidden or withdrawn versus what is open, revealed, or accessible; or (b) what is individual, or pertains only to an individual, versus what is collective or affects the interests of a collectivity of individuals. This individual/collective distinction can, by extension, take the form of a distinction between part and whole (of some social collectivity)

(Weintraub, 1997, p. 5). Employing the criteria of visibility and collectivity enables one to examine the parameters and consequences of the private/public distinction across analytical planes that are diverse and interconnected.

The public and private binary is reflective of economic, social, cultural, and political balances and imbalances of power throughout our history. For instance, during the Greco-Roman times, public life equaled civic responsibility, and the privilege of citizenship and participation in public affairs was granted to male property owners while women and slaves were disempowered by being excluded from public affairs and relegated to the private sphere. Following the Greco-Roman period, religious traditions delineated private and public rituals that reinforced power hierarchies and specific social, cultural, and political practices. In the twentieth century, feminist theorists had to claim that the personal is political, so as to emancipate the domesticated female point of view and enable it to transition from the private to the public milieu. Applying the criteria of visibility and collectivity, Bouazizi's private concerns clashed with a political culture that was inaccessible to him: a culture that lacked visibility and transparency, and that was defined by a collective that he had been excluded from. His private act of self-immolation was an attempt to inject his own point of view to a public agenda that had been determined by others. Ultimately, the publicity of his act was a claim to power. Similarly, Iman al-Obeidi, the Libyan woman who stormed a Tripoli hotel filled with Western journalists to tell them that she had been raped by Gaddafi's soldiers in March 2011, was seeking publicity as a claim to power. Under less tragic and contextually different circumstances, Kate Hanni, an exasperated airline passenger, founded the Coalition for an Airline Passenger's Bill of Rights, seeking both visibility and collectivity as a way of affording power to a viewpoint that had been excluded from public affairs. Similarly, a political analysis that an individual may post on an independent blog stands as a publicized private disagreement and a power claim that interpolates a public agenda sustained by mainstream media narratives.

I do not wish to draw careless connections between sociopolitical contexts that have little in common. But it is important to examine how visibility and collectivity suggest different modalities of the public/private binary, which then afford distinct balances of power in systems of governance. While social media— or, more broadly, technologies of convergence—alone cannot upset, interrupt, or reform these hierarchies, they are essential in challenging public/private binaries, the irony (and the premise) being, of course, that these technologies themselves thrive on blurring distinctions between the two. In the following section, I examine how this occurs and the different outcomes it may produce.

Supersurfaces and Infrastructures

In modern societies, electronic media predispose communication by suggesting a juxtaposition of private and public boundaries that human activity advances from. Meyrowitz (1986) described this as the ability of electronic media to remove, or at least rearrange, boundaries between public and private spaces, affecting our lives not so much through content, but rather "by changing the 'situational geography' of social life" (p. 6). In the seminal *No Sense of Place*, Meyrowitz (1986) likened this potential to the architectural effect that would be created were all walls physically separating rooms, houses, offices, buildings, and all concrete structures to be lifted. The result would combine several previously distinct situations, creating a paradox: an inharmonious continuum of several disconnected conversations, simultaneously aware of but potentially discordant with each other. Meyrowitz (1986) wrote mostly about television and its ability to juxtapose public and private conversations in ways that changed childhood, rearranged private/public gender discourses, and demystified politics. Information communication technologies often afford publicity without permitting the individual to provide situational context.

While it is possible for this convergence to displace the situational character of some communication, nonverbal and verbal cues afforded by technology enable the mediation of situational information. Perhaps a more apt metaphor can be located away from Meyrowitz's dramatic collapse of place to what Scannell (1996) has termed the doubling of place. Scannell explains that in late modern life, "public events . . . occur simultaneously in two different places: the place of the event itself and that in which it is watched and heard. Broadcasting mediates between these two sites" (p. 76). With converged technologies, the effect is further multiplied, creating a plurality of overlapping or mutually exclusive social realities. Consequently, social relationships are multiplied, creating the potential for multiple performances of political expression occurring on a variety of different stages (Moores, 2004). Many perceive the "doubling" or "multiplying" metaphor a more accurate reflection of the role played by technology (e.g., Couldry, 2000; Couldry & McCarthy, 2004; Moores, 2004; Ross, 2004; Scannell, 1996). The resulting space is a converged continuum made up by discordant blocks of activity that is "homogeneous, yet at the same time broken into fragments" (Lefebvre, 1991, p. 342).

As a metaphor, multiplication speaks to the *quantity* of space generated but is not descriptive of the *quality* of space multiplied. Expressive and connective spaces sustained by online media are multiplied and multipliable, but what types of activities do they tend to lend themselves to? Do they sustain public spheres, and if so, do these public spheres possess a Habermasian deliberative character (discussed below), or are they indicative of non-deliberative, yet decidedly civic, political tendencies?

Architecture employs the technique of folding to suggest the ways in which multiplied space may be fragmented and rearranged so as to present not just multiplied space surfaces, but surfaces that lend themselves to the creation of more flexible shapes. I argue that a similar effect is produced by convergent technologies. Space is not only multiplied; it is simultaneously fragmented and reassembled into structures that attain greater reflexivity. Architect and academic Sophia Vyzoviti (2001, 2003) has employed the term supersurfaces to describe the spatial possibilities enabled by the technique of folding. Using paper as an empirical model, she explains how flat surfaces can be transformed into volumes through cutting, weaving, twisting, winding, and further manipulating woven forms. The resulting supersurfaces evolve beyond the fixity of manipulated artifacts to suggest an appeal that lies in their lightness and flexibility.

Supersurfaces are appealing because they are remixed and remixable; thus they are responsive to convergent technologies that engage citizens as both audiences and producers of mediated civic content. Similarly, convergent supersurfaces describe the spatial effects of convergent technology on place. Space is disjointed, reconnected, woven, and reorganized into places light enough to rest on the outer landscapes of greater systemic structures, and not heavy enough to dissolve into the systemic core of the institutions of democracy. The concept of a convergent supersurface captures both the promise and peril of cyberspace: flexible enough to sustain a variety of conversations, too flexible to have the weight required for a lasting impact. These spaces develop upon the outer fabrics of traditional democratic institutions, a play upon space bound by its own fixity.

At the same time, unless these spaces bear distinct connections to the systemic core of democratic (or nondemocratic) institutions, their ability to effect institutional change is compromised. For example, bloggers are able to exert power to the extent that they successfully capture the attention of mainstream media or a critical mass in democratic society. This presents a necessary, but not sufficient, condition for power reversals, both in democratic and nondemocratic regimes. The concept of convergent supersurfaces communicates both the empowerment enabled via the production of multiple reflexive spaces and the challenges offered by spaces that are organically generated and thus may not always support direct systemic connections to core societal institutions. What kinds of publics do convergent supersurfaces support then?

Private Spheres and Networked Publics

It is not uncommon for scholars to rely on the concept of the public sphere when seeking to theorize the democratizing potential of new media (Malina, 1999; Papacharissi, 2002; Poster, 1995; Sassi, 2000). The public sphere in a representative democracy is where citizens engage in rational public discourse and debate on public affairs. Habermas (1973) describes it thus: "A sphere which mediates between society and state, in which the public organizes itself as the bearer of public opinion, accords with the principle of the public sphere, that principle of public information which once had to be fought for against the arcane politics of monarchies and which since that time has made possible the democratic control of state activities" (p. 351). Within a representative democracy, the public sphere serves to inject the system with a healthy dose of direct communication and debate. In the absence of a robust public sphere, it is possible that citizens may feel the distance between them and their elected representatives, which may then translate into feelings of detachment, apathy, and cynicism. Several civic uses of the internet develop in yearning for a long-lost public sphere (Papacharissi, 2010).

Habermas finds that, in contemporary democracies, the public sphere becomes a vehicle for capitalist hegemony and ideological reproduction. Thus, public life is disrupted by permeating imperatives of commodification, which interfere with transparency of process and rationality of deliberation. Several disagree with Habermas's idealized vision of a public sphere (e.g., Robbins, 1993; Schudson, 1998) and his overemphasis on rational discourse (Lyotard, 1984). Fraser (1992), one of the most notable critics of the concept, developed the alternative model of multiple coexisting public spheres, or counter-publics, that are not equally powerful, articulate, or privileged, but exist to give voice to various collective identities and interests, a model that Habermas (1992) aligned with in his subsequent work. Still, the public sphere metaphor (and it is most meaningful as a metaphor and truest to Habermas's original conception) is routinely evoked in examining the civic potential of online activities. I have argued that any assessment of the public sphere potential of online technologies must be assessed against the following criteria, as these directly affect the social and political capital generated by online media: *access* to information, *reciprocity* of communication, and *commercialization* of online space.

Greater access to information is enabled by online media but does not necessarily lead to increases in political participation or to rationally driven discourses that are modeled after the idea of the public sphere. Reciprocity refers to all parties being involved equally in mutual conversation. While the evidence suggests that meaningful conversations can occur online, it is unclear whether these fit into the deliberative model of the public sphere or engage individuals in a reciprocal manner (e.g., Howard, 2006; Kobayashi, Ikeda, & Miyata, 2006; Mitra, 1997a, 1997b; Schmitz, 1997; Uslaner, 2004). Finally, commercialization presents a primary concern for researchers who examine the public sphere potential of online platforms. While equipped with an open architecture that resists commercialization (Lessig, 2005), it is not immune to commercial objectives (Dahlberg, 2001; McChesney, 1995; Newhagen & Rafaeli, 1996). It may be more accurate to suggest that the commercial aspect of online media, however, coexists with noncommercial content, and a public interest orientation, in forming spaces of a hybrid texture. These hybrid economies of space collapse both public and private expression, but also public and private interest. The resulting spaces do not reify a Habermasian public sphere, but they do permit atomized expression to evolve into connection, which may subsequently activate ephemeral, or sustain longer-term, ties that bond a networked around a particular issue, cause, or identity.

Networked platforms for interaction like social media are frequently evocative of public sphere ideals, but typically evolve beyond that model. So it is not that networked platforms fail the public sphere test of democratization, but, possibly, the other way round. The term public sphere cannot capture the potential of the civic activities that develop around social media in its entirety. Research and practice indicate that the internet does not constitute a public or virtual sphere; if anything, it presents less of a democracy than several of the public sphere's past incarnations (Dahlgren, 2005; Noam, 2005). On the other hand, models that emphasize the pluralization enabled by digital media (Bimber, 1998), contemporary citizen needs and wants (Schudson, 1998), and the ability of the internet to amplify political processes (Agre, 2002) present more pragmatic assessments of online media potential. Finally, romanticized retrospectives of civic engagement often distort the affordances of technologies of the present.

In contemporary democracies, net-based civic actions frequently emanate from the locus of a private, not a public, sphere. This private sphere is the focal point of much civic activity that develops, whether it remains within private confines or is broadcast to publicly positioned audiences and entities. Privately contained activities with a public scope—like online news reading, lurking in on political conversation, or following opinion leaders' blogs or tweets—take place within the locus of the private sphere. Publicly oriented activities—like posting a blog, sharing a political opinion, voting on or signing a petition to support a cause, or uploading exclusive news content on YouTube—are also increasingly enabled within the locus of a digitally equipped private sphere. In past iterations of democracy, these were all activities pursued in the public realm. In contemporary democracies, however, not only do these pursuits progressively emerge out of the private realm, but it is frequently necessary for the individual to return to the private realm in order to practice these newer civic habits with greater autonomy, flexibility, and potential for expression.

This private sphere is rhetorically established by the individual by utilizing existing and imagined geographies of place. Whereas in idealized visions of democracy the citizen is enabled through the public sphere, in contemporary democracies the citizen becomes politically emancipated via a private sphere of reflection, expression, and behavior. This relocation suggests that we reexamine the spatiality of citizenship. Within this private sphere, the citizen is alone, but not lonely or isolated. The citizen is connected and operates in a mode and with political language determined by him or her. Operating from a civically *privée* environment, the citizen enters the public spectrum by negotiating aspects of his/ her privacy as necessary, depending on the urgency and relevance of particular situations. Primarily still monitorial in orientation, the citizen is able to become an agonist of democracy, if needed, but in an atomized mode.

The mobile autonomy of the private sphere is harmonious with contemporary modalities of citizenship in hyperdeveloped and hypernetworked democracies (Chadwick, 2006). First, as political power is still territorially exercised in contexts both local and global, the mobility of the private sphere potentially extends the agency of the private individual but also fragments political discourse (Garnham, 2000). Second, given the informational overload produced by fragmentized or harmonious and cosmopolitan or localized counter-publics, a mobile private sphere enables the frequently monitorial citizen to efficiently balance conflicting and potentially overwhelming civic demands. Finally, a mobile private sphere that functions as the basis of civic emancipation is concordant with values of individualism, autonomy, and self-expression that are prevalent in late modern democracies of developed societies (Inglehart & Welzel, 2005). The mobility of this private sphere further permits that everyday routines be interlaced in ways that render the individual reachable anywhere and anytime, in a way that may "revolutionalize" control of everyday life (Castells, Fernandez-Ardevol, Linchuan Qiu, & Sey, 2006; Ling & Donner, 2009). Thus, atomized gestures of civic import can sustain a monitorial citizen orientation or, depending on the context, work to mobilize networked publics.

In societies undergoing transition or political reform, the metaphor of networked publics carries greater relevance than that of a private or public sphere. In these societies, net-based civic engagement does not always observe the access, reciprocity, and rationale of the public sphere. In contrast, it serves to facilitate modes of expression and information sharing that are not otherwise available. These develop in more organic, and sometimes anarchic, flows, which are more aligned with Lyotard's (1984) critique of the public sphere, or the model of citizen-agonist presented by Mouffe (2005). The private sphere model, on the other hand, is one enabled by technologies of mobility; so, while it may be present in developing democracies and societies, it may not be representative of general tendencies.

Networked publics have been defined by boyd (2010) as "publics that are restructured by networked technologies" and therefore simultaneously are "(1) the space constructed through networked technologies and (2) the imagined collective that emerges as a result of the intersection of people, technology, and practice" (p. 39). Networked publics include civic formations that develop beyond the model of the public sphere and permit us to consider the possibilities for engagement that the affordances of convergent technologies introduce. As boyd (2010) argues, networked publics are not just "publics networked together, but they are publics that have been transformed by networked media" (p. 42). The properties of social media lend networked publics particular affordances that can be traced in the ways individuals mobilized during the recent wave of uprisings in the Middle East and North Africa. While social network sites like Twitter and Facebook certainly did not motivate the uprisings, they presented Lefebvre's (1991) ensemble of matériel, or material causes, around which conventional and innovative civic activities were structured (Tufekci, 2011).

On a primary level, social media facilitate engagement in a way that is important. Most notably, they help activate latent ties that may be crucial to the mobilization of networked publics. Because they typically involve interactions that occur on societal supersurfaces, their impact is always subject to context: to how these supersurfaces connect to the infrastructural core of a regime, be that a democracy, autocracy, or a political system in transition. Online activity cannot be confused with impact. On a secondary level, networked publics are formed around both actual and imagined communities. The connective affordances of social media, then, do not only activate the "in-between-bond" of publics, but they enable expression and information sharing that liberates the individual and the collective imaginations. This is perhaps why the influence of social media in uprisings that take place in autocratic regimes frequently persists despite attempts to shut down the networked infrastructure that supports them. Dean (2010) draws attention to the notion of affect, so as to describe the circulatory drive that characterizes networked publics, in that they become what they are and simultaneously "a record or trace" of what they are. Sustained by ongoing reflexivity that is regenerated by singular moments of expression and connection deposited by individual users, the affective flow and affective links remain and resonate with networked publics even after the specific links to content have been shut down. Affective attachments to media cannot produce communities but may produce "feelings of community" (p. 22). Depending on context, these affective attachments may either reflexively drive a movement that aims at community, or capture users in a state of engaged passivity.

Bibliography

Agre, P. E. (2002). Real-time politics: The internet and the political process. *Information Society, 18*(5), 311–331.

Akdeniz, Y. (2002). Anonymity, democracy, and cyberspace. *Social Research, 69*(1), 223–237.

Arendt, H. (1970). *Men in dark times.* New York: Harvest Books.

Bimber, B. (1998). The internet and political transformation: Populism, community, and accelerated pluralism. *Polity, 3,* 133–160.

boyd, d. (2010). Social network sites as networked publics: Affordances, dynamics, and implications. In Z. Papacharissi (Ed.), *Networked self: Identity, community, and culture on social network sites* (pp. 39–58). New York: Routledge.

Calhoun, C. (1992). *Habermas and the public sphere.* Cambridge, MA: MIT Press.

Cappella, J., & Jamieson, K. H. (1996). News frames, political cynicism, and media cynicism. *Annals of the American Academy of Political and Social Science, 546,* 71–85.

Cappella, J., & Jamieson, K. H. (1997). *Spiral of cynicism: The press and the public good.* New York: Oxford University Press.

Carey, J. (1995). The press, public opinion, and public discourse. In T. Glasser & C. Salmon (Eds.), *Public opinion and the communication of consent* (pp. 373–402). New York: Guilford.

Castells, M., Fernandez-Ardevol, M., Linchuan Qiu, J., & Sey, A. (2006). *Mobile communication and society.* Cambridge, MA: MIT Press.

Chadwick, A. (2006). *Internet politics: States, citizens, and new communication technologies.* New York: Oxford University Press.

Coleman, S. (2005). Just how risky is online voting? *Information Polity: The International Journal of Government & Democracy in the Information Age, 10*(1/2), 95–104.

Couldry, N. (2000). *The place of media power: Pilgrims and witnesses of the media age.* London: Routledge.

Couldry, N., & McCarthy, A. (Eds.). (2004). *Mediaspace: Place, scale and culture in a media age.* London: Routledge.

Dahlberg, L. (2001). The internet and democratic discourse: Exploring the prospects of online deliberative forums extending the public sphere. *Information, Communication & Society, 4*(4), 615–633.

Dahlgren, P. (2005). The internet, public spheres, and political communication: Dispersion and deliberation. *Political Communication, 22,* 147–162.

Dean, J. (2010). Affective networks. *Media Tropes eJournal, 2*(2), 19–44.

Deleuze, G. (1998). *Essays critical and clinical.* London: Verso.

DiMaggio, P., Hargittai, E., Celeste, C., & Shafter, S. (2004). Digital inequality: From unequal access to differentiated use. In K. Neckerman (Ed.), *Social inequality* (pp. 355–400). New York: Russell Sage Foundation.

Elshtain, J. B. (1997). The displacement of politics. In J. Weintraub & K. Kumar (Eds.), *Public and private in thought and practice* (pp. 166–181). Chicago: University of Chicago Press.

Fallows, J. (1996, February). Why Americans hate the media. *The Atlantic Monthly, 277*(2), 45–64.

Fraser, N. (1992). Rethinking the public sphere: A contribution to the critique of actually existing democracy. In C. Calhoun (Ed.), *Habermas and the public sphere* (pp. 109–142). Cambridge, MA: MIT Press.

Garnham, N. (2000). *Emancipation, the media, and modernity.* Oxford: Oxford University Press.

Gladwell, M. (2011, February 2). Does Egypt need Twitter? *New Yorker.* Retrieved April 2011, from http://www.newyorker.com/online/blogs/newsdesk/2011/02/does-egypt-need-twitter.html

Habermas, J. (1973). *Theory and practice* (J. Viertel, Trans.). London: Heinemann. (Original work published 1963).

Habermas, J. (1989). *The structural transformation of the public sphere: An inquiry into a category of bourgeois society* (T. Burger & F. Lawrence, Trans.). Cambridge, MA: MIT Press. (Original work published 1962).

Habermas, J. (1992). Further reflections on the public sphere. In C. Calhoun (Ed.), *Habermas and the public sphere* (pp. 421–461). Cambridge, MA: MIT Press.

Habermas, J. (2004). *The divided west.* Malden, MA: Polity Press.

Hart, R. P. (1994). Easy citizenship: Television's curious legacy. *Annals of the American Academy of Political and Social Science, 546,* 109–120.

Hassan, R. (2008). *The information society.* Cambridge, MA: Polity Press.

Herbst, S. (1993). *Numbered voices: How opinion polling has shaped American politics.* Chicago: University of Chicago Press.

Hill, K. A., & Hughes, J. E. (1998). *Cyberpolitics: Citizen activism in the age of the internet.* New York: Rowman & Littlefield.

Howard, P. (2006). *New media campaigns and the managed citizen.* New York: Cambridge University Press.

Howard, P. N. (2010). *The digital origins of dictatorship and democracy: Information technology and political Islam.* New York: Oxford University Press.

Inglehart, R., & Welzel, C. (2005). *Modernization, cultural change and democracy.* Cambridge: Cambridge University Press.

Ingram, M. (2011, January 29). It's not Twitter or Facebook, it's the power of the network [Blog post]. *Gigaom.* Retrieved April 2011, from http://gigaom.com/2011/01/29/twitter-facebook-egypt-tunisia/

Jankowski, N. W., & van Selm, M. (2000). The promise and practice of public debate in cyberspace. In K. Hacker & J. van Dijk (Eds.), *Digital democracy: Issues of theory and practice* (pp. 1–9). London: Sage.

Jones, S. (1997). The internet and its social landscape. In S. Jones (Ed.), *Virtual culture: Identity and communication in cybersociety* (pp. 7–35). Thousand Oaks, CA: Sage.

Keane, J. (1991). *The media and democracy.* London: Wiley-Blackwell.

Kobayashi, T., Ikeda, K., & Miyata, K. (2006). Social capital online: Collective use of the internet and reciprocity as lubricants of democracy. *Communication & Society, 9*(5), 582–611.

Lefebvre, H. (1991). *The production of space* (D. Nicholson-Smith, Trans.). Oxford: Blackwell. (Original work published 1974).

Lessig, L. (2005). *Free culture.* New York: Penguin.

Ling, R., & Donner, J. (2009). *Mobile communication.* Cambridge, MA: Polity Press.

Lyotard, J. F. (1984). *The postmodern condition.* Minneapolis: University of Minnesota Press.

Malina, A. (1999). Perspectives on citizen democratization and alienation in the virtual public sphere. In B. Hague & B. Loader (Ed.), *Digital democracy: Discourse and decision making in the information age* (pp. 23–38). New York: Routledge.

McChesney, R. (1995). The internet and U.S. communication policy-making in historical and critical perspective. *Journal of Computer-Mediated Communication, 1*(4). Retrieved July 22, 2013, from http://jcmc.indiana.edu/vol1/issue4/mcchesney.html

Meyrowitz, J. (1986). *No sense of place.* New York: Oxford.

Mitra, A. (1997a). Virtual community: Looking for India on the internet. In S. G. Jones (Ed.), *Virtual culture: Identity and communication in cybersociety* (pp. 55–79). Thousand Oaks, CA: Sage.

Mitra, A. (1997b). Diasporic web sites: Ingroup and outgroup discourse. *Critical Studies in Mass Communication, 14,* 158–181.

Moores, S. (2004). The doubling of place: Electronic media, time-space arrangements and social relationships. In N. Couldry & A. McCarthy (Eds.), *Mediaspace: Place, scale and culture in a media age* (pp. 21–36). London: Routledge.

Morozov, E. (2011, March 7). Facebook and Twitter are just places revolutionaries go. *The Guardian.* Retrieved April 2011, from http://www.guardian.co.uk/commentisfree/2011/mar/07/facebook-twitter-revolutionaries-cyber-utopians

Mouffe, C. (2000). *The democratic paradox.* London: Verso.

Mouffe, C. (2005). *On the political.* London: Routledge.

Newhagen, J. E., & Rafaeli, S. (1996). Why communication researchers should study the internet: A dialogue. *Journal of Communication, 46*(1), 4–13.

Noam, E. M. (2005). Why the internet is bad for democracy. *Communications of the ACM, 48*(10), 57–58.

Papacharissi, Z. (2002). The virtual sphere: The internet as the public sphere. *New Media & Society, 4*(1), 5–23.

Papacharissi, Z. (2010). *A private sphere: Democracy in a digital age.* Cambridge, MA: Polity Press.

Patterson, T. (1993). *Out of order.* New York: Knopf.

Patterson, T. (1996). Bad news, bad governance. *Annals of the American Academy of Political and Social Science, 546,* 97–108.

Poster, M. (1995). The internet as a public sphere? *Wired, 3*(1), 209.

Putnam, R. (1996). The strange disappearance of civic America. *The American Prospect, 24*(1), 34–48.

Robbins, B. (1993). *The phantom public sphere.* Minneapolis: University of Minnesota Press.

Ross, A. (2004). Dot.com urbanism. In N. Couldry & A. McCarthy (Eds.), *Mediaspace: Place, scale and culture in a media age* (pp. 145–163). London: Routledge.

Sassi, S. (2000). The controversies of the internet and the revitalization of local political life. In K. L. Hacker & J. van Dijk (Eds.), *Digital democracy* (pp. 90–104). London: Sage.

Scannell, P. (1996). *Radio, television and modern life: A phenomenological approach.* Oxford: Blackwell.

Schmitz, J. (1997). Structural relations, electronic media, and social change: The public electronic network and the homeless. In S. G. Jones (Ed.), *Virtual culture: Identity and communication in cybersociety* (pp. 80–101). Thousand Oaks, CA: Sage.

Schudson, M. (1998). *The good citizen: A history of American civic life.* New York: Free Press.

Sennett, R. (1974). *The fall of public man.* New York: Random House.

Tufekci, Z. (2011, January 15). Tunisia, Twitter, Aristotle, social media and final and efficient causes [Blog post]. *Technosociology.* Retrieved April 2011, from http://technosociology. org/?p=263

Uslaner, E. M. (2004). Trust, civic engagement, and the internet. *Political Communication, 21*(2), 223–242.

Vyzoviti, S. (2001). *Folding architecture: Spatial, structural and organizational diagrams.* Amsterdam: BIS Publishers.

Vyzoviti, S. (2003). *Supersurfaces: Folding as a method of generating forms for architecture, products and fashion.* Amsterdam: BIS Publishers.

Weintraub, J. (1997). The theory and politics of the public/private distinction. In J. Weintraub & K. Kumar, *Public and private in thought and practice* (pp. 1–42). Chicago: University of Chicago Press.

Weintraub, J., & Kumar, K. (Eds.). (1997). *Public and private in thought and practice.* Chicago: University of Chicago Press.

York, J. C. (2011, January 14). Not Twitter, not WikiLeaks: A human revolution [Blog post]. *Jilliancyork.com.* Retrieved April 2011, from http://jilliancyork.com/2011/01/14/ not-twitter-not-wikileaks-a-human-revolution/

Zuckerman, E. (2011, January 14). The first Twitter revolution? *Foreign Policy.* Retrieved April 2011, from http://www.foreignpolicy.com/articles/2011/01/14/the_first_twitter _revolution?page = full

11

SOCIAL MEDIA AND JOURNALISM DURING TIMES OF CRISIS

Axel Bruns

Introduction

Around lunchtime on February 22, 2011, the New Zealand city of Christchurch—the country's second largest city—was hit by a magnitude 6.3 earthquake. Built on a geological fault line, like Los Angeles and Tokyo, Christchurch is no stranger to tremors; indeed, it had experienced a magnitude 7.1 quake just months before, in September 2010, and technically, this new earthquake was no more than an aftershock of the earlier tremor. That earlier quake had caused significant structural damage, but no fatalities, but the February earthquake was different: with its epicenter located no more than ten kilometers from the Christchurch city center, at a depth of only five kilometers, it proved considerably more destructive—and it affected buildings whose structural integrity had already been severely compromised by the September quake, in the middle of a weekday when schools and city offices would have been fully occupied. While the full death toll has yet to be determined, it is estimated at close to two hundred.

Both recent Christchurch quakes form part of a string of major natural disasters experienced during 2010 and 2011: from the earlier September quake to the widespread flooding of several Australian states during the first weeks of 2011, through to the February earthquake in Christchurch and the magnitude 9.0 earthquake off the northeast coast of Japan on March 11, which triggered a massive tsunami and a meltdown at the Fukushima nuclear power plant. An aspect common to each of these crisis events is the role that current leading social media platforms—Facebook and Twitter, in particular—played in first spreading the word about these breaking news stories and then in helping to organize the disaster response, and this is what we will examine in detail in this chapter. What our analysis will highlight is the role of social media as an adjunct to and an amplifier of journalistic reporting, but also as a substitute for conventional, professional journalism especially in the immediate aftermath of a disaster, when journalists themselves have yet to arrive on the scene; additionally, we will also see a marked shift in attention after the first few days, as the interest of the world media in the event begins to subside and longer-term, local issues come to take center stage once again.

Our analysis here builds especially on a set of very recent, still-emerging research methodologies: what the availability of social media content through well-defined application programming interfaces (APIs) also enables is a large-scale, data-driven analysis of user activities on social media platforms that begins with a quantitative exploration of the patterns that emerge from the data, followed by a further in-depth qualitative study of key moments or of the roles of central participants.

Overview

Such work is part of a broader turn towards data-driven analysis in media and communication studies, which Richard Rogers, the founder of the IssueCrawler project that provides an important early tool for the study of network structures on the World Wide Web, has described as using "natively digital methods," rather than relying only on existing research methods that have been adopted from previous use in offline contexts. Rogers (2009) proposes "a research practice which grounds claims about cultural change and societal conditions in online dynamics, introducing the term 'online groundedness' " (p. 5). This is not to say that more conventional methods do not continue to have an important role to play, of course—however, the "natively digital" methods that Rogers highlights build more directly on the technological affordances of the online medium and can provide important and very detailed new insights.

In our present context of examining the role of social media in the immediate aftermath of a major disaster, such work also addresses a number of long-standing other themes in media and journalism research. Since the emergence of what we now call user-generated content (UGC)—and especially with the development of a special form of UGC, citizen journalism, during the late 1990s and early 2000s—the debate about user-generated reporting and commentary and its relationship to professionally, industrially produced news has continued; contributions to the discussion have ranged from a wholesale dismissal of citizen journalists as "armchair experts" to utopian visions in which user-generated journalism would replace conventional news organizations altogether.

From a more balanced perspective, what is indisputable is that user-generated news and commentary—at first in the form of dedicated alternative news websites like *IndyMedia* (Meikle, 2002) and news blogs (Bruns, 2006), but more recently also through more or less orchestrated group efforts in social media spaces—has now established itself within the overall media ecology of the news; some key sites (from the Korean *OhmyNews* to the US-based *Huffington Post* to the Australian *Crikey*) have even become important news organizations in their own right. This loose and by no means unified alliance of alternative news sites and spaces has been described by some scholars as forming a new fifth estate (Dutton, 2009)—or more modestly, Estate 4.5 (Singer, 2006)—and inherent in this description is a realization that for the most part, such alternative, largely amateur operators are unable to engage in a significant amount of firsthand reporting; they usually have neither time nor resources to be at the scene of major events or announcements. Rather, they form what Herbert Gans (1980) foresaw as a second tier of news organizations: a group of media watchdogs that critiques and comments on the content and performance of the more mainstream first tier of professional news agencies.

Their practice in doing so can be described as a form of gatewatching (Bruns, 2005), in distinction from conventional journalistic gatekeeping: where journalists, editors, and proprietors in the journalism industry have traditionally been seen as able to select from the sum total of the day's news events only those stories that they deemed suitable or important to report to their audiences—so that "all the news that's fit to print" also meant "all the news we think you need to know"—their alternative counterparts have based the core of their practices on *watching* the information that passes through the gates of the first tier of news organizations (but also through those of firsthand sources like government departments, NGOs, research institutes, think tanks, and others), and on collating and curating that information in a way that provides new insights for their readers. In doing so, of course, they benefit from the vastly greater access to primary and secondary information sources which the internet has enabled—which is why alternative news media based on such gatewatching practices have blossomed only over the past decade.

But while gatewatching is a core practice of this second tier of individuals and groups who comment on the news in online spaces, firsthand reporting is also occasionally possible for them: at times when they find themselves—deliberately or by accident—at the center of major unfolding events. This was one of the aims of the original *IndyMedia* project—set up to provide alternative reporting from the streets of Seattle during the World Trade Organization meeting (and the associated counterculture protests) that took place there in 1999 (Meikle, 2002; Bruns, 2005)—and remains important in many other protest situations, from the documentation of public opposition to the 2003 invasion of Iraq to the coverage of political unrest in Tunisia, Egypt, Yemen, Libya, and Syria during the early months of 2011; at other times, however, individuals simply find themselves, purely by chance, at the right (or wrong) place at the right time: in lower Manhattan during September 11, 2001, in downtown London during July 7, 2005, or indeed in the Christchurch city center on February 22, 2011. In such moments, even simply to take a photo or post a brief status update from the scene can become a "random act of journalism" (Lasica, 2004): it documents the unfolding event and—in combination with similar activities from other bystanders—becomes an important source of information for authorities and the wider public alike.

Additionally, during the late 1990s and early 2000s such firsthand reporting may still have been somewhat difficult—individuals would have needed access to the appropriate technology for capturing their impressions from the event (including photos or videos), as well as to the tools and platforms for dissemination, *and* they would have to have had the necessary technology literacy to use these tools to get the message out. Today, however, developments in handheld technologies (most centrally, the mobile phone), the ubiquity of mobile and wireless networks, and the rapid adoption of social networking platforms have meant that reports, images, and videos from an event can now be shared widely and instantaneously (unless, of course, the very communications infrastructure itself has been severely affected by the disaster). With Facebook claiming a total userbase of some 600 million (Williams, 2011) worldwide, chances are that any significant natural or human-made event—and certainly any event affecting a developed nation—will affect at least a considerable number of social media users, too; each of these users, in turn, becomes a potential citizen journalist providing firsthand reports from the scene, even without necessarily being aware of that fact.

Alfred Hermida (2010) points to this fact when he describes Twitter as a platform for "ambient journalism":

> Ambient journalism presents a multi-faceted and fragmented news experience, where citizens are producing small pieces of content that can be collectively considered as journalism. It acknowledges the audience as both a receiver and a sender. I suggest that micro-blogging social media services such as Twitter, that enable millions of people to communicate instantly, share and discuss events, are an expression of ambient journalism.

As Alex Burns (2010) points out in his response to Hermida, published in the same issue of *M/C Journal,* this form of journalism is also "ambient" in the same way that the style of music initiated by Brian Eno is ambient: it remains in the background, almost at the edge of perception, for most of the time but draws in its audience at particular key points, receiving their full attention. Twitter—and social media more broadly—as ambient journalism does so, too: for the most part, we may experience social media simply as a platform that is used to stay in touch with friends and acquaintances, near or far, and to exchange updates on any conceivable topic, at irregular intervals—but when a major story breaks, our (and most everybody's) attention becomes focused on the reports shared about that event.

While both Twitter and other social media spaces can operate in this way, it is nonetheless important also to note a number of key differences between them—and in particular perhaps between Twitter and the major other international social media platform, Facebook (other major social media spaces, such as the Chinese

QQ, are also of great importance, of course, but remain more regionally focused). Facebook is built more strongly around established social networks (of family, friends, friends of friends, etc.), which affects how widely information posted to the site is visible and is able to travel: unless users have made their accounts publicly visible for all of Facebook and beyond, their posts will usually only be able to be seen by already established contacts. Twitter, on the other hand, has a simpler and more open structure: on the one hand, only one form of relationship exists ("following" the updates of another user), and on the other, only one privacy setting is available (updates are either visible *only* to one's approved followers, or they are *fully* public to all Twitter users as well as published to the web beyond Twitter itself).

Further, Facebook has more sophisticated discussion functions—almost any post to Facebook can be "liked" and commented upon by other users, and lengthy discussion threads, attached to the original post, can result from this. Twitter initially had no built-in discussion threading system at all; it was its *users* who initiated the @reply system by which (nonetheless public) updates can be brought to the attention of their intended target. Even this simply provides a means of addressing another user, however, and does not constitute a formal system for organizing discussion threads in the full sense of the term. The simplicity of its underlying information architecture can also be seen as an important advantage of the Twitter platform, however, as it enables open and distributed group discussions to form *ad hoc* and quickly.

To further facilitate and coordinate such discussions, Twitter users have also introduced the #hashtag convention, which sees them include a brief topical keyword or abbreviation—preceded by the hash symbol "#"—in each update. Such hashtags then enable Twitter users to search for and follow the entire hashtagged conversation, rather than subscribing to the updates (related or not) of all participating users; indeed, to follow the hashtag discussion it is not even necessary to be a Twitter user at all, since hashtags can be searched for from the main Twitter website as well. Additionally, tweet responses to the discussion that carry the correct hashtag will themselves be visible to all participating users, regardless of whether these users already follow the sender or not.

More so than Facebook conversations, then, where widespread visibility is uncertain and established social network connections are required for individual posts to be seen by others, hashtag groups on Twitter provide an open, flexible, and quickly established platform for the group discussion of shared themes; these advantages are especially important where conversations respond to and track breaking news and unfolding events. Unsurprisingly, substantial discussion in hashtag communities has been observable for virtually any major event in recent years—from major sporting tournaments such as the 2010 football World Cup to key cultural events like the Academy Awards, from political crises to natural disasters.

The same is true for the Christchurch earthquake, of course; during the September quake, the #eqnz hashtag (short for "earthquake New Zealand") emerged as the central coordinating mechanism for tweets about the quake, and the same hashtag was used again when the major aftershock hit in February. In the analysis that follows, then, we will examine in detail how Twitter was used in the immediate and intermediate aftermath of the February tremor, and to what extent we can identify any evidence for the use of Twitter as a form of ambient journalism in the process.

Analyzing #eqnz

Gathering hashtag data from Twitter is a comparatively simple process—not least of course because of the use of the #eqnz hashtag itself. A number of research tools are available that will simply capture any tweet made under a specific hashtag; in recent times, perhaps the best-known of these has been Twapperkeeper.com, a website that enabled its users to submit specific hashtags (or even non-hashtagged keywords) for archiving, and which would make the archived data available to all users. While in late 2010 Twitter reacted against this open accessibility of tweet archives, and forced Twapperkeeper to severely curtail its functionality, an open source version of the tool, yourTwapperkeeper (yTK), is now available for internal use within research groups and organizations, and such internal use remains compatible with Twitter's current interpretation of its terms and conditions. It should be noted in this context that yourTwapperkeeper archives only those tweets that are publicly available (excluding those from accounts set to private)—but even this does not exempt researchers from considering the ethical implications of their further research activities (such as the profiling of individual users, which may be possible when processing the data).

The datasets collected by yTK contain both the individual tweets themselves and a range of further metadata, including for example the username and internal Twitter numerical ID of the originating user, their geolocation (if available—though only a very small percentage of users provide such information with their tweets), and the exact timestamp of the tweet itself. Additional metadata can be extracted from the tweets themselves: for example, we may identify any hashtags contained in the tweet that are additional to the central hashtag around which the dataset was created, or extract the names of any users that a tweet is replying to. Indeed, yTK data may contain two specific forms of such replies: on the one hand, the conventional @reply, in the form of

> Hey @user, have you heard about the earthquake in Christchurch? #eqnz

and on the other hand, a retweet of another user's message, to which the retweeting user may also have added further commentary:

> Can anyone confirm? RT @user Major earthquake in Christchurch . . . #eqnz

The latter format simply constitutes a special form of @reply, in which the letters "RT" (retweet) are prefixed to the name of the user whose original message is being shared; for most of Twitter's existence to date, such retweets represented the main way of sharing other users' updates. More recently, Twitter introduced a new style of retweet, using a "retweet button" that was implemented on its website and in most major Twitter software clients; these "new-style" retweets share the original message verbatim, and do not enable retweeting users to add their own comments to the message. At present, your Twapperkeeper does not capture such retweets, and they are therefore not included in the dataset we are examining here; many Twitter users continue to use old-style retweets, however (especially where they wish to add their own comments to the message, of course), and such "manual" retweets *are* included. Indeed, with the introduction of verbatim "button" retweets it is likely that remaining old-style retweets are *increasingly* used for this more discursive form of retweeting—since any messages that may be passed along verbatim might just as easily be retweeted using the button.

Figure 11.1, then, presents an overview of general tweeting patterns within the #eqnz hashtag. There is an immediate spike following the earthquake, unsurprisingly, as Twitter users share the news and retweet one another's messages about the event: both directly affected locals as well as—most likely—a larger number of more remote Twitter users shocked by the early reports will be involved here. Activity peaks on this first day at nearly 7,500 tweets per hour (or more than two tweets per second), resulting in a considerable volume of tweets in total; this immediate interest declines markedly over the following days, however, reducing to levels of no more than several hundred tweets per hour after the first four days. This level of activity is also linked to the number of unique users participating

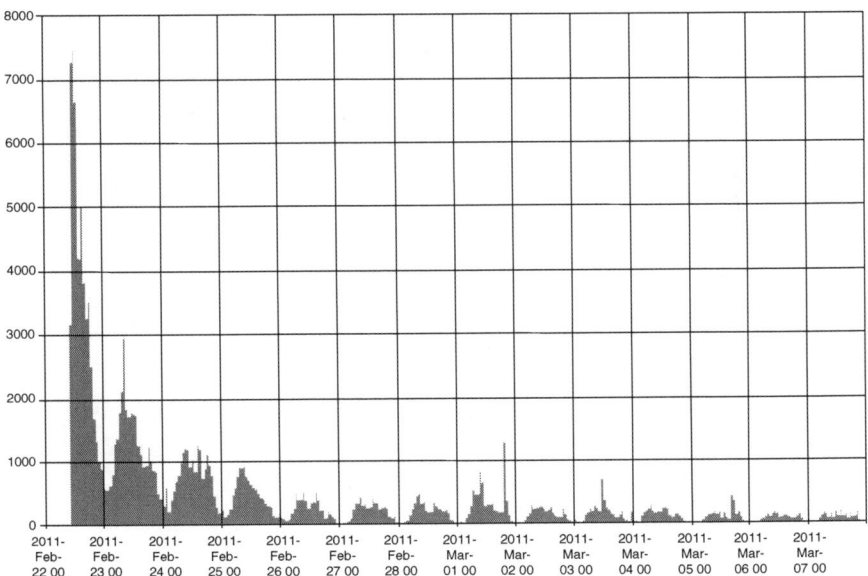

FIGURE 11.1 Number of #eqnz tweets per hour, Feb. 22 to 7 Mar. 7, 2011

in the hashtag discussion, of course: while during February 22, 2011, more than 21,000 users tweeted to #eqnz, by February 25 less than 4,300 participants remain. (This indicates the level of global attention or—less charitably—online rubbernecking that widely reported disaster events receive; similar patterns can also be observed for other natural and human-made disasters.) .

Additionally, there are also marked differences in what type of tweet is prevalent during these phases: during the early days of the disaster, retweets dominate #eqnz, as figure 11.2 indicates: of the nearly 53,000 tweets made during the first day of the crisis (or more precisely, the first half day, since the earthquake itself struck around lunchtime), over 60 percent are (manual) retweets; this percentage declines to below 50 percent for the first time six days later, on February 28. This is a clear indication that the first days of the event are predominantly concerned with sharing information and using Twitter as one element of overall information management efforts; during later stages, it may be assumed that those users left within the #eqnz discussion constitute the central core of the community affected by or addressing the earthquake and its aftermath, and that they will already be well connected to most major sources of information, so that mere information dissemination becomes less important here.

Beyond the mere volume of Twitter activity that is evident for the #eqnz hashtag, however, it is valuable to examine how the attention of the #eqnz community is

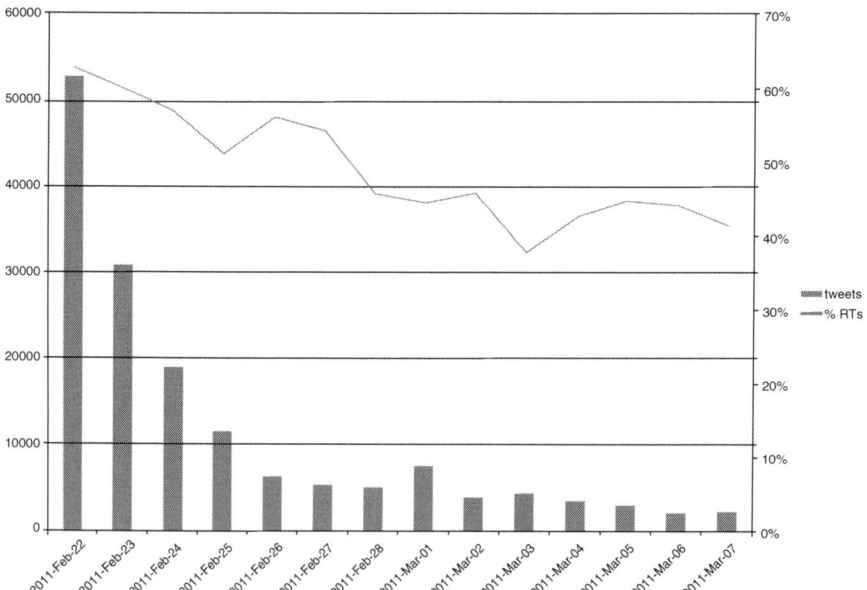

FIGURE 11.2 Number of #eqnz tweets per day and percentage of retweets, Feb. 22 to Mar. 7, 2011

distributed across different sources and participants. In the first place, the distribution of @replies (including manual retweets) provides a very useful indicator of what Twitter users discussing the Christchurch earthquake paid attention to: @ replies (a significant percentage of which were retweets, possibly with additional comments) represent a response to a previous tweet, thereby signifying not only that the replying user found the earlier message interesting, but even that it was interesting enough to reply to.

Figure 11.3 indicates a familiar pattern of attention distribution across the Twitter accounts participating in #eqnz: a handful of key accounts are complemented by a greater number of more secondary information sources. The Twitter account of the newspaper *NZ Herald* emerges as the clear front-runner over the entire period we are examining here, and a number of other media organizations (including the newsroom account of Australian Broadcasting Corporation, ABC, which also extensively covered this event in Australia's close neighbor) also appear in somewhat less central positions. Additionally, there is a well-developed system of Twitter accounts by emergency authorities, including @CEQgovtnz (the New Zealand government's Canterbury Earthquake authority; Canterbury is the region in which Christchurch is located) as the second most replied-to account, the Christchurch City Council account, New Zealand Civil Defence, and the NZ Red Cross, and two utilities—mobile phone providers Telecom NZ and Vodafone NZ—are also featured. The latter appear especially because their warnings to use the mobile telephone network only sparingly (and with a preference for SMS

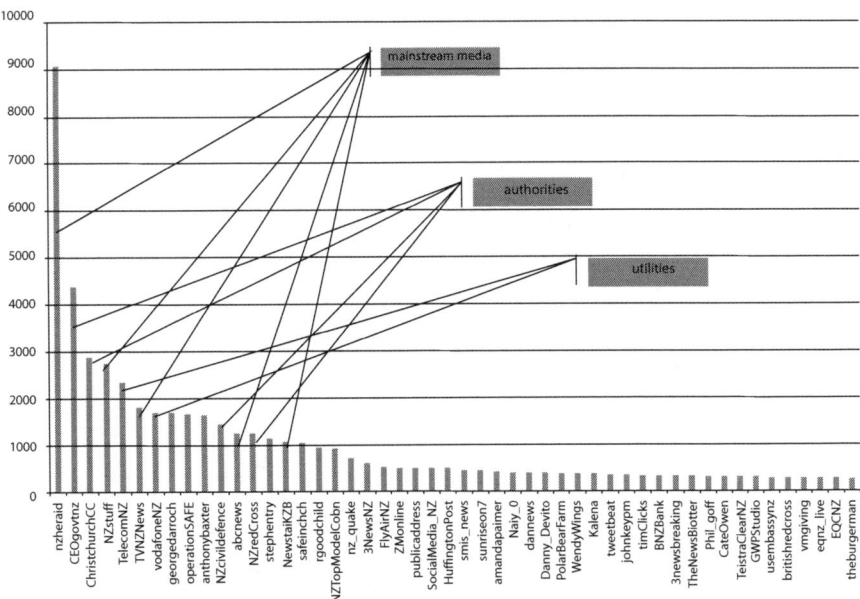

FIGURE 11.3 #eqnz Twitter accounts receiving the most @replies (including retweets), Feb. 22 to Mar. 7, 2011

messages rather than voice phone calls) were widely retweeted in the immediate aftermath of the earthquake.

Given the marked changes in #eqnz activity over time that we have already identified from the overall volume of tweets and retweets in these first two weeks following the February earthquake, however, these overall trends may obscure a more diverse day-to-day picture. Figure 11.4 breaks down this overall ranking of users, according to the number of @replies they received, into two (admittedly somewhat arbitrarily selected) periods: tweets made *before* February 25, 2011, in the immediate aftermath of the disaster, and tweets made *after* that date. Naturally, given the higher total volume, @reply numbers for the first period are significantly higher; more importantly, though, the focus of #eqnz's attention, as indicated by which accounts receive the most replies, has clearly shifted by the time the second period starts.

before 25 Feb.		after 25 Feb.	
nzherald	6239	CEQgovtnz	3439
NZStuff	2045	nzherald	2631
TelecomNZ	1882	ChristchurchCC	2070
anthonybaxter	1648	operationSAFE	918
vodafoneNZ	1576	NZStuff	711
georgedarroch	1514	nzcivildefence	545
TVNZNews	1386	NewstalkZB	475
abcnews	1240	TelecomNZ	459
stephenfry	1137	NZRedCross	451
safeinchch	967	NZTopModelColin	398
CEQgovtnz	927	nz_quake	375
NZcivildefence	802	vmgiving	286
operationSAFE	784	eqnz_live	281
ChristchurchCC	781	rgoodchild	260
NZRedCross	777	3NewsNZ	219

FIGURE 11.4 #eqnz Twitter account receiving the most @replies (including retweets), before and after Feb. 25, 2011

Where during the first period, media organizations like *NZ Herald* and *NZ Stuff* dominated, along with retweeted messages from the utilities and a number of key individuals providing firsthand updates from the scene, after February 25 there is a substantial shift in attention to the emergency authorities. The Canterbury Earthquake authority (@CEQgovtnz) as well as the Christchurch City Council (@ChristchurchCC), @operationSAFE (which provided a series of widely retweeted tips for parents in helping their children cope with disaster, but might at times have engaged in activities bordering on spamming the hashtag), @NZcivildefence, and @NZRedCross are all ranked highly, while @NZherald and @NZStuff lose their leading positions.

This shift in the comparative importance of key accounts is illustrated further by figure 11.5, which compares the number of @replies (including manual retweets) received by @NZherald, @CEQgovtnz, and @ChristchurchCC. While @NZherald is clearly leading during the first days (indeed, the about 3,900 and 1,700 @replies it received during February 22 and 23, respectively, are not pictured in the chart, to aid readability), this changes during the following days, with @CEQgovtnz first matching and then well surpassing it in the level of attention received. Perhaps understandably given the local circumstances, neither of the government authorities tweeted to #eqnz at all on February 22, and only the Christchurch City Council account tweeted briefly on the following day; this is clearly reflected in their comparative invisibility during these days. As they began to use their Twitter accounts again to provide news, information, and advice to

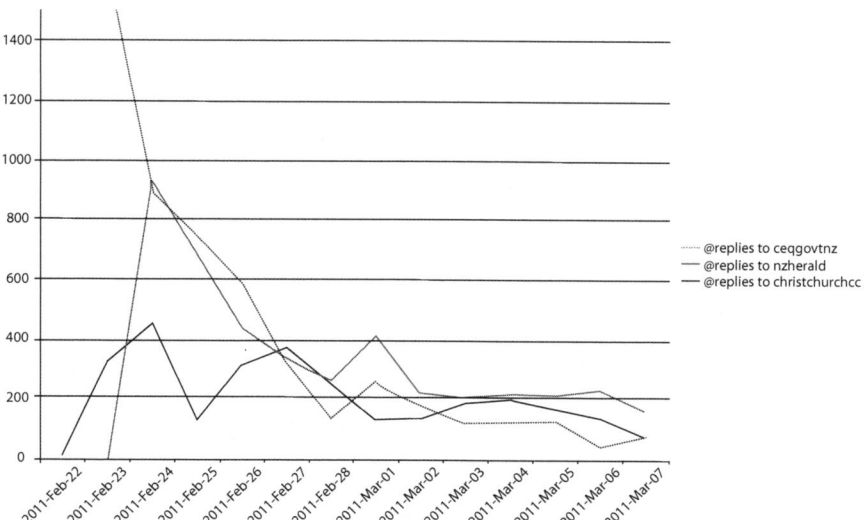

FIGURE 11.5 @replies (including retweets) to key #eqnz Twitter accounts, Feb. 22 to Mar. 7, 2011

affected residents, however, they soon became important elements of the overall disaster response on Twitter.

Overall, then, this supports Hermida's and Burns's views on Twitter as a form of ambient journalism, especially during the immediate aftermath of a disaster, while this period must be clearly distinguished from the longer-term discussion of relief and recovery that may follow it within the hashtag community. Indeed, recognizing the substantially different makeup of the userbase of #eqnz during the first days after February 22, 2011, compared to the period that followed them, perhaps it would be more appropriate to speak of two different communities: the much larger group of users that gathered around #eqnz to track news of the event and share links to the latest mainstream media stories as well as to firsthand reports, images and videos, and the smaller (and more likely far more geographically localized) community of residents and disaster relief organizations who continued beyond those first few days to share information and advice on how to cope with and address the damage and devastation that the earthquake caused.

It is likely that similar patterns can be discerned as we study the Twitter activities related to other natural disasters and similar acute events, such as the subsequent earthquake and tsunami in Japan (however, we must take into account the nature of the latter event as a continuing chain of disasters rather than one single crisis), and the approach we have taken to study #eqnz can be replicated in an examination of such other events.

It should also be pointed out that the comparatively rapid succession of major earthquakes in Christchurch, as well as New Zealand's overall familiarity with earthquakes and volcanic activity, may have prepared it (and its Twitter community) especially well for responding to the tremor. Especially following the already destructive (but far less fatal) earthquake in September 2010, the role of social media as a component of overall emergency media strategies had already been recognized, and the importance of specific Twitter accounts operated by media organizations and emergency authorities had been established. When the devastating February 2011 aftershock hit Christchurch, therefore, many interested Twitter users in the city and beyond already knew where to turn for information; similarly, they simply reused the #eqnz hashtag that had been established during the earlier event. It is very likely, too, that any future earthquakes in the country will build further on these lessons; much as most New Zealanders will know what to do, physically, in the event of an earthquake, so will most NZ Twitter users now know how to respond to it using social media.

An analysis of the #eqnz dataset reveals important activity patterns as far as key users are concerned, then; in addition to this, however, we may also extract useful information from a further examination of tweet contents. In the first place, it is possible to extract the key themes in the entire dataset through a simple keyword analysis; after a further manual processing of this list, we can determine a number of thematic keyword bundles that we may then also track over time to identify when such specific themes become important to #eqnz participants. The process here is somewhat similar to the "trending topics" that Twitter identifies on a global level, across the entire volume of tweets being made by its users; here, however, we examine what themes are trending only *within* the hashtag under investigation, and are therefore able to observe what issues exercise this specific, self-selected community.

By way of example, figure 11.6 presents an overview of the relative presence of a number of key issues in the tweets made to #eqnz. Power and water clearly are the first major concerns but further spot-checking would need to ensure that there are no false positives—such as uses of the term "power" in phrases like "powerful earthquake"—included in our count; for the purpose of demonstration, we may skip this phase. Petrol supplies, by contrast, are a clearly secondary concern and arise only on the day following the earthquake itself, as longer-term supply issues are beginning to be considered; they also appear to have been addressed quickly, as petrol is rarely mentioned at all after the end of February. Similarly, a low-level discussion of the availability of portable toilets, or "portaloos," gradually emerges during the first week after the disaster, as it becomes apparent that full water and sewage services across the city will remain disrupted for some time and longer-term alternative arrangements will need to be found. A longer-term study of #eqnz discussions beyond the period examined here may point to further community issues arising during the recovery phase.

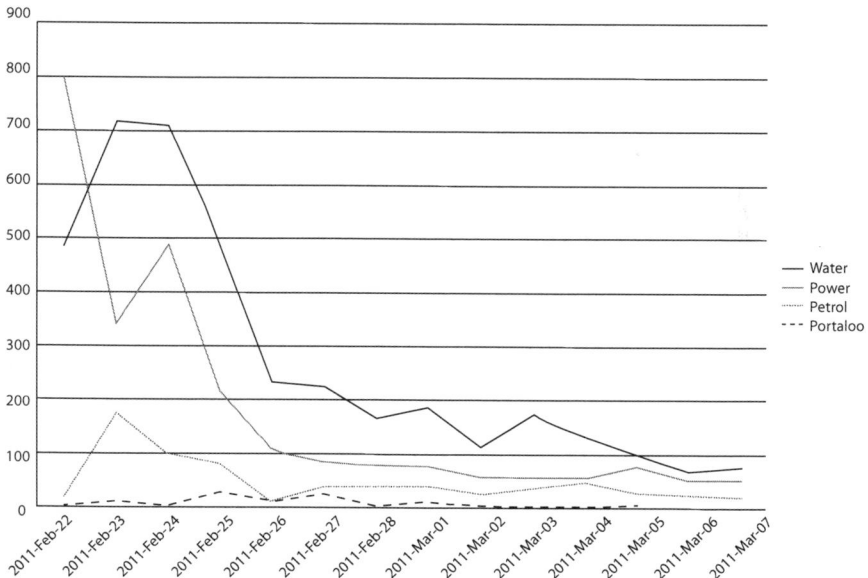

FIGURE 11.6 Key themes in the #eqnz discussion, Feb. 22 to Mar. 7, 2011

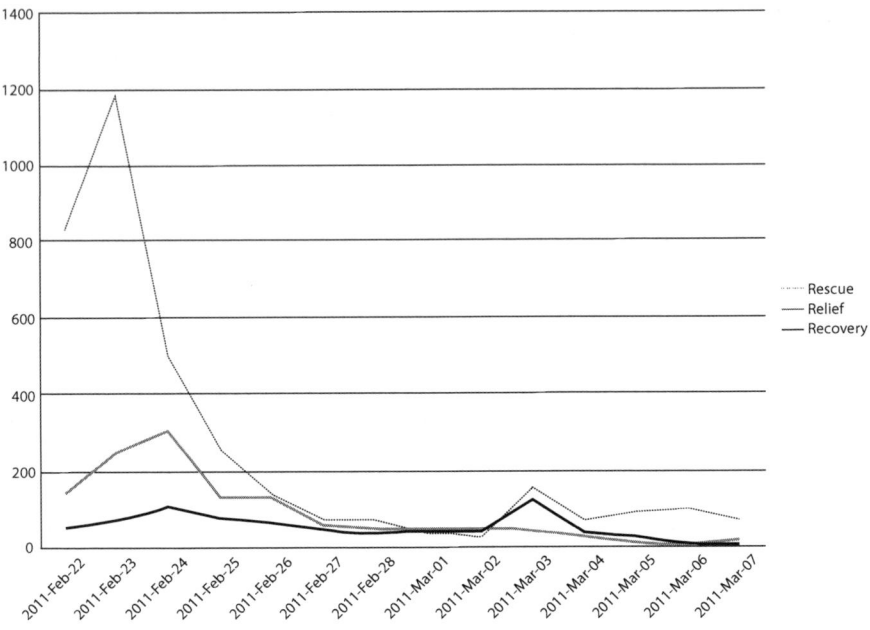

FIGURE 11.7 Changing focus in #eqnz, Feb. 22 to Mar. 7, 2011

A final striking indication of a shift in the focus of the #eqnz discussion is evident also in the incidence of a number of more general keywords: "rescue," "relief," and "recovery" (fig. 11.7). It is unsurprising that the term "rescue" occurs frequently during the first few days after the quake, especially as the focus during these days is on sharing information from the mainstream media, whose stories would themselves have been strongly centered on the continuing rescue operations. "Relief," by contrast, gains prominence slightly later, as a greater amount of support agencies begin to send their staff to the stricken city. From March 3, 2011 onwards, however, there is a marked shift in the content of tweets: "recovery" now clearly becomes the more prominent term, as the immediate emergency response operations are concluded and the lengthy rebuilding process begins. While it would be dangerous—at least without further qualitative examination—to read too much into the mere quantitative presence of these key terms in the data, this shift nonetheless makes sense in the overall context of a community emerging from the crisis event to enter a long-term phase of recovery.

Conclusion

Our brief analysis of the #eqnz hashtag in the aftermath of the New Zealand earthquake has been able to document a number of key patterns in the data; a more detailed study—which may also involve further qualitative investigation of selected subsets of the entire dataset, a closer examination of the most frequently shared links during these days, a focused analysis of the performance of specific official Twitter accounts, or interviews with the people behind these accounts or residents of Christchurch who participated in #eqnz—would generate considerably more insight. The research approach outlined here provides an important basis for such additional work.

Another avenue for further exploration is provided by the potential for network visualization that is inherent in our data. Beyond mere measures of which user accounts received or sent the most @replies and retweets, such networks of communication can also be graphically represented using a variety of approaches and algorithms, not only providing an insight into the overall ranking of attention but also pinpointing clusters of participants who were most frequently interacting amongst themselves rather than engaging with the wider hashtag community. Further, such visualizations may also track changes in the network over time, showing perhaps the gradual structuration and cluster formation processes in a community that initially emerged *ad hoc* around an acute event. In the case of natural disasters and other unforeseen events, such processes might be imagined to occur once the immediate rescue phase, where petty squabbles may have been put aside, concludes and as plans for recovery and rebuilding become increasingly politicized.

Additionally, what must also be remembered in any study of hashtag communities is that significant further Twitter activity of relevance to the topic under investigation will have taken place outside of the hashtag, involving users who either were unaware of the hashtag altogether, deliberately chose to eschew this wider visibility for the tweets, or preferred an alternative hashtag option. For example, evidence from the Japanese tsunami shows that on average, during the five days following the initial earthquake, the word "tsunami" itself appeared in over three times more tweets than were posted to the #tsunami hashtag. While a focus on the "official" hashtag of an event can be expected to capture the most engaged and committed participants in a conversation (as well as those who most want to be seen by others), it does not cover the entire Twitter audience for that event.

Twitter's current restrictions on access to larger tweet datasets, even for publicly funded research that addresses issues of significant public interest, also make it very difficult to put the findings from hashtag studies into a broader context. While we know, for example, that some 21,000 users posted to #eqnz during the day of the earthquake, and while a further examination of their Twitter user profile information could reveal with some degree of accuracy what percentage of these users were based in New Zealand, what is missing to date is reliable information about the total size of the New Zealand Twitter population—a measure that would enable us to determine what percentage of the local userbase became directly engaged in discussing the disaster on Twitter. What estimates are publicly available for any one nation (or for the total Twitter userbase) tend to vary wildly and derive from a variety of research methodologies—or more often, mere guesswork; reliable scholarly work on such questions has been largely blocked by Twitter's policies. That said, the situation here still remains more manageable than in many other social media platforms, and not least on Facebook, where the far more complex system of content types and applicable privacy restrictions means that even comprehensive access to basic public content is both technologically and ethically problematic.

What will be more easily possible for most researchers is to compare the coverage of an event by the hashtag community with the contemporaneous coverage of the same event by the mainstream media. Conventional content coding approaches as well as computer-aided content analysis methods may be brought to bear on a corpus of mainstream media reports covering the period under investigation, to compare the presence of key themes and key actors as well as the overall level of coverage on both sides. Such comparative approaches return us to some more fundamental questions about the relationship between user-driven new and social media on the one hand and more traditional, industrially produced media forms on the other: do they pursue the same themes with the same level of attention, or are there marked differences between the two? Is their framing of events and stories comparable, or are they differently biased? Can we detect any signs of the mainstream media agenda influencing that of the online discussion, or vice versa?

Whatever the answers to these questions, both for individual case studies or more generally, what is already apparent is that social media of various forms clearly do have a role to play in covering and responding to crisis events—much as conventional mainstream media continue to do; indeed, both frequently act in conjunction with one another and at times serve as mutual amplifiers: social media by disseminating key breaking news stories, mainstream media by picking up on firsthand information reported by immediately affected locals. The research approach outlined here can contribute significantly to a better understanding of this complex interaction between the two, as well as provide greater detail and documentation of the specific use of social media during disasters; in doing so, it may also contribute to further improvements in the disaster response mechanisms by emergency authorities, media organizations, and individual citizens.

Acknowledgements

This work was supported by the ARC Discovery project "New Media and Public Communication" and the ARC Centre of Excellence for Creative Industries and Innovation at Queensland University of Technology. For more information on this work, see http://mappingonlinepublics.net/.

Recommended Readings

danah boyd, Scott Golder, & Gilad Lotan. (2010). *Tweet, Tweet, Retweet: Conversational Aspects of Retweeting on Twitter.* Paper presented at HICSS-43. IEEE: Kauai, Hawai'i, January 6, 2010. Available from http://www.danah.org/papers/TweetTweetRetweet.pdf
Courtenay Honeycutt & Susan C. Herring. (2009). *Beyond Microblogging: Conversation and Collaboration via Twitter.* Paper presented at the Forty-Second Hawai'i International Conference on System Sciences, Los Alamitos, CA. Available from http://ella.slis.indiana.edu/~herring/honeycutt.herring.2009.pdf

Bernardo Huberman, Daniel Romero, & Fang Wu. (2008). Social Networks That Matter: Twitter under the Microscope. *First Monday, 14*(1). Available from http://firstmonday. org/htbin/cgiwrap/bin/ojs/index.php/fm/article/view/2317/2063

Akshay Java, Xiaodan Song, Tim Finin, & Belle Tseng. (2007). *Why We Twitter: Understanding Microblogging Usage and Communities.* Paper presented at the Proceedings of the 9th WebKDD and 1st SNA-KDD 2007 Workshop on Web Mining and Social Network Analysis, San Jose, California, August 12, 2007. Available from http://ebiquity.umbc. edu/get/a/publication/369.pdf

Marcelo Mendoza, Barbara Poblete, & Carlos Castillo. (2010). *Twitter under Crisis: Can We Trust What We RT?* Paper presented at Social Media Analytics, KDD '10 Workshops, Washington, DC, July 25, 2010. Available from http://research.yahoo.com/files/mendoza _poblete_castillo_2010_twitter_terremoto.pdf

Richard Rogers. (2009). *The End of the Virtual: Digital Methods.* Amsterdam: Vossiuspers UvA. Available from http://www.govcom.org/publications/full_list/oratie_Rogers _2009_preprint.pdf

Richard Rogers. (2010). Internet Research: The Question of Method. *Journal of Information Technology & Politics, 7,* 241–260. Available from http://www.govcom.org/publications/ full_list/rogers_internet_research_question_of_method_2010.pdf

Shaomei Wu, Jake M. Hofman, Winter A. Mason, & Duncan J. Watts. (2011). *Who Says What to Whom on Twitter.* Paper presented at WWW '11, Hyderabad, India. Available from http://research.yahoo.com/files/twitter-flow.pdf

Bibliography

Bruns, Axel. (2005). *Gatewatching: Collaborative Online News Production.* New York: Peter Lang.

Bruns, Axel. (2006). The Practice of News Blogging. In Axel Bruns & Joanne Jacobs (Eds.), *Uses of Blogs.* New York: Peter Lang.

Burns, Alex. (2010). Oblique Strategies for Ambient Journalism. *M/C Journal, 13*(2). Available from http://journal.media-culture.org.au/index.php/mcjournal/article/view/230

Dutton, William H. (2009). The Fifth Estate Emerging through the Network of Networks. *Prometheus, 27*(1), 1–15.

Gans, Herbert J. (1980). *Deciding What's News: A Study of* CBS Evening News, NBC Nightly News, Newsweek, *and* Time. New York: Vintage.

Hermida, Alfred. (2010). From TV to Twitter: How Ambient News Became Ambient Journalism. *M/C Journal, 13*(2). Available from http://journal.media-culture.org.au/index .php/mcjournal/article/view/220

Lasica, J.D. (2004). Blogs and Journalism Need Each Other. *Nieman Reports,* Fall 2003, 70–74. Available from http://www.nieman.harvard.edu/reports/03–3NRfall/V57N3.pdf

Meikle, Graham. (2002). *Future Active: Media Activism and the Internet.* New York: Routledge.

Rogers, Richard. (2009). *The End of the Virtual: Digital Methods.* Amsterdam: Vossiuspers UvA. Available from http://www.govcom.org/publications/full_list/oratie_Rogers_2009_ preprint.pdf

Singer, Jane B. (2006). Journalists and News Bloggers: Complements, Contradictions, and Challenges. In Axel Bruns and Joanne Jacobs (Eds.), *Uses of Blogs.* New York: Peter Lang.

Williams, Dave. (2011, March 25). Of Course Social Media Works—If You Measure It Right. *AdAge.* Available from http://adage.com/article/digitalnext/measure -facebook-social-media-click-throughs/149588/

CONTRIBUTORS

Axel Bruns is an Associate Professor in the Creative Industries Faculty at Queensland University of Technology in Brisbane, Australia, and a Chief Investigator in the ARC Centre of Excellence for Creative Industries and Innovation. He is the author of *Blogs, Wikipedia, Second Life and Beyond: From Production to Produsage* (2008) and *Gatewatching: Collaborative Online News Production* (2005), and a coeditor of *Twitter and Society* (2013), *A Companion to New Media Dynamics* (2012), and *Uses of Blogs* (2006). His current work focuses on the study of user participation in social media spaces such as Twitter, especially in the context of acute events.

Francesca Coppa is Professor of English at Muhlenberg College and a founding member of the Organization for Transformative Works, a nonprofit established by fans to provide access to and to preserve the history of fanworks and culture. She is currently the Wolf Professor of Television Studies at the University of Pennsylvania.

Katie Ellis is Senior Research Fellow in the Department of Internet Studies at Curtin University. Her research focuses on disability and the media, extending across both representation and active possibilities for social inclusion. Her books include *Disability and New Media* (2011; with Mike Kent) and *Disabling Diversity* (2008) as well as the forthcoming *Disability, Ageing and Obesity: Popular Media Identifications* (2013; with Debbie Rodan & Pia Lebeck), *Disability and the Media* (2013; with Gerard Goggin), and *Disability and Popular Culture* (2014).

Gerard Goggin is Professor and Chair of the Department of Media and Communications at the University of Sydney. He has published widely on disability and media, as well as internet and mobile media, including the books *Disability* *and the Media* (2013; with Katie Ellis), *Locative Media* (2014; with Rowan Wilken), *Global Mobile Media* (2011), *Internationalizing Internet Studies* (2009; with Mark McLelland), *Cell Phone Culture* (2006), and, with the late Christopher Newell, *Disability in Australia* (2005) and *Digital Disability* (2003).

Alexander Halavais is an Associate Professor in the School of Social and Behavioral Sciences at Arizona State University, where he researches ways in which social media change the nature of scholarship and learning, and allow for new forms of collaboration and self-government. He serves as the president of the Association of Internet Researchers, and is affiliated with the Digital Media and Learning Hub at the University of California and the Learning Sciences Institute at ASU. His most recent book was *Search Engine Society* (Polity, 2008), and he is working on a book tentatively titled *Participatory Surveillance*.

Andrew Herman is Associate Professor of Communication Studies at Laurier University. He has appeared in journals such as *Cultural Studies, Critical Studies in Media Communication, South Atlantic Quarterly,* and *Anthropological Quarterly.* Among his many publications are his book, *The Better Angels of Capitalism: Rhetoric, Narrative and Moral Identity among Men of the American Upper Class* (1999), and his edited collections, *Mapping the Beat: Popular Music and Contemporary Cultural Theory* (1997) and *The World Wide Web and Contemporary Cultural Theory* (2000). His edited book *Materialities and Imaginaries of the Mobile Internet* is forthcoming from Routledge.

Jeremy Hunsinger is an Assistant Professor in Communication Studies at Wilfrid Laurier University. His research agenda analyzes the transformations of knowledge in the modes of production in the information age. His current research project examines innovation, expertise, knowledge production, and distributions in hacklabs and hackerspaces. He coedited the *International Handbook of Virtual Learning Environments* (2006) and the *International Handbook of Internet Research* (2010) and has edited or contributed to several other volumes.

Angus Johnston is a historian. He teaches at Hostos Community College in New York City, writes and speaks widely on student activism, social movements, and higher education policy, and can be found online at studentactivism.net. He is currently writing a book about campus organizing.

Alice Marwick is an Assistant Professor of Communication and Media Studies at Fordham University and an Academic Affiliate at the Center for Law and Information Policy at Fordham Law School. Her work investigates online identity and consumer culture through lenses of privacy, surveillance, consumption, and celebrity.

Safiya Umoja Noble is an Assistant Professor at the University of Illinois at Urbana-Champaign. She conducts research in critical digital media studies, including feminist, historical, and political-economic perspectives on computing platforms and software. Her research and teaching are at the intersection of culture and technology in design of the internet.

Zizi Papacharissi is Professor and Head of Communication at the University of Illinois at Chicago. She has most recently authored *A Private Sphere* (2010) and edited *A Networked Self* (2011), among other work on the social and political consequence of new media. She is presently working on *Affective Publics* (2014).

Toni Sant is Director of Research at the School of Arts and New Media at the University of Hull, Scarborough Campus. His writings on performance/art have appeared in various academic journals, and he is also the author of *Franklin Furnace & the Spirit of the Avant-Garde* (2011).

Theresa Senft is the author of *Camgirls: Celebrity & Community in the Age of Social Networks* (2008) and the coauthor of *History of the Internet: A Chronology, 1843–Present* (1998). She coedited a special issue of *Women & Performance* devoted to the theme "sexuality & cyberspace." Her work has appeared in numerous anthologies and popular press outlets like *The New York Times*. Formerly a Senior Lecturer at the University of East London, Terri now teaches in the Global Liberal Studies Program at New York University.

INDEX

The annotation of an italicized "f" indicates a reference to a figure on the specified page.

Facebook: art on 51; breaking news stories on 159; communication through 55; data ghosts 13; data implications 8; demagoguery in 13; disabilities and 134–5, 138; electronic leviathan and 5; emergence of 24; identity on 49; New School occupation 28; as online home 25–6; overview 2, 145–6, 162–4; person-to-person relations on 1, 94; politics and 154; privacy settings on 96; spatiotemporal configuration of 41; teaching with 93, 97; ubiquity of 30–1; video distribution over 67
Facebook News Feed 45
fan art 3, 52–3, 55, 82, 86
fandom: conclusions 89–90; defined 76–7, 85; early internet 79–82; before the internet 78–9; introduction 3; management and moderation 87; online 82–4; overview 76; science fiction fandom 78, 79–80; social network ownership by 87–9; Web 2.0 and 84–7
FanLib 87
Fanlore wiki 82
Fanon, Frantz 109
fans, defined 77
fanzines 79
Fausto-Sterling, Anne 61
fetch, defined 54
File Transfer Protocol (FTP) 80
Fisher, E. 41
Flickr site 38, 50
Flora, Liz 119
Florini, Sarah 114
Foley, A. 137
"Fordist" model of cultural production 33–5, 38
Frankfurt School of Critical Theory 32
Freedom (Suarez) 13
Free/Open Source software development 69
Friendster 24, 26, 38
Fukushima nuclear power plant 159
Furnace, Franklin 49

The Gamma Group 5
Gans, Herbert 161
gender and sexuality: future research 69–70; introduction 59–60; online and offline 64–6; online participation 66–7; performative gender online 62–4; social media and 64; understanding of 61–2
Gernsback, Hugo 78

Gershon, Ilana 70
globalization 112
Gochenour, P. H. 24
Goffman, Erving 46, 47, 49
Goggin, G. 138–9
Google 5, 8, 10
Google+ 51, 94
Greco-Roman period 149
Gregg, Melissa 41
Grindr app 64
Grusin, R. A. 52
Grzanka, Patrick 117, 119
Guggenheim Museum 46

Habermasian deliberative character 150
habitual audiences 77
Hage, Ghassan 109
Hamlet (Facebook News Feed Edition) (2008) 45
Hanni, Kate 149
Haraway, Donna 63
Harlequin romance novels 77
Harris, Stewart 45
Harry Potter fandom 89–90
hashtag convention 163–74, 165*f*–169*f*, 171*f*–172*f*
Heap, Imogen 51–2
Hellekson, Karen 86–7
Henderson, Maureen 60
Hermida, Alfred 162, 170
Herring, Susan 65, 67
heteronormativity 61–2
heterosexuality 61–4, 66, 112
Hilton, Paris 59
Hing, J. 111
Hispanic women 107
Hobbes, T. 5
Hoffman, Anthony 68
Holland, Sharon Patricia 116
Holmes, Sherlock 78, 85
Holzer, Jenny 54–5
Horkheimer, Max 32–3
Horn, Stacy 50
Howard, P. 147
human community 21
human interface 10
Hurley, Erin 118
Hyatt, Glenda Watson 134
hypertext transfer protocol (http) 9

Illich, Ivan 94, 96
imagined communities 2
Imagined Communities (1983) 21